Understanding Peace Research

This textbook offers an overview of different methods and sources for information gathering for peace research, as well as the challenges presented by such work.

Research on conflict-ridden societies carries special challenges for the collection and evaluation of information about the conflict and its actors. First, due to the nature of conflict, parties have incentives to misrepresent information and propaganda is common. News coverage is sometimes poor and reporting is often incomplete, selective and biased. Second, the sensitivity of the topic and the questions posed in peace research means that access to and the security of informants can be a problem.

Peace research as a discipline encompasses a number of different approaches for obtaining empirical information which serve as a basis for analyzing various research topics. This book provides a comprehensive overview of different methods and sources of information gathering for students and researchers, as well as the challenges presented by such work. It offers:

- tools for evaluating sources and information
- suggestions on where different types of information can be found
- advice on using different types of sources, including news reports and written narratives
- practical guidelines for constructing large-scale datasets
- insights and guidelines for comparative fieldwork, in-depth interviews, focus groups, and surveys
- reflection and discussion on important ethical concerns in peace research.

This book will be of much interest for students and researchers of peace studies, conflict resolution, war studies, development studies, security studies and IR, as well as for NGO workers/researchers.

Kristine Höglund is Associate Professor at the Department of Peace and Conflict Research, Uppsala University. She has a PhD in Peace and Conflict Research from Uppsala University Sweden (2004). She is author of *Peacemaking in the Shadow of Violence*.

Magnus Öberg is Associate Professor at the Department of Peace and Conflict Research, Uppsala University, and Associate Editor of the *Journal of Peace Research* (since 2006). He has a PhD in Peace and Conflict Research from Uppsala University (2003) and is co-editor of *Resources, Governance, and Civil Conflict* (Routledge, 2008).

Understanding Peace Research

Methods and challenges

Edited by
Kristine Höglund and Magnus Öberg

LONDON AND NEW YORK

First published 2011
by Routledge
2 Park Square, Milton Park, Abingdon, Oxon OX14 4RN

Simultaneously published in the USA and Canada
by Routledge
711 Third Avenue, New York, NY 10017

Routledge is an imprint of the Taylor & Francis Group, an informa business

Typeset in Times New Roman by
Saxon Graphics Ltd, Derby

British Library Cataloguing in Publication Data
A catalogue record for this book is available from the British Library

Library of Congress Cataloging-in-Publication Data
Höglund, Kristine.
Understanding peace research: methods and challenges/Kristine Höglund and Magnus Öberg.
p. cm.
Includes bibliographical references.
1. Peace–Research. 2. Peace–Research–Methodology. 3. Conflict management–Research. 4. Conflict management–Research–Methodology. I. Öberg, Magnus. II. Title.
JZ5534.H64 2011
303.6'6072–dc22
2010039813

ISBN13: 978-0-415-57197-5 (hbk)
ISBN13: 978-0-415-57198-2 (pbk)
ISBN13: 978-0-203-82855-7 (ebk)

To Mats Hammarström and Peter Wallensteen

Contents

Boxes, figures and tables

About the contributors

Karen Brounéus is a Lecturer at the Centre for Peace and Conflict Studies, University of Otago, New Zealand. Her research focuses on the psychological aspects of truth and reconciliation processes after civil war, the effects of interethnic dialogue in intractable conflict, and the psychological well-being of soldiers returning from peacekeeping operations. Her work has been published in journals such as *Journal of Conflict Resolution* and *Security Dialogue*.

Tomislav Dulić is the Director of Research at the Hugo Valentin Centre, Uppsala University. He is the author of *Utopias of Nation: Local Mass Killing in Bosnia and Herzegovina, 1941–42* (Acta Universitatis Upsaliensis). He has also published articles in *Holocaust and Genocide Studies, Europe-Asia Studies, Journal of Genocide Research* and *Journal of Peace Research*. He is currently leading two research projects: one on local mass violence in Bosnia and Herzegovina during the war of the 1990s, and one on nation and state building in Montenegro.

Kristine Eck is an Assistant Professor at the Department of Peace and Conflict Research, Uppsala University and an affiliated researcher with the Uppsala Conflict Data Program (UCDP). Her research focuses on civil war dynamics and the processes of rebel recruitment. She has published in *International Studies Quarterly, Journal of Peace Research* and numerous anthologies. She is currently involved in a survey project concerning exposure to conflict violence in Nepal.

Lotta Harbom is Project Leader for the Conflict Data Collection component of the Uppsala Conflict Data Program at the Department of Peace and Conflict Research, Uppsala University. Harbom has many years of experience with data collection in the UCDP and her publications include book chapters, reports, and several articles on conflict data in *Journal of Peace Research*.

Kristine Höglund is Associate Professor at the Department of Peace and Conflict Research, Uppsala University, Sweden. Her research has covered issues such as the dilemmas of democratization in countries emerging from violent conflict, the causes and consequences of electoral violence, the importance of trust in peace negotiation processes, and the role of international actors in dealing with crises in war-torn societies. Her work has been published in journals such as *Democratization, Review of International Studies, Negotiation Journal, International Negotiation* and *International Peacekeeping*. She is the author of *Peace Negotiations in the Shadow of Violence* (2008, Martinus Nijhoff).

Frida Möller is a Research Assistant at the Folke Bernadotte Academy. She has previously worked for the Uppsala Conflict Data Program. Her extensive experience with data collection includes collecting global data on third-party interventions, conflict prevention, conflict management and coups d'état. Recent publications include book chapters and articles in *Negotiation Journal, Conflict Management and Peace Science,* and *International Interactions.*

Magnus Öberg is Associate Professor at the Department of Peace and Conflict Research, Uppsala University. Öberg is Associate Editor of *Journal of Peace Research.* He has extensive experience with large-N data collection and statistical analysis. His research focuses on the causes and dynamics of civil war and his publications have appeared in, inter alia, *European Journal of International Relations, Conflict Management and Peace Science,* and *International Interactions.*

Johanna Söderström is a PhD Candidate at the Department of Government, Uppsala University and research coordinator within the Uppsala Forum on Peace, Democracy and Justice. She has performed extensive research in Liberia with ex-combatants using focus groups, particularly concerning their political reintegration. She has also taught extensively in methodology courses at all levels of instruction (BA, MA and PhD) in Uppsala and in Ann Arbor, Michigan, including courses dealing with focus group research.

Margareta Sollenberg is a researcher at the Department of Peace and Conflict Research at Uppsala University and a Senior Adviser to the Uppsala Conflict Data Program. Sollenberg has had a leading role in the Uppsala Conflict Data Program since 1994 and has published more than two dozen articles and book chapters on conflict data. Her current research focuses on governance, aid, and civil war.

Ralph Sundberg is a PhD candidate at the Department of Peace and Conflict Research, Uppsala University, and has worked as a Project Leader for the Human Security component of the Uppsala Conflict Data Program. Sundberg has extensive experience with collecting data on, inter alia, peace agreements, power sharing, one-sided violence and non-state conflicts. His publications include book chapters, reports, and an article in *Third World Quarterly.*

Peter Wallensteen is Dag Hammarskjöld Professor of Peace and Conflict Research, Uppsala University (since 1985) and Richard G. Starmann Sr Research Professor of Peace Studies, Joan B. Kroc Institute for International Peace Studies, University of Notre Dame, IN, USA (fall semesters, since 2006). He is the director and founder of the Uppsala Conflict Data Program (UCDP), a leading provider of systematic data on armed conflicts and related issues. He has written in renowned international journals and has published more than 40 monographs and edited volumes including the textbook *Understanding Conflict Resolution* (2007, second edition, Sage Publications) which is used worldwide.

Acknowledgements

The Department of Peace and Conflict Research at Uppsala University has been devoted to the systematic study of issues related to peace and violent conflict for more than 40 years. This book has grown out of this unique and stimulating environment, where collegiality marks the workday. The core of the research team who have contributed to the book are affiliated with the department in one way or another. We thank the contributors for their cooperation, time and effort, without which this book would not have been possible. Marcus Nilsson has provided excellent assistance in cleaning up the manuscript, putting together the index, and helping us with all sorts of practical matters related to the finalizing of the manuscript.

We are grateful to all those who participated in a workshop in Uppsala, in March 2010, where we had a first chance to discuss the book as a whole. In addition to the contributing authors, we received high-quality feedback from Louise Olsson, Manish Thapa and Katrin Uba who had scrutinized the manuscript. Anders Nilsson and Mats Hammarström have given constructive comments on individual chapters. We also appreciate the effort by Jonas Baumann, Thimna Bunte and Nynke Salverda – students from our MA programme – who took the time to review the manuscript from a user's point of view. The valuable feedback from all these people has undoubtedly served to improve the end product.

We also gratefully acknowledge research grants from the Swedish Research Council, the Swedish International Development Cooperation and Riksbankens Jubileumsfond, which made production of the book possible. We are grateful for permission from Catarina Fabiansson to use her photograph in Chapter 9.

We dedicate this book to Mats Hammarström and Peter Wallensteen, who in different ways have been instrumental in creating and developing the Department of Peace and Conflict Research at Uppsala University. Their dedication to the field and to the scientific study of peace and conflict has been a source of inspiration for us, and for several generations of students and researchers at the department.

Kristine Höglund and Magnus Öberg
August 2010, Uppsala, Sweden

Part I
Introduction

1 Doing Empirical Peace Research

Kristine Höglund and Magnus Öberg

Introduction

Truth is often said to be the first casualty of war. Indeed, conflict brings with it incentives to control and misrepresent information. Fear, severe trauma and other psychological processes have profound influences on people's recollections and on what issues they can discuss openly. At the same time the ability of third parties to observe and report is reduced and sometimes severely restricted during and after armed conflicts. Warfare also tends to damage infrastructure and disrupt the keeping of records in various ways. Thus, gathering accurate and reliable information about violent conflicts and their aftermath is a challenging but also a critically important undertaking. The development of empirically-based knowledge about the causes, dynamics and resolution of armed conflicts is contingent on researchers' ability to gather useful information.

But how do you actually do empirical peace research? What sources can be used and how can they be evaluated? How can information about sensitive and contentious issues be accessed with safety for both yourself and your sources? Information is a limiting condition for peace research as it is for any other empirical science. Yet many types of methods used to collect data are barely addressed in the methodology literature and the particular problems relating to collecting information in or about countries in conflict are even less well covered. With the notable exception of survey and interview techniques, the existing literature has surprisingly little to say about information gathering. Those that do exist almost exclusively pertain to field research and qualitative research methods (Lee, 1995; Nordstrom and Robben, 1995; Smyth and Robinson, 2001; Sriram *et al*, 2009; Yin 1994; see also Galtung, 1967a).

In this book we address the promise and pitfalls of different methods and sources for information gathering. Our aim is twofold: first, to raise methodological awareness of problems related to information and evidence; and second, to help students and researchers to develop better data-gathering skills. The book has a unique perspective by focusing on the information-gathering process as it pertains to research on and in conflict-ridden societies. It is rooted in experienced-based knowledge and entails both qualitative and quantitative data-gathering methods.

The contributors to this volume share a belief in the importance of careful empirical investigations for the development of theories about peace and war. Peace research as a discipline encompasses a number of different approaches for obtaining empirical information that serves as a basis for analyzing various research topics. For this reason, we investigate a range of different methods for gathering data in conflict situations, including survey methods, interview techniques and systematic large-scale data collection. We pay special attention to the challenges that arise from the conflict situation and that in various ways affect each method and the various types of sources used. We cover the potential sources of error and bias in the information-gathering process, and provide guidelines for assessing information using source criticism. We also address practical and ethical problems confronting different techniques and peace research in general. The sensitivity of the questions posed in peace research means that access to and the security of informants is a key concern for field research. In short, we have attempted to put together a book that will introduce researchers and students to different challenges of doing peace research and point to ways in which to cope with these challenges. It is primarily an introduction and resource for those collecting and evaluating information for research purposes, but can also be used by those who analyze existing data, allowing them to better understand the information-collection process that underlies the information they analyze.

In the following sections we introduce the overall themes of the book. We begin in the next section by situating information gathering as one important step in the research process. This section outlines how empirics are interconnected to the other parts of the research design and to the research problem. We thereafter provide a brief introduction to the different types of sources and information available for a peace researcher and the different methods used for collecting them. In the penultimate section we bring attention to the ethical considerations involved in doing peace research especially relating to information gathering. Finally, we provide a chapter-by-chapter overview as a guide to the reader.

What this book is about

Peace research has developed in response to a set of formative events in history – the World Wars, Hiroshima, the Cold War, the ethnic wars in the post-Cold War era and most recently September 11 2001. It is therefore strongly normatively driven by a concern to understand how violent conflict can be prevented and how peace can be made durable (Wallensteen, Chapter 2 in this book). As a scientific discipline it has also been stimulated by theoretical and philosophical debates on the ideas about central concepts such as peace, just war and violence. Progress has been spurred by empirical studies which have taken these ideas and put them to test.

We use the terms 'data' and 'information' synonymously, although there is a preference to use 'data' in quantitative studies and 'information' in qualitative research. The shift from theorizing to theory-driven empirical investigation introduces the demand for information upon which theories can be evaluated and explored. Our approach to research falls into the mainstream of peace research with theory-driven empirical studies that seek to explain and understand specific research problems. In these studies, theory and empirical enquiry go hand-in-hand. Empirical evidence is needed to substantiate theoretical positions. Theoretical arguments are needed to make sense of the empirical patterns or observations within and across cases.

In essence, the research process consists of several distinct but interlinked parts: 1) the formulation and specification of a *research problem*, 2) the identification or formulation of a relevant *theory*, 3) the *methods* used, 4) the gathering of *data*, and 5) the *analysis* of the data and the results. The research design determines the structure of the study by linking the research problem to a theory and a method, which in turn has implications for what types of data is needed and how it will be gathered, as well as for what types of conclusions it will be possible to draw. A research design, thus, has to be judged from the criteria of whether it will be meaningful and effective with regard to the posed problem and the inferences the researcher is interested in making. An important consideration is also what is practically achievable with regard to time and data availability.

Each step in the research process involves a number of choices about the theoretical approach, methodology, the type of data to be used, and so on. Box 1.1 introduces a series of questions involved in the research process that relates to these different steps. These choices are very similar regardless of whether you are writing an undergraduate, Master's or PhD thesis, or are involved in a research project that spans several years. In a term paper or a conflict analysis that includes an empirical analysis, the research problem or research task may already be formulated, but there is still a need to attend to other elements in the research process.

This book provides only one piece of the puzzle of understanding the processes and different steps involved in doing peace research. It should be read in combination with other textbooks that focus on other aspects of the research process. The first step in any research project entails the important task of identifying, formulating, and motivating a research question. One excellent guide to formulating a research question and to the practice of writing scientific papers is *The Craft of Research* by Booth *et al* (2008). Standard methodology textbooks also provide insights into finding research questions and problems, but mainly focus on issues related to the other steps in the research process, such as choice of methodological approach, case selection, analysis and inference. Useful textbooks include *Doing Research: Methods of inquiry for conflict analysis* (Druckman, 2005); *Theory and Methods of Social Research* (Galtung, 1967a); *Designing Social Enquiry: Scientific inference in qualitative research* (King *et al*, 1994); and *Case Studies and Theory Development in the Social Sciences* (George and Bennet, 2005). Few textbooks discuss the construction of theory, but one useful example is *The Fundamentals of Political Science Research* (Kellstedt and Whitten, 2009). There are also a number of specialized books and articles that address specific problems and techniques on qualitative and quantitative data analysis.

This book is primarily concerned with the fourth step in the research process – data/ information – which is usually not so well covered in standard textbooks. It focuses on how choices about information gathering can be improved and how the uncertainties in our inferences can be better evaluated. It also highlights the interlinkages between data and choice of method, as well as the importance of theory for the choice of methodology and information-generating process. We discuss the *type of sources and information* available for peace researchers: what information do you find where? And what are the strengths and limitations of different types of sources, such as news media sources, surveys and interview-based material? We also discuss the challenges related to the *process* of research and information gathering. These challenges relate both to how the choice of method (for instance national survey versus in-depth interviews) shape the information that can be obtained and to how practical and ethical aspects of research in violent societies (for instance access and security for the researcher and informants) influence the study of conflict. The process of research includes a number of elements, determined and influenced by the purpose of the research. The process of gathering information will appear very different depending on whether you are doing desk research or if the study also entails a field research component to collect information via interviews, focus groups, surveys or other techniques. The main distinction between

---

Box 1.1: The Research Process

1. RESEARCH QUESTION

What is the research gap that motivates my study?
What is the purpose and research question of my study?

2. THEORY

What are the common theories in previous research dealing with or related to my topic?
What is my theoretical framework/causal story/main argument?
What are the definitions of key concepts in my theoretical framework/causal story/main argument?
Can I formulate a hypothesis (hypotheses) from my theoretical framework/causal story/main argument?

3. METHODS AND CASE SELECTION

What are the reasons behind choosing the method(s) that will be in the study?
How can I describe how the method(s) will be used (applied) to analyze the empirical material of my study?
How do I translate my key theoretical concepts into terms that can be observed in the material I will analyze (operational definitions)?
What are the criteria for selecting my cases?
What time period have I selected for my analysis and what are the reasons for the focus?

4. DATA/INFORMATION

What kind of information do I need to answer the research question and to explore/test my theories?
How will I go about gathering such information?
How do I assess the information I have gathered?
What are the main problems relating to the information I have gathered?
How will I structure and present the empirical part(s) of my study?

5. ANALYSIS

How do I present and interpret the main results?
Are there interesting variations in my results?
How do I interpret additional relevant observations emerging from the analysis and the material?
What objections can I identify to the results reported and to my interpretations of the results?
What has my study contributed to the general field?
What are the implications of my study for future research and policy?

Source: Adopted from teaching material by Mats Hammarström, Department of Peace and Conflict Research, Uppsala University.

---

desk research and field research relates to the interaction with research subjects and the research context. While desk research builds on existing sources (both primary and secondary), field research entails direct observation and interaction with humans as research subjects and thus has an influence on the information-gathering process itself.

Generally, data collection and evaluation are improved by a *systematic and transparent approach*. The very essence of good scientific practice is to be systematic in the data-gathering process, to be clear about how the information was obtained, and to report on the procedures. A systematic approach in terms of procedures and information gathering allows for assessment of the potential biases and uncertainties. In addition, a systematic and transparent approach ensures a degree of protection against subjectivity. Research may never be fully free from bias. As students and researchers we are influenced by our pre-existing understanding of the world. But with explicitness in terms of the choices made and the procedures used, problems can be reduced and comparisons with alternative approaches are made possible.

Different types of sources and information

Different types of sources provide different types of information and are accessed using different methods. Consequently, the methods required to gather information depend to a large extent on what type or types of information are to be collected. In this section we provide a rough guide to where and how different types of information about conflicts can be found. In our experience, these are the types of information that you will typically find using the methods and sources described in this book. We cover the most commonly used methods and sources, but it is by no means an exhaustive list. There are, moreover, considerable overlaps and many types of information can be gathered using a variety of methods and sources and it is often a good idea to combine them. Combining sources is important to ensure that different aspects of the same phenomenon are covered, thereby improving construct validity (see more in Chapters 4, 6 and 8). Even if only one type of source or information-gathering method is used (for instance news reports or interviews), it is always important to have more than one original source to establish the veracity of the information (see Chapter 3). Using more than one original source and combining different sources are both commonly referred to as *triangulation* of information.

Descriptions of reality and events unfolding in a conflict situation are almost always contested and there are many potential sources of bias and error. News articles, reports and memoirs are written with an intended audience in mind. For this reason, researchers always have to be critical and question the authenticity of the source, its potential biases, whether it is first-hand or second-hand information, and so on. These issues are dealt with in detail in subsequent chapters in the book. Here we provide an outline of and guide to where different types of information can be found.

Conflict behavior, actors, events and issues

Who does what to whom, where and when? News media generally provide the most extensive and up-to-date information on conflict behavior, actors, events and issues. Given that you make use of a wide variety of different types of media sources, there are few if any sources that can rival the scope of coverage provided by news media concerning these issues. Written narratives provided by scholars and NGOs are also good sources for this type of information, but their coverage tends to be more selective than the news media coverage. However, certain types of information, such as information on sexual violence and human-rights abuses are often better covered by reports issued by specialized organizations, such as monitoring agencies and human rights NGOs.

Moreover, while news media are fairly good at covering the top of the decision-making pyramid and what transpires on the ground, they are typically not so good at covering mid-level decision-making – the critical connection (or sometimes disconnection) between top-level decision-making and events on the ground. Interviews and surveys can provide supplementary, and sometimes critical, information on conflict behavior, actors, events and issues. It is not uncommon in conflicts for controversy to surround what actually transpired and news media coverage may be unclear, incomplete, or contradictory on critical issues. In such cases interviews with the actors themselves or other first-hand observers may be the only way forward. Interviews and surveys can also often be used to clarify and provide more detail and nuance where news media coverage is limited, unclear, or simply provides insufficient detail.

Perceptions, motivations and attitudes

Perceptions, reasoning, motivations and assessments of the parties to a conflict and the public in general are less well covered by news media, and other sources need to be consulted. In many instances, new primary data needs to be collected. In addition, many of these aspects, like motivations and intentions of groups and individuals, cannot be observed directly. We can only learn about them indirectly by making assumptions about their observable manifestations, and inferences from statements and behavior.

To obtain information about the actors involved in the conflict, interviews with decision makers and first-hand observers can be useful. Written narratives in the form of biographies and memoirs can also be informative. Conflict actors often provide information about their goals and state their motivations on websites or issue statements and information via political offices. When dealing with partisan sources, issues related to authenticity and bias are especially important to consider.

The archives, diaries and communications of conflict actors are more rarely used by peace researchers because they are usually unavailable in recent or ongoing cases, and because most peace researchers are not trained as historians.[1] These types of sources avoid many of the problems inherent in news media coverage and interviews, as well as in scholarly and NGO reports and can provide types of information that may be difficult or impossible to find elsewhere. Examples include the actors' perceptions, reasoning, motivations and assessments at the time of important decisions. Archives, diaries and communications are also good sources of information on mid-level decision-making.

Another area where the news media coverage tends to be less extensive is public opinion. Although surveys are often reported in the news media, surveys are rarely carried out in conflict areas. Instead, statements in the news media about public sentiments in conflict areas are often based on little more than the – hopefully well-informed – opinion of a reporter or the statements of political or social leadership figures in the conflict area. There are many voices that will typically not be heard in the news media and local leaders cannot be relied upon to accurately reflect public opinion. Thus, surveys are an important tool for establishing what people in general or in particular sub-groups actually think and feel about conflict-related issues. Interviews and focus groups can also be used to gather information about grass-roots perceptions, motivations and assessments, as well as about small scale grass-roots activities. Although interviews and focus groups usually target a more limited number of individuals in comparison to surveys, a well-designed study can provide new insights as well as heuristics for theory development.

Structural conditions

Information about structural conditions can be found in official statistics provided by governments, international organizations, researchers and NGOs. Unfortunately, countries ridden by conflict are usually those with the poorest coverage in official statistics. This is unsurprising because conflict, and in particular intrastate conflict, makes it very difficult or impossible to keep good public records, conduct surveys and to otherwise collect information in a systematic fashion. Conflict countries often also have weak and poorly functioning state apparatuses to begin with. This means that coverage is often uneven across the globe and over time. Even so, there is a surprising wealth of information on a wide variety of issues including social, economic and political conditions, as well as on public health, geography and infrastructure, among other things. There are also large data compilations on various types of political and conflict events within and between countries. Some of these large data compilations are listed in Box 1.2.

Ethical considerations

Social science research is usually developed within a framework of ethical standards that is more or less clearly formulated. Specific guidelines may be issued by funding bodies, the university or other professional bodies. In some countries there is a legal framework to protect human research subjects. This means that research proposals have to be exposed to ethical review that is based on an assessment of the needs and expected rewards to society versus potential harm to research subjects.[2]

Peace research raises important ethical dilemmas through its very focus. Several ethical questions may come to the fore in relation to the information-gathering process. The topics of research are often sensitive both to the participants in a study and to the governments that experience the conflict. Ethical dilemmas for researchers are most acute in field situations and when research subjects are directly involved. A key issue is the potential risk for informants and collaborating partners who assist or participate in the study. Box 1.3 highlights some of the most pertinent questions that need to be considered when conducting fieldwork.

While the main ethical concern for peace research should be with the research subjects, it is important to acknowledge that the exposure to common themes in peace research such as violence, death and other traumatic experiences may influence the emotional wellbeing of those conducting the research and gathering the information (including transcribers, local assistants, etc) and should also be considered in desk research. There are risks of becoming oversensitive to viewing or reading about violence, whether documentary or fictional, or of developing a cynical and or pessimistic outlook on the world.

In sum, the information-gathering process entails several ethical dimensions – for the student or researcher, for the research subjects, and for collaborating parties – that need to be considered and which will be addressed in this book (see Chapters 7–10 in particular).

Box 1.2: Useful Sources in Peace Research

This box lists a sample of different types of sources useful for peace research. Most of them are available on-line.

News databases	• BBC Summary of World Broadcasts (www.monitor.bbc.co.uk) • Factiva (www.factiva.com) • Open Source Center (www.opensource.gov) • Keesing's Record of World Events (www.keesings.com) • LexisNexis (academic.lexisnexis.com)
Reports issued by specialized NGOs and IGOs	• Global Witness (www.globalwitness.org) • Human Rights Watch (www.hrw.org) • International Crisis Group (www.crisisgroup.org) • Integrated Regional Information Network (www.irinnews.org)
Surveys	• Afrobarometer (www.afrobarometer.org) • Households in Conflict Network – HiCN (www.hicn.org) • World Values Survey (www.worldvaluessurvey.org)
General country information	• World Development Indicators (data.worldbank.org) • UN Data (data.un.org) • The Quality of Government Institute, Göteborg University (www.qog.pol.gu.se) • Gapminder (www.gapminder.org)
Conflict data programs	• Centre for International Development and Conflict Management, University of Maryland (www.cidcm.umd.edu) • Correlates of War (www.correlatesofwar.org) • Uppsala Conflict Data Program (www.ucdp.uu.se)

Organization and overview of the book

The book is organized as follows. Part I includes two chapters that serve to introduce the reader to the book and to peace research more broadly. Following this introduction, Chapter 2, by Peter Wallensteen, traces the origins and developments of peace research since World War I and highlights how new research questions and themes have come into focus as a result of a set of formative events.

Part II (Chapters 3–5) provides the reader with a set of chapters that point to basic tools for evaluating information. It also highlights the different advantages and disadvantages of various types of sources, primarily for desk research. In Chapter 3, Tomislav Dulić explains how to use source criticism to estimate the extent to which the information provided by a source is likely to be fraught with uncertainty and bias. Regardless of which information-gathering method is used, a critical task is to evaluate the veracity of the information obtained. While we may never be able to establish the

---

Box 1.3: Ethical Considerations – Examples

- Are there potential risks for the participants (interviewees, informants, survey respondents) from their involvement in the study?
- If so, how can I ensure the anonymity of my informants?
- How do I inform potential participants in my study about the purpose of it so that they can make an informed decision on whether to participate?
- How are my collaborating parties affected by the study I am doing?
- How can I ensure that the data I collect is securely stored?

---

facts with certainty, we can and should systematically attempt to identify and reduce uncertainty and bias.

Chapter 4, by Magnus Öberg and Margareta Sollenberg, analyzes the main advantages and problems with using news media to gather information about armed conflicts. It discusses problems inherent in news reporting on armed conflict in general and how it affects different types of media, and media with different geographical coverage. The chapter also discusses how to search for and retrieve information from electronic news databases.

In Chapter 5, Frida Möller evaluates and compares two different types of material – news reports and written narratives. The chapter shows that news reports generally locate the events that key actors define as significant, but also include a wider set of events such as day-to-day activities that narratives leave out as they tend to focus on high-profile events and cases. Narratives supply information on the context and the strategies used and thus provide valuable insights that news reports fail to do.

In Part III, we turn to the practice of collecting information in different types of studies (large-scale data collections and comparative field work) and with different types of methods (in-depth interviews, focus groups and surveys). Chapter 6, by Ralph Sundberg and Lotta Harbom, maps the experiences of the Uppsala Conflict Data Program (UCDP) in creating global datasets and outlines the necessary and sometimes difficult choices that have to be made when turning an idea into a useable dataset. The UCDP has, since the 1980s, been dedicated to creating global datasets on organized violence and peacemaking for use by students, scholars and policymakers.

In Chapter 7, Kristine Höglund focuses on comparative field research and highlights the importance of case selection to avoid unnecessary bias, but also to assess practical and methodological challenges in field research. In comparative studies, the local conditions and the timing of the research may determine how insecure the research setting and how sensitive the research topic is and can vary substantially between different research locations. As a result of such differences, the research strategies may need to be adapted to the different cases.

Chapter 8, by Karen Brounéus, analyzes the in-depth interview as a method for gathering information. The chapter concentrates on how to build an in-depth interview, how the skills of listening can be refined through evidence-based techniques, and also on field research ethics. It emphasizes the importance of creating a comfortable and encouraging atmosphere in which the interviewee feels respected and safe, to improve the quality of the interview and ensure that it is ethically sound.

In Chapter 9, Johanna Söderström discusses focus groups as an under-used method for data-gathering in peace research. She highlights the particular advantages of focus groups (such as creating a safe environment where sensitive topics can be easily discussed) and the disadvantages (such as the issue of anonymity within the group).

Chapter 10, by Kristine Eck, focuses on issues concerning the design and implementation of surveys in conflict and post-conflict settings. It places particular focus on how these aspects are affected by the special considerations of the conflict environment. Topics like trade-offs between feasibility and theoretical aims, personal security for researchers and respondents, and censorship, are discussed.

In Part IV, which consists of a concluding chapter, we summarize the main themes emerging from the book. Chapter 11 brings out key lessons for improving the methods and practices for collecting and evaluating information in peace research and bases its conclusions on the insights from the preceding chapters.

The book includes a number of features to guide the reader. The end of each chapter includes a summary which highlights the key points made in the chapter. Each chapter also includes suggested 'Further reading', which lists some of the key works relating to different methods or issues. When relevant, chapters will also include informational boxes: definitions and case studies or empirical illustrations that often draw on the author's own research and practical experiences.

Further reading

Booth, W.C., Colomb, G.G. and Williams, J.M. (2008) *The Craft of Research*, 3rd edn, Chicago, IL: University of Chicago Press.

Druckman, D. (2005) *Doing Research: Methods of inquiry for conflict analysis*, Thousand Oaks, CA: Sage Publications.

Galtung, J. (1967) *Theory and Methods of Social Research*, Oslo: Universitetsforlaget.

George, A.L. and Bennett, A. (2005) *Case Studies and Theory Development in the Social Sciences*, Cambridge, MA: MIT Press.

Gustavsson, B., Rudén, L., Tibell, G. and Wallensteen, P. (1984) 'The Uppsala Code of Ethics', *Journal of Peace Research*, 21 (4): 212–6.

Kellstedt, P.M. and Whitten, G.D. (2009) *The Fundamentals of Political Science Research*, Cambridge: Cambridge University Press.

King, G., Keohane, R.O. and Verba, S. (1994) *Designing Social Enquiry: Scientific inference in qualitative research*, Princeton, NJ: Princeton University Press.

Lee, M.R. (1995) *Dangerous Fieldwork*, Qualitative Research Methods Series Vol. 34, London: Sage Publications.

Smyth, M. and Robinson, G. (eds) (2001) *Researching Violently Divided Societies: Ethical and methodological issues*, London: Pluto Press

Yin, R.K. (1994) *Case Study Research: Design and methods*, 2nd edn, London: Sage.

Notes

1. While these types of sources are not directly covered in this book, there are several useful books that address archival methods. See, for instance Hill (1993) and Howell and Prevenier (2001).
2. In Sweden, an Ethical Review Board appointed by the government is responsible for reviewing research on humans in accordance with the Ethical Review Act, which came into force in 2004. Amendments to the act in 2008 mean that most social science research, including that involving human research subjects, is to be vetted (see more on www.epn.se). For reference, see also the code of ethics of the American Political Science Association (www.apsanet.org)

and the codes developed by the British Economic and Social Research Council (www.escrsocietytoday.ac.uk). Another example is the Uppsala Code of Ethics, which was formulated in the 1980s by a group of scientists who were concerned with how research would be put to use in society (Gustavsson *et al*, 1984: 313).

2   The Origins of Contemporary Peace Research[1]

Peter Wallensteen

Introduction

Peace research grew as a critical and constructive analysis of basic tenets of 'conventional wisdom' of violence, much of which was well formulated in the advice of the Florentine politician and diplomat Niccolo Machiavelli to the Renaissance rulers of 16th century Europe. Guidance on war and peace appeared earlier as well – for instance, in the writings of Arabic (Ibn Khaldun), Indian (Kautilya), Chinese (Sun-tzu), and Greek (Thucydides) thinkers – often emphasizing the role of power and interest. Indeed, in many cultural traditions there have been continuous reflections on war and peace, notably in India (Upadhyaya, 2009). Certainly such ideas were prevalent in European discourses on strategic studies during the 19th and 20th centuries, specifically within the so-called realist school. Some pillars were formulated even earlier by Thomas Hobbes, summarized in Latin as *Bellum omnium contra omnes* – everybody's war against everybody (Hobbes, 1651/1996). Peace research emerged as a criticism of these ideas. Its contribution, however, is not only criticism. Its strength has been to logically challenge and empirically examine whether Machiavellian ideas are in fact founded in reality: are realists realistic, or is that only what the thinkers think they are?

Machiavelli and his legacy are only one stimulus for peace research. There is also another, less easily captured but still significant source of inspiration: research drawn from Utopian ideas. There has been considerable thinking on peace throughout history. Many 'realists' are not entirely realist. Many in fact discuss matters of morals, ethics and values in connection with the exercise of power, as concerning ideas of 'just war'. Alternative ideas have been derived from secular and philosophical traditions, as well as religious, ideological and other normative sources. Together, these sources provide a rich pool from which ideas can be developed. Utopianism is an input to peace research that is different from the one generated by the Machiavellian heritage. The underlying idea is not only to ask what the world 'really' looks like and how it works; it is also to say that the world has to be improved – no matter how we describe it today – as the present condition of our planet is far from most meaningful definitions of peace. Utopia means 'no place' (More, 1516/1997), so these are ideas that have not necessarily been tried as full-scale experiments. Still, hope as well as trauma drives people. Paraphrasing Hobbes, the Utopian source of thinking strives for *Pax Omnium Inter Omnes* (everybody's peace with everybody; Wallensteen, 2008). Such a peace research strand is located in a tradition of peace philosophers, exemplified by Tolstoy and Kant, and practitioners such as Gandhi, King and Hammarskjöld, unnamed citizens resisting repressive regimes, and humanitarian action aimed at reducing civilian suffering during war (as exemplified by Henri Dunant).

The critique of realism and utopist thinking are complementary sources and there is no broad division within peace research along these particular lines. They are two different sources for inspiration to research questions. Still, when analyzing the origins and growth of peace research, the distinction provides insight into what type of research appears at which moment in time. As each type is associated with different methodological approaches this is a way of understanding the plurality of peace research approaches.

Peace research grew together with modern scientific methods of inquiry. What began as an intellectual struggle with Machiavelli developed into innovative approaches to the study of violence and understanding of conflict. Ideas developed from the Utopian tradition have inspired research on the conditions for peace and cooperative approaches to achieving peace. This chapter will discuss the main sources of inspiration for peace research and outline the main historical events forming the discipline and its contemporary peace research agenda. It highlights how the discipline has been driven forward by a number of formative traumas – from World War I to recent developments in the wake of September 11 2001. These traumas have generated new research questions, which in turn have resulted in the development of new methods and a search for data to inform, develop and test theory. The chapter also exemplifies how methodological development and data gathering relate to the underlying intellectual development of peace research. It does not present a full survey of peace research around the world, but provides examples of research that typify theoretical and methodological innovations.

Peace research, violence and peace

Peace research is concerned with the question of violence. The concepts of peace and violence relate to one another. The most common definitions of peace include the notion of absence of war, armed conflict or threat of violent action. These are definitions of peace that state what should be *removed* from a relationship for it to be defined as peace. This can be contrasted to positive peace, which stipulates what should be *added* so as to change society and make it more peaceful. This would include, for instance, the use of conflict resolution, equal integration and/or justice for all partners in society. There is a multitude of possible definitions, which enlarge the research agenda. This makes it important to limit the field for any researcher or institution in order to be able to penetrate particular aspects more thoroughly. One may say that peace research has come to deal with organized violence in societal conflicts in particular. This focus makes peace research unique. Although this aspect of society might also be considered in other fields of inquiry, it is not a central issue in theory building. It is for peace research to answer the questions of 'why?' and 'what to do?' The definition of violence, consequently, is an important object of discussion and analysis in peace research, not only for thinking about causes of war but also for peace-building after a violent conflict (for a recent contribution, see Höglund and Söderberg Kovacs, 2010). Let us look at some of the definitions.

One definition focuses the instrumental, conscious use of violence by one actor against another when at least two actors find themselves holding incompatible positions. This definition is closely connected to the analysis of open conflict: armed conflicts, wars, genocide, civil conflict and the use of sexual violence in war. It is what peace research pioneers Johan Galtung and others have labeled 'direct violence': one actor deliberately uses violent means against another to achieve particular goals. This concept of violence also connects to an understanding of peace as the absence of war (or armed violence): if violent behavior ceases then there is peace. Galtung has labeled this 'negative' peace (Galtung, 1964). While early peace research focused on the danger of world war, attention today is more on the occurrence and recurrence of civil war.

There are also more indirect forms of violence, where the implicit use of violence is inherent in situations of repression, occupation, colonialism and deterrence. The threat of violence by dominant actors – whether explicit or implicit – can also affect relationships; the potential for violence and its unpredictability can be enough to keep populations at bay. Thus, the Cold War actually froze relations and created insecurity on both sides. The threat of nuclear war affected top-level decision making as well as ordinary people. Fear of war is a powerful tool of intimidation. The fear arises if one side has more powerful weapons than the other. Certainly, present-day terrorism uses a similar logic: the unpredictable use of violence against unprotected civilians generates fear. Fear is also a means used by repressive governments.

However, taking the distinction one step further, there is also 'structural violence': a situation in which killing occurs not through the individual use of arms but through the organization of society – for example, humans dying from starvation in a country that is rich in food. It is significant that discussions of this meaning of violence have taken place within the field of peace research itself rather than in other disciplines (Derriennic, 1972; Galtung, 1964, 1969; Gronow and Hilppo, 1970; Pontara, 1978; Schmid, 1968). Also, the concept of structural violence has found application elsewhere, for instance, in medical anthropology (Farmer, 2004). Studies that connect structural variables to direct violence are sometimes drawn from structural violence conceptions and also from a study of justice and quality of peace as seen in questions such as: does inequality generate violence and war within and/or between states? Is durable peace conceivable in a relationship characterized by one dominating the other?

Historically, the distinction between direct and structural violence has given rise to parallel research traditions. For instance, peace research at Uppsala University, Sweden, is pursued in the Department of Peace and Conflict Research, implying a focus largely on matters of causes of war and peace processes aimed at ending large-scale violence. Peace research at Göteborg University, Sweden, is organized in a milieu for Peace and Development Research, with a focus on structural issues, such as economic conditions, international dependencies and strategies for peaceful development.

Empirical peace research and social ethics

When dealing with issues of violence, peace research has demonstrated a preference for empirical investigation. Important theoretical contributors often explicitly invite empirical confirmation or suggest ways of substantiation. This preference unites the two sources of peace research. Discussions on realist issues, sooner or later, require empirical corroboration (Which examples are there? How many? Are they relevant? What can be learnt from them?) but also Utopian thinking – however untried it may be – requires evidence in modern history or in contemporary conditions (thus inviting comparisons between situations). A logically coherent argument against or in favor of a particular theoretical position is not enough: it will only gain credence once it can be demonstrated to have a counterpart in reality, in whole or in part. Theory is incomplete without evidence, as noted by J. David Singer, one of the peace research founders (Singer, 1969).

This element in peace research means that methodological innovation is of great interest and importance to peace researchers. For a traditional analyst, who largely is repeating what is already paradigmatically known, there is little need for methodological creativity as there is little expectation of finding something different or new. In contrast, peace research has been receptive to new methodologies and has been quick to draw on natural science methods, quantitative data, statistics, comparative approaches, experimental designs, surveys and new developments in geographical analysis such as geographic information system (GIS), as well taking ideas from behavioralism, game theory, future studies, neo-Marxism, environmentalism, constructivism, feminism, identity studies, etc. In terms of methods and approaches, peace research has been open and pluralistic, in short, interdisciplinary. Ideally, this situation means that results can be replicated by using different techniques, a possibility that has been explored too little.

The interest in methods results from an additional ambition of peace research, namely to be able to make generalizations and, in a certain sense, predictions about social realities. In this regard, peace research is part of a natural and social science movement to understand what is general and repetitive, to learn from reality something that is applicable and useful for society's development. Peace research aspires to say something about the conditions that can advance the attainment of peace.

A consequence of this focus is that peace research has developed an awareness of social values in research. Obviously, values will affect scholarship – the more so the less conscious the researcher is of the value problems – but values constitute a major issue in peace research. Peace researchers are not simply interested in empirically understanding the extent of violence in the world. They also hope to contribute to the *improvement* of the human condition. For many peace researchers, the medical profession is an important parallel. Medical sciences are interested not only in understanding disease but also in developing methods to cure and eliminate 'unhealth' (Galtung, 1965). Other research fields have similar ambitions, for example psychology. Indeed, value statements abound in all research, such as business administration and economics (studying the efficient uses of resources for the benefit of firms or nations) and education (to improve teaching practices to benefit students and society). Peace research exists in order to contribute significantly to the reduction of latent and manifest, present and future, uses of violence within and between societies, not to predict under what circumstances a war is successfully launched. This emphasis means that peace research does not want to contribute to the advance of a particular actor (be it a state or a movement), but to a system as a whole. It is only methodologically solid work that will have a chance to contribute to an improvement of the human condition, because to be respected among peers in the research community is a first requirement. It is upon this basis that peace researchers can play a role in societal development.

Global traumas and the development of peace research

The development of the field of peace research can be described with respect to some particularly formative traumas: World War I, Hiroshima, the Cold War, the civil wars following the end of the Cold War and the less obvious developments after the trauma of September 11 2001. These traumas have generated research into the causes of war, armaments, identity-based conflict and terrorism with a search for new approaches and, eventually, solutions without the use of violence. They are also connected to methodological developments. Let me here highlight the impact of some of these global traumas on the course of international peace research.

The World War I trauma, causes of war research, and international organizations

Machiavelli's assumptions concerning the instrumentality and omnipresence of violence were dominant in Western thinking and political practices until World War I. Objections were raised by philosophers and pacifists – by liberal, socialist, religious, humanitarian and women's movements – without affecting the decision makers in leading states. World War I began in the spirit of traditional thinking that can be summarized thus: 'Violence is inevitable; if I don't strike first I will lose. I control events sufficiently to know what the outcome will be; my country will support me.' All centrally placed decision makers expected the war to run according to previously established timetables (see for instance, Tuckman, 1962), but the war became devastating and took a course nobody anticipated. The initiators of the war were defeated, their kingdoms were overturned and their states were reduced, without the victors being able to celebrate. The traditional thoughts on war and the reality of World War I contradicted each other. New thinking was required, and from this intellectual and moral trauma sprung what is today peace research.

Thus began the systematic historically-oriented study of patterns and causes of war. During the 1920s and the 1930s several comprehensive projects were initiated. In effect they criticized the inevitability and instrumentality of violence. Certain systematic studies of war in history had already been made before World War I (Bloch, 1899), but the true pioneering efforts were made after 1920. Sorokin (1937) collected statistics on wars during Greek and Roman times as well as in the world after 1100 AD, Wright (1942) studied the world following the end of the European Middle Ages, and Richardson (1960) analyzed 'deadly quarrels' since the Napoleonic age.

The statistics gave a different picture of history. Violence appeared to be not continuous or omnipresent but varied in time and space, and the researchers began to look for periodicities and correlations. Some states had been more involved in wars than others. In other words, violence and war had causes and, in principle, it would be possible to influence and control them. These investigations also gave a picture of the destruction caused by the many wars before World War I, and it seemed apparent that many of these had also been more devastating than the decision makers had anticipated. This suggestion provided more material for discussion on the instrumentality of war and violence.

The period immediately after World War I saw many peace efforts. The trauma gave rise to hopes for an effective international organization, and ideas from the 19th century were brought to bear on the actions of statesmen and politicians. Kant's thinking on perpetual peace again became relevant (Kant, 1795/2003). Thus, the trauma also sparked a search among leaders, researchers and the broad public for alternative solutions. Untested ideas became relevant and the idea of an international organization emerged as a way out of a repetitive trauma. There were a few precedents, such as the Rhine Commission and the International Postal Union successfully focusing on narrower issues. After the war there was strong support for something untried, leading to the creation of The League of Nations as well as an emphasis on international law as roads to peace. An entire field of inquiry and practical implementation emerged, with a strong emphasis on law, and this type of investigation has remained a field of its own. Of the earlier peace researchers, Wright was probably the one most open to such influences, and he made suggestions about the effectiveness of the League of Nations. The ideas of world order had, of course, been around before, with a focus largely on the sovereignty of the states as the ultimate cause of war. International organization and international law would contribute to reducing the independence of states, in the interest of general peace. However, there were no precedents to draw on, and little empirical basis for knowing if and how such organizations would work. The organizations were created by political leaders without any previous research, although the main proponent of the League of Nations, Woodrow Wilson, was not only the US President but also a former university president (Macmillan, 2003, ch. 7).

The tradition of studying the causes of war that emerged in the 1920s and the 1930s is still vigorous. The Correlates of War (COW) project, initiated by J. David Singer at the University of Michigan, is one manifestation of this field of inquiry. By using clear definitions and carefully collecting information on inter-state relations since the Napoleonic times, the project assembled widely used data for further investigation (Small and Singer, 1982). It inspired other work, notably research initiated by historian Istvan Kende in Budapest and continued by K. J. Gantzel in Hamburg (Gantzel *et al*, 1986; Kende, 1971). The focus was not, however, exclusively on inter-state war and the period was shorter, covering the world since 1945. Later, in the 1990s the Uppsala Conflict Data Program emerged as a strong contender, covering inter-state as well as intra-state conflicts, and using new technology for searching and organizing information as well as for making the information available to the public (notably through the freely accessible web-based conflict database, www.ucdp.uu.se). By 2010 it was probably more frequently used in teaching and research, than COW (Dixon, 2009).

The causes of war studies utilize a research approach that is fairly typical of peace research: violence is the central issue, stringent hypotheses are developed and empirically tested, with the hope that this increased understanding will result in useful proposals on how to prevent wars from erupting. This approach allows for analysis and methodological development, but the political impact of studies using this approach has been limited. Demonstrating the number of conflicts and scale of violence in the world has a strong educational effect but will not change the world. There was a need to sharpen the methodologies and raise more pertinent questions. Such improvements have been made in some of the post-World War II studies. Building on COW data, for instance, the work by Michael Wallace (1979) demonstrates the dangerous combination of an arms race and smaller conflicts between nuclear-weapon states. It would make the experience of 1914 a repetition with more devastating consequences. The evidence, however, was not entirely conclusive (Diehl, 1983).

In the 1990s, the work by Bruce Russett most clearly challenged the realist notion by demonstrating that democratic states very rarely are at war with other democratic states. War and violence was not omnipresent or always a useful tool. This work suggested that the quality and form of government matters, and thus there would be concerns other than narrowly defined national state interests that motivate states. States can at least restrain themselves when they face states that are similar in governance. It may even suggest that there are other driving forces than pure self-protection (Russett, 1993; Russett and Oneal, 2001). These findings, which also included the observations that trade and shared institutions matter for reducing the occurrence of war, squared well with the experience of the European Union. The results, in other words, were not only statistically and academically convincing, they also supported and incorporated real-world examples.

Causes of war studies addressed fundamental assumptions of the realist paradigm but left others unexplored. Clearly, the data show that violence is neither omnipresent nor inevitable. The instrumentality was also challenged: the results of a war were not necessarily those that the initiator had expected. In fact, initiators of large wars often ended up losing, as evidenced by World War I and other major conflagrations. This means that the violence did not 'solve' the underlying problems and space was opened for alternative ideas.

This strand of research underscored the importance of building an international system that did not continuously generate new wars between states. The exact nature of such a system, however, remained to be carefully mapped out. The possible alternatives were still many: was it an integrated world, was it one where all units were democratic, or was it enough that all were drawn into the web of one, legitimate international organization? Certainly it suggested that a world of completely independent states was not going to generate peace, although that would have been the logical conclusions from the Machiavellian assumptions. Reality seems to suggest a different story.

The trauma of World War II and disarmament research

The devastation of World War II was even greater than that of World War I. The second war again underscored the inability of the power holders to predict the effect of their actions. Also in this war, the initiators were all defeated; the attacked became the victors. The need to understand the causes of war remained important. But World War II also gave rise to two new dangers: nuclear weapons and the dangers of rivalry between major powers, even though they had been united and victorious in recent wars. From these problems disarmament research and conflict theory emerged.

The nuclear explosions over Hiroshima and Nagasaki were fundamental challenges to the research community, particularly to natural scientists and physicists. The basic civilian and humanitarian orientation of science was dramatically contradicted. Research, seen by its practitioners as theoretical and abstract, was suddenly and rapidly applicable and concrete in the most devastating way. The political failure to control nuclear energy and to make it freely available, as well as the onset of the nuclear arms race, led to a movement among scientists to contribute to arms control and disarmament. Few political leaders mastered the technological questions involved, and too many of them depended on expertise that was motivated by other desires. In the Einstein-Russell manifesto of 1955, the need for scientists to work to prevent a nuclear catastrophe was expressed. One result was the international Pugwash movement, which drew together scientists from East, West and South. It was awarded the Nobel Peace Prize in 1995. Another outcome was the creation of IAEA, an international agency for the peaceful use and control of nuclear energy; it received the same prize 10 years after the Pugwash movement. However, the fear of nuclear weapons did not only involve the major powers but became a concern of specific regions: Northeast Asia, South Asia and the Middle East all had nuclear weapon states or states with such ambitions (whether officially acknowledged or not).

In the development of peace research, the ethics and practicalities of the nuclear problem resulted in disarmament and arms control research. In this field, studies focus on the twists and turns of arms technology, as well as on proposals for preventing further armaments. This tradition of peace research is now institutionalized, one example being the Stockholm International Peace Research Institute (SIPRI) founded in 1966. The basic premise of this work is the need to control (some types of) violence and to question the instrumentality of (some types of) violence and armaments. Nuclear weapons seemed to generate more fear than security.

As the nuclear threat was tied to the conflict between East and West, disarmament research had to be global and great-power oriented. The aspiration was to influence disarmament negotiations under UN auspices or in bilateral talks. Interestingly, many disarmament agreements were concluded directly between the major powers themselves, rather than through international treaties and organizations. The verification regimes that emerged in the 1980s and 1990s were vested in bilateral agreements. In remarkable contradictions to Machiavellian assumptions, major powers were actually willing to restrict themselves in the acquisition of weapons. States were not maximizing weapons arsenals, but preferred to increase security by reductions of weapons, again a more Utopian idea. Research input became more technical, generating ideas for inspection regimes building on how to discover actual and potential new weapon technologies. The peace researchers dealing with nuclear disarmament were not concerned with the theoretical development of peace research as such. On the other hand, these researchers may have had more impact on policies in this field.

Issues concerning test bans and non-proliferation were subject to global agreements. Utopian ideas of building confidence through small steps aimed at gradually changing relations were attempted, for instance, in the European security process during the 1970s and 1980s (Etzioni, 1967; Osgood, 1962). Practice showed that Utopian ideas could work. At the Stockholm Conference in 1986, East and West agreed to an 'arsenal' of such confidence-building measures, all largely being implemented in the following years. Thus, there is now a reservoir of regional confidence-building measures, but almost no research has followed up on their significance or asked whether such measures could work under different regional contexts than the European one.

Nuclear weapons were not the only weapons to pose concerns for the scholarly community. Equally important were the conventional, chemical and bacteriological weapons and their production and trade. The non-nuclear arms questions have received attention but have not been strongly linked to arms control efforts, as international arms negotiators during most of the post-1945 period have concentrated on nuclear issues. Instead, this type of research has had a more important role in national debates, in which the purchase, transfer and production of arms have often been contentious issues. A related series of questions concern the importance of armaments for economic issues such as unemployment, industrial profits, regional development and inflation. Such questions have seldom received penetrating analyses among economists, but in peace research they played a role early on. Research showed that armament decisions do not necessarily follow military logic; partly they also had to do with the role of the state. The label 'military-industrial' complex was a telling description for the complicated influences on a government constraining its decisions.

Thus, disarmament and peace would require a break with the logics of arms races and the influence of military industry. International treaties for arms control and measures of converting military industry into civilian uses were avenues for moving towards peace. An expression of such ideas was the creation the Bonn International Center for Conversion (BICC) in Germany in 1994. It related to the needs of dismantling the large Cold War arsenals accumulated in East and West Germany, but also to what to do with a military production that was no longer needed. Initially, the end of the Cold War meant a reduction of such industrial investments, but it was replaced with the problems of small arms and the international arms trade.

The peace research methodologies in this field have had more to do with unearthing documentation, finding information in archives and in public sources, and making compilations not found elsewhere. Institutes such as SIPRI and BICC recruited researchers with deep insights into military technology and the sciences connected with nuclear, chemical and biomedical sciences. As the ambition was to find ways out of the dilemmas created by arms races, the concern tended to be practical, although there were attempts at understanding the connections of military expenditures, industrial concerns and political decisions (Melman, 1974; Nincic and Cusak, 1979; Rundquist, 1978). This strand of research has moved away from a focus on Western industrial countries to new economies (Conca, 1997), is rich in information, but remains weak on general theory.

The Cold War trauma and conflict theory

The disarmament research contrasts a third field of inquiry arising as an additional consequence of World War II: the rapid polarization of the conflict between the victorious allies. After only a couple of years, much of Europe was divided into East and West. The joint interest forged during the war against Germany, Italy and Japan was not sufficient to bridge issues of contention among the allies. Furthermore, the new conflict was defined in general terms (democracy versus totalitarianism according to the West, socialism versus capitalism according to the East). Actions were explained in terms of historical lessons, in particular the fear of being deceived by the other and the danger of yielding to an opponent that had only one ambition, namely to establish its own hegemony over the world.

   The Cold War and the policies of deterrence – becoming nuclear deterrence during the 1950s – influenced the relations among the major powers. The frequent use of historical analogies, particularly Hitler and the agreement in Munich, served to underline the need for a historical study of the causes of war. Also, the generalizations made by the various parties suggested the need to understand how conflict works. Thus, theories of conflict emerged. Through the study of other conflicts and their dynamics, it was hoped that knowledge would be gained to bridge or contain contention between East and West. Much hope was placed in game theory, in particular its ability to illuminate situations in which two parties have difficulty reaching optimal outcomes (such as the security dilemma or stag hunt, and the so-called prisoner's dilemma). Game theory seemed to suggest that conflicts do not necessarily have to be zero-sum situations, according to which the victory of one is the defeat of the other (Rapoport, 1961). Other approaches involved the use of sociological interaction theory, drawing on Homans and Parsons (Deutsch *et al,* 1957), and the social functions of conflict (Coser, 1956). In the peace research journals and centers founded at this time (*Journal of Conflict Resolution* and the Center for Conflict Resolution, University of Michigan, *Journal of Peace Research* and the Peace Research Institute, Oslo) considerable thought was given to conflict theory and conflict analysis (Galtung, 1959, 1964; Schelling, 1960).

   The development of conflict theory and conflict analysis was also the result of an interest in integration. Integration could be studied empirically in Western Europe, but it was also regarded as a way of transcending conflicts between East and West. The concept of a 'security community' was used to investigate how former rivals had been able to eliminate the danger of war among them (Deutsch *et al,* 1957). Theories of détente were developed from integration and conflict studies. Confidence-building measures were practical applications of such insights.

   These new developments of peace research were also a reaction to the narrow intellectual climate during the Cold War years and the simplicity of the deterrence postures. The researchers worried that the origin of wars was to be found in the way the conflicts themselves worked. A fear was that decision makers and public opinion would be trapped in the dynamics of conflict. Thus, deterrence would lead to escalation rather than to containment. Other ways of handling conflicts had to be found. In the models of integration, an underlying idea was that societies would become so strongly intertwined that violence and conflict could be 'tamed' – an idea that involved battles with some other issues in Machiavelli's legacy: the view of violence as the 'ultimate' determinant of power and as a way of resolving conflicts. Peace researchers suggested that the dynamics of conflict could be the ultimate determinant and that a state/government might not be in control of the forces released by sharp antagonism. In addition, integration ideas pointed to ways in which economic, cultural and social links could reduce the independence of the state, something that would in turn decrease the likelihood of devastating conflict.

One way to transcend the security dilemma was to generate new sources of information. If the parties know what the other side is up to, they can make counter-moves based on knowledge. Thus, a theoretical foundation was found for confidence-building measures that also interested researchers in arms control and nuclear disarmament. It was a way to signal to the opposing sides that 'we are not planning a war, only doing measures of defense'. This included inviting the other sides to maneuvers, publishing schedules of major military movements and removing certain weapons from border areas.

Thus, conflict theory turned out to be a fertile approach, even resulting in special handbooks to bring together the many facets of inquiry (Gurr, 1980). The hypotheses drawn from conflict theory were precise and the requirement for data and confirmation led to the need for discussing indicators, measurements and data sources. Thus conflict theory became a significant breakthrough in research and it has found applications far beyond Cold War tensions.

In some of the leading countries, the peace researchers of this era were closer to decision-making bodies in some of the leading countries than had been the case previously. The studies of conflict theory and cooperation were in line with the desire to reduce tension during the 1950s and the 1960s, described as times of 'détente'. It was even proposed that there should be peace specialists, recruited from among the peace researchers, to advise the decision makers (Galtung, 1967b). However, little came of such ideas except in rather special circumstances. Instead, peace research milieus that built up education and training may have had a stronger impact. Students of peace research could later be located in the higher decision echelons, particularly in the Nordic countries.

The trauma of the Vietnam War and asymmetric conflict

The war in Vietnam changed this situation. Many of the peace researchers, as well as many social science researchers, had serious difficulties in analyzing the Vietnam War. In that war a superpower was in conflict with a very poor state, ostensibly for the sake of some not very clearly defined general principles of social order (anti-communism or pro-democracy) as well as for some general principles of social behavior (maintaining credibility of commitments), neither of which had much to do with Vietnam itself. For peace researchers, the Vietnam War became both an intellectual and a moral challenge. It was the most devastating war since peace research had become institutionalized, and it showed that many of the models of peace research were flawed.

For instance, peace research theories often assumed that decision makers did not want war but were drawn into it because of uncontrolled escalation and conflict dynamics. It was often taken for granted that decision makers were interested in solutions that would be satisfactory for all involved parties. Leaders were expected to search for the common good, but turned out to pursue their own course without regard to such consequences. The political leaders were, indeed, more Machiavellian than the critics expected and thus the critique did not gain support at the top level. Other forms of influence had to be considered, notably public opinion, popular movements and media. It seemed that democracy was a necessary framework for giving peaceful alternatives a hearing.

The Cold War models also assumed that the parties (be they superpowers, alliances, states or regional groupings) were about equal in strength and in responsibility for conflict. Such assumptions were probably largely correct for the East-West conflict, even during its coldest phases (such as the crises over Germany, Berlin and Cuba), but the Vietnam War was different in all respects; for instance, both parties pursued the war to win, not to reach a compromise. Also, how could two unequal parties be treated equally? Perhaps this question was to have the most lasting effect on peace research as it revealed a theoretical emphasis on symmetry between contending parties in a world full of asymmetries. For many researchers the matter of importance became influencing the stronger of the parties, that is the United States, to change its goals. For others, there was not necessarily a contradiction between these two positions.

With regard to the development of peace research, the Vietnam War gave rise to a whole set of new questions. How are parties shaped? How do the interests they pursue emerge? What are the relations between different types of interests, for instance, class versus nation? What does sovereignty mean in a world of asymmetric economic dependencies? Studies were made on the links between economic dependency and war, military interventions and other military actions. From neo-Marxism as well as classical Marxism, new ideas could be extracted and put to empirical test (Galtung, 1971). In this way, the trauma created by the Vietnam War could be turned into a new phase of development for peace research. A lasting effect has been a widening of the agenda of peace research (Wiberg, 1988) as the studies of dependence have led to inquiries into the possibility of creating more self-reliant and independent societies. Thus, issues of development theory became linked to peace research, particularly with regard to questions on the role of the military in the development process and on conflict-inducing economic dependencies.

For conflict theory, asymmetric conflicts still pose unresolved problems. It is hard to determine how such conflicts could be separated from other conflicts or how they affect the analysis of conflict resolution. Even obvious cases like major power interventions in Third World conflicts could be difficult to define as asymmetrical. The big power could often claim it was 'assisting' a legitimate side in an internal conflict, for instance. Thus, it was even suggesting it was redressing an asymmetry in the country. The study of asymmetric conflicts, such as issues between a Global North and Global South, both supplement and contradict some earlier tendencies of peace research. The emphasis on economic factors takes integrationist arguments one step further. Not only are states and governments restrained by economic interests; rather the ultimate power, in some analysis, is located in the economic sphere. What then does the state do? Does control over weaponry provide a state/government with an independence of its own, or does it only make it a more important target for others to control?

The question of sovereignty became another subject of debate for peace research. In the study of international organization and integration, there was an underlying assumption that the independence of the state is an important part of the problem. If only this independence could be restrained, devastating conflicts could be avoided. But the opposite conclusion emerges from studies of dependence and imperialism: peaceful relations can be established only if states are more independent. According to this perspective, dependency results in imbalances that give rise to internal as well as to external conflict, revolutions and interventions. From a conflict resolution perspective, furthermore, independence could be a perfectly plausible solution to some conflicts, for instance ethnic contention.

Can this debate be solved simply by saying that integration promotes peace when the parties are equal and leads to conflict when they are unequal? How, then, do we distinguish between symmetric relations and asymmetric ones in a way that makes it possible to predict what solution will have what effect? We could also ask: what is the record? In contemporary Third World societies, which are assumed to be very dependent, we can still see that leaders behave in a highly independent way, in spite of the cobwebs they are entangled in. Coupled to the observation that external powers often are reactive rather than active in many conflicts in Africa and Asia, the issue of the autonomy of states and their leaders comes into a new light. Is it actually possible for major powers to depose a leader if he or she becomes inconvenient? The sovereignty issue remains paramount in the way many former colonies view international relations. Thus, even leaders with disturbing records (Amin in Uganda, Mengistu in Ethiopia, Mugabe in Zimbabwe, the military junta in Burma/Myanmar, the Islamic Republic in Iran or Bashir in Sudan) can still count on support from other Third World countries. Indeed, many such leaders display traits in their exertion of power similar to their counterparts in the 1500s.

The record of intervention and different forms of intervention is open to analysis, however. There are now a number of databases on such actions, leading to studies of when intervention takes place by whom with what means and with what outcome (Regan and Aydin, 2006; Tillema, 1989). The debate continues, particularly as issues of humanitarian intervention came forth during the 1990s, in view of the experiences of genocide, which gave new arguments for international action.

Still, the normative as well as empirical merits of change through outside intervention were not convincing. The challenge to power, in other words, was more likely to come from inside a society than from outside. Thus, the search for alternative strategies for social change had to turn to unexplored sources. A central concern early on was non-violent resistance. The study of non-violence has been stimulated by the experiences of India and Mahatma Gandhi, which played a role for studies in Europe in the 1950s (Galtung and Naess, 1955) and remain important in India. During the 1960s, the civil rights movement in the United States gave rise to studies in many parts of the Western world (Sharp, 1973). The Czechoslovakian resistance to the Soviet invasion in 1968 stimulated interest in the notion of civilian defense strategies (Roberts, 1986), and in the 1980s, inputs have come from, for instance, the experience of Solidarity in Poland (Wehr, 1985[2]). These were all highly publicized events that directly or indirectly involved major states, but there were also other events. Cases of great societal transformation such as the reformist labor movement in northern Europe have seldom been identified as examples of non-violence, and thus such cases have not played the role they perhaps should in stimulating research. Attempts to bring this research to life are witnessed in work recently published by David Cortright (2008; 2009).

This is, of course, only one more reminder that several major social changes have come about through peaceful means, notably the decolonization movement as well as the break-up of the Soviet Union. Only a few projects have been devoted to the use of non-violent actions for social change, such as at the Heidelberg Institute for International Conflict Research in Germany (Pfetsch and Rohloff, 2000; Stephan and Chenoweth, 2008). In the same way, inspiration for alternative forms of action can be found in other emancipatory movements, notably for promoting civil rights, ecological sustainability and feminism. The methods often stemmed from non-violent examples, but there was a constant evolution of techniques, innovation being part of media coverage, success and lately a factor in forming a global civil society (eg, Smith, 2007; Wehr 1979, 1985).

As this suggests, these movements were often elements in major transformations of societies, for instance turning away from authoritarian rule to civilian systems. To this category belong studies of protests against war, military regimes, arms production and confrontation with others. It also suggests a major additional field for analysis, namely studies of the developments that follow such transformations (for instance democracy, civilian production, détente-type relations) as well as their durability. Largely, the field has been ripe with cases studies and sometimes with little theoretical coherence. Recent attempts at creating large-scale data collections or doing systematic comparative studies bode well for the future of the field. It is particularly significant as it challenges a Machiavellian emphasis on armed force.

Furthermore, there has been limited focus on the regional level. Low-tension areas such as the Nordic and the Pacific regions still need exploration. A regional comparative approach might illuminate the specific Latin American experience of the past 50 years, which has included considerable violence within nations and in relations with extra-continental actors but less among Latin American nations. The idea of a new regionalism (Hettne *et al,* 1999) captures this need, as do ideas on 'regional security complexes' (Buzan and Waever, 2003; Wallensteen and Sollenberg, 1998).

The same is true for the global level, where the dependency theory emanated, but which has often been left outside the analysis. The international asymmetries are striking, however, with a few countries commanding most of the world's military resources. There is some study into the use of collective decision making (for instance in the UN or the EU) on the use of coercive, but still not directly violent means such as economic sanctions, but these measures have to be compared to military actions for a complete evaluation.

Asymmetric conflicts on global, regional, inter-state and intra-state levels remain intellectual and real-life challenges that require further methodological and theoretical development.

The post-Cold War period and peace-building research

The end of the Cold War created a new twist to the problem of sovereignty. The reduction in major power rivalry led to a decrease in external control over particular countries and regimes. Conflicts prolonged by the actions of the West, East and, to a limited extent, China, could be removed from the agenda: peaceful changes took place in Eastern Europe, the Caucasus and Central Asia. Peace agreements were negotiated in Indochina, Southern Africa and Central America. The Middle East saw a peace process of unprecedented quality and commitment (the Oslo process). It seemed like a post-Machiavellian moment. Reasonable conversations were possible to end protracted conflict. In a way the 1990s were reminiscent of the 1920s, when conferences managed to deal with a number of the post-World War I issues resulting from the creation of new states in Eastern Europe.

At the same time, however, a whole set of new conflicts emerged involving genocide, ethnic cleansing and other vicious deeds (Rwanda, Srebrenica, Darfur). There were experiences of state failure, ethnic antagonism, greedy actors looking for lootable resources, and humanitarian disasters. The state machinery seemed to collapse or lose territorial control. The international community, in a completely novel way, took on the responsibility of managing human-induced disasters. Peacekeeping operations were sent into new complicated situations. Peace agreements were fostered at a historically unprecedented rate. For peace research this posed new challenges, almost having to start from the beginning, but this time dealing with intra-state conflict. What were their causes and how did they compare to what was already known about inter-state relations?

The Uppsala Conflict Data Program (UCDP) was well placed to be a data resource as it focused on all conflicts, not just inter-state conflicts that were the chief concern of COW. UCDP data demonstrated that there were more intra-state conflicts than any other form, but also that there was a strong regional involvement. Neighbors often had interests in conflicts across the border. Peace agreements became more frequent, but also had a problem of durability (Harbom *et al,* 2006). Such protracted and wide challenges of conflict resolution and conflict prevention had few historical counterparts. The need for knowledge made peace research important. The number of centers focusing on intra-state conflict quickly expanded. By the early 2000s there were more than 400 centers doing peace research and teaching programs around the world (PJSA, 2010). Issues of negotiation, prevention, mediation, peacekeeping and peace-building entered into the research agenda, but also became part of the daily schedules of international institutions, regional organs and civil society organizations. They were part of a new global society, and globalization became the catchword. To some extent this trend reduced the independence of states, but in another way it increased the state's significance, since collective state actions (for instance in the UN, NATO or EU) also had an impact beyond their own borders. The independence of the state began to take on a completely novel meaning, where the resort to violence no longer was the ultimate source of power, but equally much attention was given to legitimacy, justice, quality and skill in negotiations.

In sum, post-Cold War developments challenged the Machiavellian legacy. First, it did so by questioning the inevitability of violence. Negotiation options were often provided, while victory was increasingly uncommon. Second, the instrumentality of violence and 'hard' power were challenged and notions of 'soft power' gained acceptance (Nye, 2004). Wars were increasingly seen as human disasters for the international community to act on, with sympathy for victims, not for political gains. Similarly terrorism did not generate popularity or sustained power to terrorists. Third, violence did not end the wars; instead many seemed protracted or prone to recur. Fourth, the state's resort to violence was neither determining the outcome nor resolving the conflicts. Fifth, the uniqueness of the state was questioned. Often, popular movements, ethnic or religious groups, commercial companies and non-governmental organizations seemed stronger than the governments. Sixth, this brought attention to a novel phenomenon of state failure and the importance of 'good' governance issues. The idea of an international responsibility to protect populations, also against their own governments, served to question the meaning of sovereignty and the independence of the states.

The Machiavellian assumptions built on the idea of a sovereign, functioning state with stronger coercive, fiscal, territorial and ideological power than any other actor in a society. State failure was not part of the picture. In earlier times, a collapsing state was immediately gobbled up by its neighbors. In the post-Cold War world, however, the prohibition of interference in internal affairs made only collective action legitimate, and it was not always forthcoming or sustainable. Somalia since 1991 became a symbol of an area 'governed' without a legitimate and functioning state. Turkey's invasion of Cyprus in 1974 or Russia's conflict with Georgia in 2008 resulted in the announcement of new states, but without credibility and thus with little international recognition. The prohibition of intervention remained strong, even if powerful neighbors sought to cover their designs in a more modern disguise.

The study of the causes of war had to make a new, fresh start: the study of the origins of internal wars became a new issue. In absolute numbers these wars were more frequent than inter-state conflicts, but it was also more difficult to argue that they all would stem from the same causes, resting in the operation of an inter-state system. The data made cross-national comparisons possible and the first debate posited tensions between studies of greedy actors versus those who saw actors motivated by basic needs or social grievance. Later the debate expanded to include creed (Zartman, 2000) into more complex models of multidimensional entrapment (Collier, 2009). The methodological richness was also wide, ranging from statistical work to well-selected cases studies, from global and regional concerns to national, ethnic, local and tribal dimensions. But in a way this was full circle from the World War I trauma. There was again a need for data as well as for questioning the established paradigms. The causes were sought with parallel theories, although applied to internal conditions; the Utopian elements had to do with the ways peace agreements and peace processes were done.

In the late 1990s and early 2000s the concept of peace-building after war emerged as a novel point for peace research. The Kroc Institute for International Peace Studies formulated this as a strategic concern for its research (Philpott and Powers, 2010). However, the concept and practice of peace-building also sparked a debate within peace research on its meaning and justification (Paris, 2004; Richmond, 2009). In the same way that the causes of international war studies wanted to avoid a repetition of world wars, the study of intra-state conflict was concerned with the prevention of renewed wars in the same state. Similarly, the hope was vested in making agreements among the parties, with the help of negotiations, mediation, arbitration or other means.

A particular focus was on conflict prevention and preventive diplomacy. If the causes of intra-state wars were known, it would be possible to develop strategies for structural prevention. Even if the causes were not understood, diplomatic, political and economic actions might be taken to prevent disputes from escalating to armed conflict. Indeed, it was soon shown that there were considerable possibilities of preventive action (Lund, 1996), but it remained to demonstrate how much activity actually took place and what the effects were. Several studies at Uppsala University showed that there was more activity than many anticipated (Öberg *et al*, 2009). The effectiveness of preventive activities by third parties remained to be decided, however.

Peace-building was seen as the actions after a war, prevention as the measures before a conflict escalates. For either concern, armaments were important. Arms trade would be an indication of brewing trouble, before a conflict and definitely during one. Arms embargoes would be a way of dealing with conflicts throughout these phases. The record was still not overwhelming (Brzoska, 2008; Fruchart *et al*, 2007). Establishing intra-state peace would require programs for dealing with disarming rebels and transparency of the security sector. Thus, studies on these issues began to emerge, generating new insights of importance for strategic peace-building (Humphreys and Weinstein, 2007; Nilsson, 2008; Weinstein, 2005).

Peace-building issues also involved a gender dimension (Olsson, 2007). Women were part of the population that had generally been overlooked in previous research and their role as victims and as part of conflict actors (female combatants) was highlighted. Women also had a legitimate security concern. With the concept of security equality, Olsson sought to bring attention to this, not least by studying how international peacekeeping missions were striving to achieve protection for all citizens, not just a select few. There are strong reasons to incorporate gender analysis into peace research as well as practical strategies, since gender equality in society is generally connected to durable peace and human rights (Melander, 2005).

The concern of intra-state peace led to a remarkable enlargement of the peace research agenda. Entirely new phenomena came under scrutiny, such as violence and peace processes (Höglund, 2008), reconciliation (Brounéus, 2008), involvement of rebel groups and civil society (Nilsson, 2006) and the quality of government (Fjelde, 2009). Notions of ethnic security dilemmas (Melander, 1999) and the rationale behind rebel strategies (Hultman, 2008; Kalyvas, 2006; Lilja, 2010) seemed to rely on the Machiavellian assumptions for understanding intra-state politics. But the focus was on finding routes to peace, in a broad sense. All the studies were contributions to understanding the creation of a society that would be less conflict prone. For peace researchers there was a hope to prevent further traumas, for policy makers a concern to avoid further humanitarian tragedies. The many ways to peace that were embarked upon, however, suggested that there was not one overarching idea that has – as of yet – crystallized as the crucial one. Different approaches remain to deal with a multi-faceted complexity not previously faced by social and political sciences: which were the factors that made a society at the same time stable and dynamic?

The attacks on the United States on September 11 2001 came as a surprise given the strong emphasis on negotiations and preventive actions. It provided a new global trauma that affected the peace research agenda. It rapidly led to renewed military actions by the US and the US defense budget again began to rise. The US proclaimed war on terrorism and the invasion on Iraq in 2003 followed a different logic than the typical post-Cold War actions that world had witnessed hitherto. It was a return to some of the Machiavellian dictums. The new political consensus was a throwback to the assumption about the inevitability of violence. The maxim seemed now to be: 'it is better to use force first; strike hard early and you will win; remain firm and you will prevail', but the critique was there: using force invites more opposition, victory today is more difficult than ever. To remain on the same course makes you not only appear determined, but also stubborn without necessarily providing the conditions for success. Machiavellian thinking returned, but under new circumstances. Force was again seen as the final arbitrator, and there was no space for negotiation. The state had to be strong and forceful, using all necessary means, ranging from war to deceit.

Intellectually and politically this resulted in an analytical bifurcation. There were now two worlds. One dealt with internal armed conflicts as local issues, solved through negotiation and dialogue, involving as many actors as possible. This was a continuation of the approach developed during the first post-Cold War period. The other one dealt with conflicts defined as part of the campaign against terrorism, where none of these features mattered, only victory and security (in particular for the state hosting the conflict). Policy making in conflicts defined to be part of the struggle between the USA and al-Qaida (and copycats) was uncompromising, while international policy making in all other conflicts followed an approach of third-party negotiations, mediation and agreements. The bifurcation seemed to exist also in the academic communities. The terrorism researchers appeared as a distinct group with their own logics, methods and rules for providing evidence. Peace researchers' focus on finding constructive solutions was different, but seemed less relevant in facing terrorism. In fact, it was not.

It was left to well-trained researchers to determine what might be the real origins of terrorism. The questions were many: could the causes be found in a legacy of unsolved conflicts, flawed agreements, economically skewed development, repressive regimes, easy access to weapons and finance? These were factors that seemed to explain other internal wars. Or were there some other factors as well, such as the psychology of the perpetrators, fanaticism, ideological postures, sect-like networks, or rational calculations that were indifferent to human suffering? The effect of September 11 2001 on peace research was, perhaps, not as strong as might be expected. The underlying problems were already defined. But in the public discourse, it provided a return to Machiavellian assumptions.

Traumas, hopes and the future of peace research

Peace research has had its inspiration from two different sources. On the one hand, analyses of some of humankind's major disasters have prompted a reconsideration of some of the basic, traditional explanations. Conventional thinking has been challenged and new sets of research topics have appeared. On the other hand, futuristic and Utopian ideas – formed by thinkers, politicians, and researchers alike – have provided a pool of ideas for theoretical and empirical study. Increasingly, peace research is forming its own traditions and finding its own way forward. Theories, data and methods are being developed to increasingly sharpen the questions under investigation, the rules of providing evidence and the conclusions. The history of peace research suggests that the traumatic experiences of humankind have come first and formed the agenda. The unique feature of peace research is, however, the immediate search for alternatives, thus invoking Utopian ideas, making them researchable and possible as options for policy.

The traumas associated with the major wars and conflagrations of the 20th century have enlarged the scope of peace research by forcefully drawing attention to different types of conflicts. This attention has led to debate and a reconsideration of older propositions and assumptions of peace research. The widening scope means an increased awareness of complexity. A pertinent question is how wide peace research should become.

The hopes provided by the positive developments in the world have given inspiration to research on the conditions for peace, which have also developed into major and long-term research projects. Again, new traditions of scholarly inquiry are being created. In this case, the two strands might be suitable 'correctives' to one another: to make sure that scholarly standards are kept but also that a larger perspective is maintained.

During this first century of peace research, considerable developments have taken place. Peace research has demonstrated that peace is researchable. It requires new methods, new ways of collecting data and new ways of analyzing them. Peace research has been in the forefront of generating information on wars, peace efforts, preventive actions, sanctions and nonviolent measures. It has been the basis for moving research forward into the strengths and limits of the peace-building qualities of democracy, international integration and international organizations. Still, many issues have not been penetrated at all; some have only been approached lightly and research has concentrated only on certain fields. The need for peace research can no longer be questioned. One message has been clearly demonstrated. There were a number of researchable questions that were left untouched in universities and other research milieus throughout the world until the advent of the peace researcher. This has been true for each of the periods we have looked at, including the latest ones, where questions were raised on peace-building. Peace research has taken a place within higher education and frontline research. Modern universities now include a special department for peace and conflict research. This institutionalization of peace research has led not only to students with BAs and MAs leaving university with a solid training in the subjects of peace and conflict. The doctoral programs have resulted in the turning of more stones. Empirical research continues to challenge conventional wisdoms.

Summary

- Peace research has now existed for almost a century as a separate and identifiable academic activity.
- Peace research has been particularly open to the use of the most recent methodological developments.
- Peace research interacts with practical concerns for peace, which means it has expanded its range of topics, largely as an expression of concerns over large-scale traumatic events.
- The past century has been strongly marked by violent conflicts such as World War I and II, Hiroshima, the Cold War, the Vietnam War, and the challenges of the post-Cold War era, which means that peace research deals with the fundamental issues shaping the course of the planet.
- Peace research has been an arena where many policy issues have first found scholarly analysis, as is seen in concepts such as causes of war, conflict theory, confidence-building, conflict resolution, democratic peace, targeted sanctions, conflict prevention and peace-building.

Further reading

Bercovitch, J., Kremenyuk, V. and Zartman, I.W. (2009) *The SAGE Handbook on Conflict Resolution*, London: Sage.

Brown, M.E. *et al* (1998) *Theories of War and Peace*, Cambridge, Massachusetts: The MIT Press.

Crocker, C.A., Aall, P.R. and Hampson, F.O. (2007) *Leashing the Dogs of War: Conflict management in a divided world*, Washington, DC: USIP Press.

Diamond, L. (2001) *The Peace Book. One hundred and eight simple ways to create a more peaceful world*, Berkeley, CA: Connan.

Galtung, J. (1996) *Peace by Peaceful Means: Peace and conflict, development and civilization*, London: Sage.

Geller, D. and Singer, J.D. (1998) *Nations at War: A scientific study of international conflict*, Cambridge: Cambridge University Press.

The Global Directory of Peace Studies and Conflict Resolution Programs, 7th edn, 2007, online
    edition continuously updated.
Vasquez, J.A. (ed.) (2000) *What Do We Know about War?,* Lanham, MD: Rowman & Littlefield.

Notes

1. This is a revised and updated version of Wallensteen (1988).
2. See also *Journal of Peace Research* (1982) 19 (2), which is a special issue on Poland.

Part II
Evaluating Information

3 Peace Research and Source Criticism

Using historical methodology to improve information gathering and analysis

Tomislav Dulić

Introduction

The 19th century German historian and important co-founder of modern historical science Leopold Ranke once defined a historian as a person who 'merely wants to show how it really was' in history (Ranke and Wines, 1981). For the present-day reader, his words might sound ambitious, even presumptuous. As of late, the mere idea that there is an objective 'truth' to be discovered by scholars has been subjected to considerable challenge by a reaction to positivist views on historical events and processes. Although it is relevant to question the validity of 'reality' as an objective concept, this chapter is based on a set of premises that are opposed to overly relativistic approaches to hard facts. The first is that we can make truthful claims about events that have come to pass, which means that truths do exist and are more than mere reflections of our perceptions of reality; the second is that it is the historian's task to search for that type of truth; the third is that the sources we base our conclusions on are not guaranteed to be truthful, either because the agents could or would not tell the truth (Jarrik, 2005: 219). This is not to deny that we all live in a time and space that is influenced by specific cultural, social, political and other contexts. These will influence our *interpretation* of events or historical processes to varying degrees. However, to say that our interpretations are products of a *Zeitgeist* does not mean that truth is nowhere to be found or that we are inherently unable to understand or explain historical events or processes.

The great contribution of Ranke and other historians of his age was that they created a set of criteria for how sources should be handled and interpreted. Thus, they effectively established source criticism as a distinct methodological approach to the analysis of historical documents. During the latter part of the 20th century, however, historical scholarship saw a trend by which source criticism gradually appears to have lost some of its previous prominence in research, a process which one can attribute to the above-mentioned tendency to downplay objectivity and reality for the benefit of perceptions of history; if there is no truth in the objective sense of the word, then it may seem futile even to strive for objectivity in the analysis. This is a troublesome development, not least since the great leaps forward in information technology during the last couple of decades have produced previously unheard of opportunities to collect, streamline and analyze, but also manipulate, data. Hence, scholars are in dire need of more, not less, prowess in source criticism.

The purpose of this chapter is to introduce peace researchers to source criticism, a methodological tool designed to improve information gathering and analysis. The purpose of information gathering is to establish facts about specific historical events, but researchers also need to place the present in relation to the historical processes that have taken place in a given country or region. Source criticism provides criteria and guidelines for identifying and evaluating authenticity, uncertainty and bias in sources, thereby improving the ability to increase the accuracy of the analysis. The chapter therefore focuses on the theory and practice of source criticism, discussing how the specific problems with data processing that peace researchers face can be addressed by a systematic approach to historical method. The first section begins by clarifying the distinction between primary sources, secondary sources and artefacts. The subsequent sections concern external and internal evaluation of sources, biases and the relationship between various types of sources. The chapter finishes with a summary note and recommendations. Throughout the text, examples are given from how sources have been used in historical analyses, with a couple of more in-depth analyses of specific problems. Each section also contains some hands-on examples and points pertaining to how to conduct source critical analyses and the questions that need to be posed to the material. The final section summarizes the main points and provides a set of general recommendations.

Primary and secondary sources

In historical research, one usually distinguishes between *primary sources, secondary sources* and *artefacts* (see Table 3.1). The latter are basically non-written sources (such as mass graves, trenches, potholes or wrecks) that provide some information on events. However, historians have generally attributed less attention to artefacts than to archival documents such as minutes from meetings, private communications, classified documents and other written pieces of information (generally speaking, it is primarily the task of archaeologists and not historians to analyze artefacts through, for instance, excavations).

Archival documents, diaries, interviews and other frequently unpublished sources usually fall into the category of *primary sources* in historical research. *Secondary sources* are books, reports and other materials that are authored by scholars, journalists or other individuals who describe events that they themselves have not taken part in or witnessed. Hence, secondary sources are generally considered less useful than primary documents. At the same time, however, one has to remember that the borderline between primary and secondary sources is fluid and depends on the question that one poses to the material. While most historians treat history books as secondary sources, for historians that specialize in historiography – in other words the study of the writing of history – books and narratives are considered primary sources. The reason is that those interested in historiography try to capture societal change by studying how historians have *perceived* a particular subject over time and are less concerned about establishing *what actually happened.*

This chapter deals mainly with printed sources; because they are widely used in peace research and also because of space constraints. Nevertheless, one should bear in mind that current technological developments have made it much easier to analyze non-printed materials. This trend is probably going to continue for the foreseeable future, for instance through the massive influx of audiovisual material on the internet and a concurrent improvement in computer software for qualitative analysis of textual and other information. Moreover, the fact that anyone can publish information on the internet is a double-edged sword, since it can be almost impossible at times to ascertain

Table 3.1: Categories of sources and types of source material

Categories of sources	Types of material
Primary sources	Archival documents; minutes from discussions and judicial proceedings; agreements/statutes; statistics; interviews
Secondary sources	Books; reports; dissertations; newspaper articles; television/radio news; documentaries
Artefacts	Ruins; mass graves; trenches; wrecks; mine fields; drawings; tools; weapons, etc

Note: The delineation between the categories is fluid and largely depends on one's approach to the material. Moreover, there is also a difference in categorizations in different countries and scholarly traditions. This table should therefore only be understood as a general suggestion on how to differentiate between sources.

whether an internet document in fact is authentic or not. It is therefore of paramount importance to handle all sources, whether they are primary documents from archives or reports by NGOs, with the highest degree of care possible.

Concurrently with this trend, we also see that the amount of printed sources that are kept on paper may be diminishing. The fact that people write emails rather than letters presents a challenge to historians, since over time it may result in the number of available letters, diaries and similar documents diminishing in archives. Unless general agreement is reached on how to collect, preserve and validate official records that exist in electronic form, the time may come when it will be much more difficult to reconstruct decision-making processes. Another problem in this context is that globalization has led to an increasing number of decisions being made on supra-national levels such as various organizations like the UN and EU. Since most regulations pertaining to access to archival records only concern the national level, an increasing amount of important historical records may become more difficult to access in the future.[1]

Agency

Understanding the distinction between primary and secondary sources is important for peace researchers, since their material frequently does not fulfill the *proximity criterion.* By this is meant that the source is close in time and space to the depicted event, in other words that the person describing what happened had direct information as a witness or by being involved in the decision-making process. Most news reports, for instance, are filtered through the eyes of journalists, who apart from having their own 'angle' on events often relate to information that they received from others. As an example, one might have a situation where a bomb explodes in Baghdad at the time of a high-profile official visit from the UN. A journalist rushes to the scene, views the debris and corpses and reports that the attack was perpetrated by an organization with close links to al-Qaida in order to disrupt the UN visit. In fact, most of what the journalist said is speculation; he/she saw the effects of the bomb, but he/she cannot know for certain who was responsible; neither can he/she claim that the agent behind this particular act planted the bomb with the specific aim of disrupting a political visit. For all we know, the perpetrator may not even know that the visit was underway.

These and similar problems with news reports are difficult to handle, since it is sometimes impossible to know from a particular news report what is established fact and what is speculation. Frequently, journalists try to be careful by adding modifiers into the text, such as 'allegedly' or 'purportedly'. The problem is that they may be overlooked or be interpreted as meaning 'probably'. Moreover, such caveats are often difficult to reconcile with quantifications, particularly insofar as one needs to code the data according to binary criteria such as 'yes' or 'no'. Hence, it is even more important to devise strict rules about how to code pieces of information that display ambivalence. A peace researcher doing event coding, for instance, can establish the fact that people were killed, but he/she will have much more of a problem when trying to code who did what and for what purpose.

This aspect brings us to the issue of *agency*. By *agency* is meant the scope within which an actor can think and act, where structural factors such as, for instance, culture and ideology set up the outer limitations of action, by influencing the actor's perception of reality. Somewhat differently put, it is the actor and his/her associates that nurture ideas and motivations for action and it is by having access to information about such deliberations and ideas that one can give a true picture of *why* somebody made a specific decision. Journalists can report *that* something happened, but they are frequently not in a position to answer the question *why* as they are not privy to the internal communication and deliberations of the belligerent parties. Most minutes from meetings in general staffs or among political elites, particularly in war situations, are regarded as state secrets for decades, which means that they are not accessible until long after the events transpired (usually 30 to 50 years, sometimes more depending on the regulations of specific countries). Hence, journalists are forced to conduct their analysis on the basis of incomplete data and the external manifestations of, for instance, violence.

External evaluation

The above-mentioned note about the relationship between actor and action points to the importance of proper analysis of sources. The first thing the historian has to do when encountering a new source is to *identify* and *classify* it by ascertaining when it was made, where it came from, who wrote it, where it was kept, how it came about and with what purpose. This part of the source analysis is frequently referred to as the *external evaluation* of the sources, and basically aims at establishing the *provenance* (the origin) of the source and its intended audience.

As previously mentioned, a source that is written the same day or in a relative sense very close in time to the event is considered more reliable than a source that is not. However, this can sometimes be misleading, particularly insofar as the information is derived from a secondary source or a primary source that tries to make an assessment on issues that it cannot possibly have information on. Aggregated death tolls during conflicts are such pieces of information, where post-conflict demographic or other calculations frequently arrive at different results than aggregated 'guesstimates' made at the time of conflict.

Students who conduct research and data gathering can use a hands-on approach to the external evaluation when approaching their sources. One way of doing so is by asking specific questions such as:

- What type of source is it (book, newspaper article, report)?
- Who is the intended audience?
- Who authored the document?
- Is the author a third party or a belligerent in a conflict situation?

- When was the document produced?
- Does the source contain a signature, stamp or other piece of information that can serve to validate it?
- Is the source an original or a copy?
- Is the source in its original language or has it been translated?

One should of course remember that the external evaluation of the source is usually not a very complicated issue, because sources are only rarely to be considered outright forgeries. On occasion, however, one can arrive at rather intricate issues pertaining to the claim that a particular actor places in respect to the sources. Usually, one tries to solve similar problems by 'triangulation', in other words by collecting information from three independent sources. Frequently, however, this is not possible since all media outlets refer to the same source. In such situations it is advisable simply to explain the problems and give one's own interpretation of the facts.

An interesting example of the problems that can arise due to insufficient external evaluation of sources relates to the Kosovo War of 1999. Just like the war in Iraq, the bombing campaign against the Federal Republic of Yugoslavia that began in March 1999 lacked a mandate from the UN Security Council. This presented a particularly sensitive problem for Berlin, since the Kosovo War was the first time since World War II that Germany went into offensive military action outside its own borders. The situation became even more dramatic in late March, when tens of thousands of Albanians started amassing in Macedonia and Albania and critics began arguing that the bombing campaign provoked rather than prevented violent expulsions of civilians and refugee flows.

At the height of the critique in early April, world media reported that German Minister of Defence Rudolph Scharping and Foreign Minister Joschka Fischer had evidence of a Serbian plan dubbed 'Operation Horseshoe', which aimed at the expulsion of the Albanian population from Kosovo. Scharping claimed that the plan 'was organised in the end of November/beginning December last year, and it was implemented since January of this year' (BBC, 1999). The dating was of crucial importance for Scharping, since the claim that the expulsion would have happened irrespective of the bombing campaign helped nullify internal German criticism of the war.

Although Scharping or Fischer did not openly claim to be in possession of a document from the Serbian military, *Le Monde* immediately followed through by writing that Joschka Fischer had received from the authorities of a non-specified neighboring country of Serbia a copy of a plan from the government in Belgrade, detailing the policy of ethnic cleansing implemented in Kosovo (*Le Monde,* 1999). On the following day, *The Times* referred to *Le Monde* and talked about a 'chilling document' which was 'significant, too, because of the written evidence it would provide against the Yugoslav leader should he be brought before an international war crimes tribunal'. The article further argued that 'the German Government has confirmed that it is studying the document, but has yet to decide whether to make it public' (*The Times,* 1999).

However, the German government never produced a Serbian document and Scharping soon found himself accused of misleading the German public. During a parliamentary inquiry in April 2000, Scharping reiterated that the 'Horseshoe Plan' indeed existed. When pressed on the point of the provenance of the information, Scharping answered: 'Do you expect that someone could photocopy a military plan in the general staff in Belgrade?' (Das Parlament, 2000). This statement essentially confirmed German Brigadier-General Heinz Loquai's assertions in a book, where he argued that the whole affair was a sham designed by people from within the German military establishment. He also claimed that there were no Serbian documents while those that appeared were German translations of reports from the Bulgarian or Austrian intelligence services (Loquai, 2000: 142–3). This was finally corroborated by Joschka Fischer in 2007, when he explained that he received the information from Bulgarian Foreign Minister Nadezhda Mihailova (Политика, 2007).

The debate surrounding Operation Horseshoe has continued ever since the war and this is not the place to provide a final settlement to that dispute.[2] Instead, the aim is to see whether the documents that were published by the German MoD, and the subsequent claims by world media, could have passed a critical scrutiny. Two key issues stand out as particularly important in that context. One is to test whether there is support for Scharping's claim that the expulsions of civilians were planned and initiated months and weeks before the bombings and the other the claim and/or insinuations that the information was based on Serbian military documents. By returning to the guidelines on external evaluation, we may conclude that the document presented by the German MoD contained no signatures, stamps or other pieces of information that could ascertain its origin one way or another, and we know that it was not written by the Serbian military establishment (nor for that matter do we know whether it was a copy). The fact that the document had a horseshoe drawn on top of it with the opening towards Albania, while being written in the Latin alphabet without diacritics adds to the problem with its provenance. Moreover, the actual content confirms Loquai's argument and casts serious doubt on the credibility of the claims in media, since the authors do not disclose any sources and confirm that 'the elements of this plan, … are still not known in their details' (Bundeswehr, 1999). In conclusion, the researcher would find that some plan might well have existed, but that the only information about the specificities of the 'Horseshoe Plan' comes from one belligerent party in a conflict. Consequently, there is little support for Scharping's claim that the expulsions of civilians would have happened irrespectively of the war (which, as the ICTY concluded, in no way reduces the culpability of those perpetrating crimes *after* the initiation of the bombing campaign).

Internal evaluation

The previous discussion touched upon the internal evaluation of documents, which generally speaking is a more difficult process than the external evaluation. The reason for this is that the internal evaluation involves analyzing the *content* of the document itself, its wording and the reliability of the information, as well as trying to identify biases. In order to conduct such analyses the researcher frequently has to read up on a region's history, and some of the information (such as, for instance, commonly used linguistic codes and expressions) cannot be acquired without language skills. Additionally, it often becomes necessary to compare the facts presented in the source to descriptions from other sources, which is a painstaking and time-consuming task particularly insofar one is involved in archival research.

One should also remember that the internal evaluation is closely related to the external one, since it is the provenance of the source that helps the researcher identify the questions that he/she needs to pose to the content of the document. One of the most important tasks in this process – at least insofar political history is concerned – is to identify whether the fact that the source was intended for a particular audience or aimed at achieving a specific effect may have influenced its content, presentation and wording. Military and other intelligence services, for instance, usually wish to have as accurate information as possible on a particular event, but the information that is gathered can in another situation be slanted in a way to serve political purposes. The by now classical example is of course US Foreign Minister Colin Powell's claim regarding the existence of facilities for the production of weapons of mass destruction in Iraq (AFP, 2003). Although analyses made by the UN inspectors Hans Blix and Muhammad Baradei produced very little hard evidence that there were any such facilities in the country, the US administration used the little data that was provided by the CIA in a way as to motivate an attack on Iraq. Whether or not this was the result of a misunderstanding or a conscious manipulation of world opinion on the part of the Bush administration remains a debated issue to this day.

Frequently, the researcher does not have to assess whether or not something is true. Instead, as mentioned previously, he/she has to ask whether and to what extent a source actually has the capacity to say something about an event or influence a process. This is an aspect related to the proximity criterion that concerns the issue of *agency*. By this is meant that the usefulness of a source increases insofar it originates with a person that is privy to the decision-making process and has the capacity to influence the developments through his/her own actions. Such aspects are not least important for researchers involved in the analysis of diplomacy and high-level political decision-making, which is perhaps best illustrated by the seemingly endless discussions among historians pertaining to the outbreak of World War I and Germany's 'war guilt'. If one, for instance, is studying German Chancellor Theobald Bethmann Hollweg's decision-making during the July Crisis, one has to have access to his own communication or the communication of his close associates when assessing motives and his perception of threat. Documents from the British Foreign Office will not do by themselves and neither will the official statements that were made with the intention of influencing public opinion or Germany's adversaries. On the other hand, British documents do provide important additional information, not least about how the British actors *perceived* that the German actors reasoned (which, needless to say, is an important piece of the overall puzzle).

To conduct a proper internal evaluation of documents one of course needs to have considerable background information about a particular conflict region and it is therefore difficult to provide an exhaustive list of questions that need to be addressed. Among the general, however, one may consider the following:

- Did the person who wrote the source witness the event him or herself, or did he/she relate to information from a third party?
- Does the source contain its original wording or has it been changed by a third party (for instance, a news agency in the case of news reports)?
- If the text has been translated, are there any words that can have a different meaning in the original language than in the translation?
- Did the author represent a particular agency, organization or institution?
- Did the author have a particular agenda when making the statement, and how may it have affected the wording and presentation of the data?
- How do the facts that are presented in the document relate to other pieces of information from other sources? Can the claims be corroborated or refuted?

Bias

Another important task of the internal evaluation is to assess bias in the information, which is particularly important to keep in mind when one is using secondary sources or news reports. This is a tricky task though, since biases can result either from manipulations with the sources, because of the journalist's lack of knowledge about a particular event, or because the sources themselves are biased but the journalist or other reporter does not know this. There is also the problem that researchers do not have enough language skills and knowledge about historical context to be able to assess possible sources of bias.

Rudolph Rummel's large study on 'democide' serves as an interesting example of how such inadequacies may affect large-N datasets in a negative way. In *Death by Government*, Rummel used data on death tolls from secondary sources to test a set of hypothesis relating to the 'liberal peace' model. Among the most important were that democracies are less prone to commit mass atrocities and genocide than non-democratic states. The Yugoslav communist regime of Josip Broz 'Tito' was one the 218 case studies. Rummel argued that Tito's regime caused the death of 600,000–2,000,000 Yugoslavs during the period 1944–47. Thus, Tito belonged to the 'megamurderers' of the 20th century, since the death toll attributed to his regime reached a mid-estimate of 1.072 million people (Rummel, 1997: 339).

In 2004, the present author published a detailed analysis of Rummel's dataset pertaining to Yugoslavia. The analysis showed that there were rather serious problems with the raw data that Rummel had used. The vast majority of those who wrote on the massacres perpetrated by Tito's forces at the end of the World War II, for instance, based their accounts on hearsay and pure speculation. In addition, some of the sources used by Rummel had the character of pure propaganda, some originating with highly biased political groups. In addition, a demographic analysis showed that the population deficit for Yugoslavia in 1948 reached 1.8, while those of Rummel's deaths that were attributable to the same period of time (1941–48) reached 2.6 million.[3] Through the addition of demographic data, it was thus shown that Rummel grossly overestimated Tito's Yugoslav death toll. This was due to methodological deficiencies on the part of the author, most importantly poor evaluation of the secondary sources. As a result of this and other methodological problems, Rummel ended up with a skewed dataset that favoured high death toll estimates for Tito's Yugoslavia (for our debate, see Dulić, 2004a, 2004b; Rummel, 2004).

It was not the point of the present author's critique to claim that Rummel is necessarily wrong in the hypothesis of 'democratic peace', but to show that there is no foundation for his claim in respect of Tito's death toll on the basis of the sources he used (hence, Tito in all likelihood did not belong to the 'megamurderers' of the 20th century). Moreover, the analysis touched upon yet another issue concerning the difference between the source and the data itself. What Rummel did was to treat all authors as equally culpable in terms of possible bias, merely assuming that high death toll estimates would be taken out by low ones (an assumption that overlooks the fact that low estimates are truncated at zero). In fact, however, one can run across data that is reliable, even if the source itself is biased. It is therefore not appropriate to say that a piece of information is unreliable merely because it comes from a source we otherwise 'know' is biased, or because 10 other sources say it is incorrect. Conversely, one cannot simply assume that the data is reliable because we 'know' that the organization providing it is benevolent (which frequently happens when representatives of western governments, the EU or the UN make various claims). Instead, one has to assess the value of the information on the basis of its own merits and compare the information with other sources. One way of doing so is through triangulation. As indicated above, however, this might become a serious problem in those cases where all news reports relate to information that is gathered from the same, often undisclosed source. In such situations one may be forced to make one's own assessments or conduct more detailed and specialized enquiries into specific subtopics. One should also not be afraid to contact 'area specialists' for input.

Finally, one has to remember that sources may report on a *perception* of events without seeking to distort the facts, but the information nevertheless is biased. This risk is frequent in the case of interviews, where informants who sometimes have suffered traumas and other severe stress may generalize on the basis of their own experiences, or try to place their own suffering in a narration that seeks to create a rational explanation for, for instance, violence. As a researcher, one therefore needs to look into the local event specifically, while constantly placing the violence in the perspective of events on the macro level. To avoid these and similar problems, one needs to address the following issues:

- Only use aggregated data that has been properly calculated by the source and avoid information that is based on unsubstantiated claims.
- Always try to disaggregate the data into particular events and sub-phases.
- Beware of the provenance of the source when assessing the data.
- Try to learn as much as you can about the actors, since such information is crucial for you to be able to assess whether the source can be considered credible.
- Do not automatically discard the sources even if they are biased, since the information can nevertheless be sound. Check the reliability of the data by 'triangulation' if possible.

Legal documents

Various types of legal documents from court proceedings are another type of source that are frequently difficult to handle. While legal documents are an invaluable source for any analysis of local violence and other events, one has to remember that judicial proceedings are a sort of 'boxing game' between the prosecution and defence. Indictments, for instance, are produced by the prosecutor, who alleges something about the accused and therefore are *not* to be considered objective assessments of what actually happened (neither could it be so, since the prosecutor is a party in the debate that wishes to prove the culpability of the accused). Conversely, the defence frequently focuses on a refutation of details, by which the aim is to undermine the general argument of the prosecution. One way of doing so is by casting doubt on the correctness of local death tolls, or by arguing that the prosecution has not proved beyond reasonable doubt that a general was privy to information about an event that transpired locally. In such situations, one must be careful to understand the goal of the defence and not over-interpret the argument as meaning that a local massacre did not happen.

The case of Tihomir Blaškić, a general in the Bosnian Croat armed forces (Croatian Defence Council, HVO) during the war of the 1990s serves as an interesting illustration of the problems that may arise when one uses legal and newspaper material when assessing criminal responsibility. In 2000, the International Criminal Tribunal for former Yugoslavia sentenced Blaškić to 45 years in prison for crimes perpetrated against the Bosniak population in central Bosnia. The indictment contained many charges, but the most severe ones concerned the village of Ahmići, where a group of Croatian paramilitaries committed a massacre of 117 Bosniaks. The prosecution argued that Blaškić was guilty of war crimes in this locality, since the forces perpetrating the crime were under his command. The defence, on the other hand, put forward the claim that there in fact was a parallel line of command surpassing Blaškić and that he therefore did not have command responsibility (ICTY 2000).

Following the death of Croatian president Franjo Tudjman, however, information was leaked (probably from within the Croatian security services), which suggested that Blaškić in fact was right: there indeed appeared to have existed a parallel line of command that went not from the perpetrators to the HVO, but to the political leadership of the self-proclaimed Bosnian Croat statelet of Herceg-Bosna. Consequently, it appeared that Blaškić might have been used as a scapegoat to avoid allegations being levelled against the political leadership of Herceg-Bosna and beyond that to Tudjman himself. In 2003, the appeals chamber of the ICTY overturned the previous ruling in respect to Ahmići and lowered Blaškić's sentence to nine years (ICTY, 2004).

The Blaškić case serves as an interesting illustration of the difficulties facing peace researchers who use legal documentation. Should one use the indictment as a source at all, considering its function during court proceedings? How does one assess the validity of the arguments put forward during the court proceedings, considering that the prosecution and defence have the task of arguing from a position of proving their point rather than exploring the matter without any preconceived notions? Should one at all rely on the minutes from proceedings, or make an analysis of one's own on the basis of the evidence material itself? The best way in which to handle legal documents is to be aware of these problems, the salience of which depends on the level and unit of analysis. If one wishes to establish that people were killed at a specific time in a specific locality, then legal documents provide much more reliable detail than is the case with media reports. If one is interested in the organization of violence locally, the issue becomes much more complicated, particularly as one moves up the chain of command. The fact that a massacre happened in Ahmići is indisputable, but it might be relevant to know exactly who perpetrated the crimes and one might therefore find it prudent at least to await the ruling before using the data.

Conversely, one can also decide to make a different interpretation than a court, since a researcher only needs to make a statement plausible, while a court has to prove a fact or the guilt of a person beyond reasonable doubt. When making a different interpretation from a court, however, it is essential to explain the reasons for one's opinion and how and why it differs from the court's decision. These differences between law and research are important, since a court's position on guilt may have a profound effect on human lives, while a researcher's analysis has a different aim.

Recommendations

The foregoing discussion has shed some light on source criticism as method in historical research, but it should in no way be seen as an exhaustive account of the details. As any scientific method, source criticism entails not only theoretical analysis but must be accompanied by hands-on experience through trial and error. If properly trained, historians gain a 'gut feeling' almost by looking at a source and automatically pose the critical questions to it. If and when one has become well acquainted with source criticism and views it as a crucial aspect of any scholarly endeavour, one internalizes it to a point of not thinking about it when applying it.

A proper understanding of source criticism as a method seems to be of particular importance for peace researchers dealing with conflict data coding or similar scientific activities. More so, since the peace researcher and his/her analysis remains highly susceptible to external influences and a dearth of useful data (the 'garbage in, garbage out' point), while not having the 'protection' of historical distance from the problem at hand. In such situations, the researcher might be tempted to overstretch the analysis and make inferences that, for instance, muddle the issues of agency and temporal or geographic proximity to action.

To avoid these pitfalls, the peace researcher needs to use stringent criteria when collecting the data, regardless of whether one is involved in event coding for the purpose of large-N studies, or doing fieldwork in a conflict zone. Source criticism comes in as a handy tool in this process, since it can help improve the quality of analysis.

As was shown, there are certain categories of sources, each of which can tell us something about the subject matter. These are generally divided into the three categories: *primary sources, secondary sources* and *artefacts*. While the two first categories are distinguishable from the last one because they are printed sources or contain words in some form or another, they are mutually distinguishable on account of the fact that primary sources are closer in time and space to the described events.

To ensure that the quality of analysis can be maintained on a high level, peace researchers may adhere to a set of principles relating to source criticism. These include taking due account of issues such as the evaluation – both internal and external – of sources, which is done in a systematic and coherent way. Ultimately, source criticism is not only about striving to unearth the 'truth' in the sense of establishing exactly what happened in a given situation. Even more important, it is about increasing the reliability of data and thus also of research. In that sense, peace researchers, historians and other scholars have much in common and can learn from each other.

Summary

- Always keep a critical distance from any piece of information that is acquired, including information that comes from democratic states with free media. This is particularly true if they come from individuals that in one sense or the other are belligerents in a conflict.
- Be particularly systematic in the external assessment of sources and always strive to ascertain where a source comes from, who wrote it, which audience it is intended for and whether or not the person writing the source has access to information that makes it possible for him or her to claim facts.
- Strive to learn as much as possible about the historical, cultural and political context in which a source came about. This is important because contexts will help explain not only the role and meaning of linguistic codes, but also how such statements should be interpreted in a given situation. If you do not have enough information about a region or event, do not hesitate to contact historians, anthropologists or other 'area experts' for their input.

- Always make a careful analysis of the words contained in a source, particularly if you are working with translations.
- Try to avoid bias by checking the data. One way to do this is through 'triangulation'; another is by removing one source from the data and seeing whether that will affect the overall results.
- Try to disaggregate statistical information as frequently as possible, as aggregated data is often a source of error.
- Finally, always be open about problems with the dataset if you encounter them, since that will help others improve upon the information.

Further reading

Howell, M.C. and Prevenier, W. (2001) *From Reliable Sources: An introduction to historical methods*, Ithaca, NY: Cornell University Press.

McCulloch, G. (2004) *Documentary Research in Education, History and the Social Sciences*, London: RoutledgeFalmer.

Tosh, J. (1984) *The Pursuit of History: Aims, methods, and new directions in the study of modern history*, 3rd edn, London: Longman.

Tosh, J. (2008) *Why History Matters*, Basingstoke, Hampshire: Palgrave Macmillan.

Williams, R.C. (2007) *The Historian's Toolbox: A student's guide to the theory and craft of history*, Armonk, NY: M.E. Sharpe.

Notes

1. Another problem in this context can be found in the different national regulations. Since 1766, Sweden has had a very liberal law concerning public access to official records. At the time of Sweden's entry into the EU in 1994, several countries within the union that apply much more strict rules were concerned that journalists and others would gain access to Swedish documents that could give information on the decision-making processes in their respective countries. To date, however, Sweden has been able to retain its liberal constitutional law in this respect.
2. During the court proceedings against Milošević and the former president of Serbia Milan Milutinović, a former employee of the Serbian intelligence, Ratomir Tanić (who in the autumn of 1999 left Yugoslavia after being interrogated and accused of spying for the British intelligence service), claimed that the term 'Operation Horseshoe' had been a colloquial term for an entirely different military contingency plan in socialist Yugoslavia concerning a NATO invasion from southeastern Europe. It is rather unclear from his statement how that plan – if it existed at all – related to the war of the 1990s, but he claimed to have received this piece of information from General Momčilo Perišić (the commander of the Third Corps of the Yugoslav Army who today stands trial in the Hague for war crimes perpetrated during the wars in Croatia and Bosnia and Herzegovina). The value of Tanić's statement is difficult to assess, considering that his words could not be corroborated by the Hague (ICTY, IT-2005-87, T. 20061115: 6642–43; T. 20061117: 6807) and no documents were provided in support of it. Conversely, several other expert witnesses could not confirm that the patterns of violence coincided with the admittedly sketchy evidence presented by the German Ministry of Defence.
3. The population deficit is calculated by the deduction of the estimated population for 1941 from the population figure established at the census in 1948. To establish the death toll one would need to deduct refugees that left the country. According to the most reliable research in former Yugoslavia, the death toll reached 1–1.2 million people.

4 Gathering Conflict Information Using News Resources

Magnus Öberg and Margareta Sollenberg[1]

Introduction

Every minute of every day, hundreds if not thousands of journalists around the world are working to collect and disseminate information on matters related to armed conflicts. Journalists provide 'a first rough draft of history that will never really be completed about a world we can never really understand'.[2]

An accurate description of what transpired in a conflict is fundamental to any type of conflict analysis. Therefore news reporting is an indispensible resource for peace research. News reports provide detailed accounts of what happened, who did what to whom, when and where in conflicts around the world. For current or recent conflicts (post-1989) news resources provide unrivalled coverage and amounts of information. News resources are still very useful in earlier periods, but the amounts of information and the scope of coverage declines, and the need for complementary sources of information increases the further back in time we go. Complementary sources include biographies, historical case studies, war diaries, archives, NGO reports and so on. These alternative sources of information are always important complements to news reports because they often contain types of information that are less well covered in news reports.

In this chapter we elaborate and analyze the main advantages and problems with using news resources to gather information about armed conflicts. We begin with the news industry, very briefly describing how it is organized today – functionally and geographically. We then discuss what types of information are found in different types of news resources, and what types of information are typically either not found there or better covered elsewhere. In the subsequent sections we analyze problems inherent in news reporting on armed conflict in general and how it affects different types of news resources, and news resources with varying geographical coverage and audiences. We provide several illustrations of how different factors affect how events are reported. We also discuss how coverage varies across countries and over time and what this implies for data gathering over time and across cases.

Throughout the chapter we suggest strategies for minimizing or overcoming problems inherent in news reporting on armed conflict. Having a good understanding of how news is made on the ground and then filtered through the chain leading from the reporter to the news consumer will help the data gatherer avoid or ameliorate many problems and pitfalls. There are also a number of recurring problems in news reporting that are useful to be aware of when gathering conflict information. For example, different labels are often attached to the same events or facts in different conflicts or in the same conflict in different news resources and generalizations made in news reports are often unsubstantiated. We also use examples to illustrate how source criticism can help identify problems with bias or reliability of the facts reported. Finally, we provide some practical guidelines on how to avoid common pitfalls when searching for information in international news databases and on the web.

The news industry

For the purposes of this chapter the news industry can be divided into two important sections: *news agencies* and *news organizations*.[3] News agencies, often referred to as news wire services, are producers of news reports. The main role of news organizations is to disseminate news to the public typically in broadcast or print media. Simplified, news wire services can be thought of as the news suppliers or 'wholesalers' and the news organizations as news 'retailers'.

News agencies, or news wire services, provide news reports on particular events on the ground. They are the ones recording events providing a first account of what transpired in a particular place. Reporters working for such agencies may at times be primary sources actually witnessing a conflict event, but mostly they are secondary sources reiterating what they learn from the parties to the conflict or witnesses to the event. The largest news agencies today are Reuters, the Associated Press (AP) and Agence France-Presse (AFP), and in addition to these there are numerous news wire services all across the world. In the case of Reuters, by far the largest current news agency, some 2,500 field staff operate in about 150 countries. Reuters, as many other news agencies, also relies to a great extent on so-called 'stringers' or freelance journalists that sell individual reports to the agency. News wire services generally operate without restrictions in terms of how many reports are produced per day. One consequence of this is that vast numbers of reports are produced each day on all kinds of topics from all across the world. To get an overview of the most important events, selections must be made and this is where the news organizations come in.

The news reports generated by news agencies such as Reuters, AP, AFP and others are bought by national news agencies or directly by news organizations. The national news agencies select, compile, edit and translate news from foreign news agencies and then sell the stories to news organizations in their country. They also gather national news that they sell to news organizations and to foreign news agencies. News organizations base most – or all – of their foreign news on news agency reports, selecting news items that they consider newsworthy (concerning newsworthiness, see further below). The reports bought from news agencies are then edited and some form of analysis, commentary or opinion is often added before they are published (print or broadcast) to the general public. News organizations may also have their own foreign correspondents that produce original news reports. A few of the largest news organizations like the British Broadcasting Corporation (BBC) and Cable News Network (CNN) produce significant amounts of foreign news.

Students or researchers typically have access to numerous news organizations – both broadcast and print media – at home, on the internet, and in libraries. University libraries also often provide access to news wire services through information databases like Factiva (www.factiva.com) or LexisNexis (www.lexisnexis.com). When collecting information about what transpired in a particular conflict, news agencies or news organizations can be consulted. It is important to appreciate the difference between them in order to understand what kind of news they provide and the process through which the news item came about.

The foreign news in newspapers and news broadcasts are generally at least one step farther removed from the actual event. Compared to the original news wire report they have gone through an additional filter and have often been subjected to substantial editing and language changes. News organizations often also add analysis and commentary of their own. In order to avoid distortions and biases it is important to stay as close to the original source as possible. This speaks clearly in favor of using international news agencies as well as national news agencies and news organizations in or close to the conflict country. The large international news agencies often have elaborate policies to maintain objectivity and neutrality in reporting. News organizations and national news agencies often proclaim similar goals but in comparison to the international news agencies, they tend to be less objective and neutral both in what they select to report and in how they report it.[4] The large international news agencies cater to a worldwide audience of news professionals so striving for neutrality and objectivity in reporting makes good business sense. That does not mean that they report on everything or that reporting is never biased or false, but it does mean that when the international news agencies report on events, there is generally no conscious bias. Language is more neutral, information is provided on the identity of the primary sources from which they gathered the information, and some indication of the level of certainty of the obtained information is generally also provided. This greatly facilitates source criticism (see Chapter 3) and thus proper assessment of the information. The disadvantage of using news agencies is the sheer number of reports produced. Using news agencies requires from the user an ability to sift through enormous volumes of news reports in order to locate what he or she is after. We will discuss advice on how best to do this below.

Most large national news organizations have their own foreign correspondents and they produce some original material of their own. But since maintaining a network of foreign correspondents or war correspondents is expensive, they often have one correspondent covering several countries or whole regions of the world. By necessity then, much of what they do is recycling news that they have picked up from news agencies and local or national news organizations. For example, it is not uncommon to see or hear the TV or radio network correspondent report on events in one country sitting in the capital of another country in the same region. Only a few news organizations have sufficiently large networks of foreign correspondents to actually cover major events in a large number of countries around the world with reporters on the ground on a regular basis. BBC, CNN and Al Jazeera are among the news organizations that fall into this category, but neither come close to matching the largest international news agencies.

The news landscape

In this section, we discuss – in very general terms – the strengths and weaknesses of various news resources depending on their location and coverage. Having this overall picture of the news landscape is helpful in searching for and locating information on particular conflicts, regions, or conflict-related phenomena. These resources complement each other and each has its strengths and weaknesses.

News organizations and national news agencies based in the conflict country often have the most detailed and in-depth coverage of the conflict. These local news sources tend to have a national focus in their reporting and cater primarily to a national audience. They often have unrivalled background knowledge and access to various original sources in a given country. However, national news agencies are typically state-owned and news organizations in the conflict country are often also either state-owned or associated with a party to the conflict. This means that news resources based in the conflict country are often biased. But, it should not be taken for granted that a news resource is biased just because it is based in the conflict country, and even if it is, it may be useful nonetheless. As always, the researcher should be aware of the risk and use source criticism to evaluate the potential bias. Another limitation of local news sources is that freedom of the press may be more restricted than for international news media.

Furthermore, if comparisons are made between different conflicts for which different local news sources are used, the comparability between cases is compromised by the fact that local news sources, including national news agencies, may operate in different ways in different countries and thus not cover the same types of events the same way. For some countries, especially those where freedom of the press is limited or non-existent and news resources are state controlled (for instance Iran, China and Eritrea), there is very little independent reporting by local news sources, in some cases none at all.

Finally, local news sources are not always available to an outsider, either because of language barriers or because they are not distributed internationally. The primary problem is usually language barriers. News organizations and news agencies in most countries maintain web pages in the local language and the large news databases Factiva and LexisNexis contain news items from news organizations and news agencies around the world. If one does not have access to Factiva or LexisNexis, identifying and finding in-country and regional news resources can be difficult. However, several helpful websites offer country-by-country lists of news resources around the world, including links to newspapers, television networks, news agencies and radio stations.[5] The BBC Monitoring service, moreover, publishes transcripts of local radio and TV broadcasts, as well as press, internet and news agency sources from around the world in over 100 languages, all translated into English. BBC Monitoring is very useful, especially when language is a problem. It is included in Factiva and LexisNexis, but is also available as a separate news database (www.monitor.bbc.co.uk).

Outside the conflict country, news organizations and news agencies in neighboring countries often have relatively extensive and detailed coverage. These news sources are particularly valuable when searching for information on conflicts in countries with little or no press freedom or on conflicts in countries with little or no local news sources. For example, Al Jazeera (based in Qatar) is a useful source for many countries in the Middle East and Central Asia, and the *Bangkok Post* can be a source for information on conflicts in Myanmar.

Regional powers often have news agencies with a regional coverage (for example the Xinhua News Agency in China). These news agencies sometimes provide in-depth coverage and often provide information on regional implications of the conflict. However, the country in which the news agency is based may have stakes in a particular conflict and may thus be biased toward one of the warring sides. Moreover, regionally-focused news agencies may not have the same longevity as some of the largest international news agencies, limiting the time period for which reporting is available.

Moving further away from the conflict country, most out-of-region news organizations have very little coverage and most of it comes from the large international news agencies. There are a few news organizations that have substantial international coverage of their own and also serve an international audience. The BBC stands out among these news organizations, operating both as a significant international news agency and a news organization with a global audience, broadcasting in over 30 languages to a weekly audience of nearly 200 million people.

As discussed in the previous section, the largest international news agencies (Reuters, AP and AFP) have several advantages not least in regard to their unrivalled breadth of coverage. It should be noted that international news agencies are especially useful when the aim is to compare different conflicts – or conflicts over time – since the same type of information is available across various regions of the world and over time. What is gained in terms of coverage, however, may be lost in the amount of detail and in-depth knowledge provided for single conflicts. In addition, although objectivity is often strived for in these sources, there are still processes at work that may produce bias in the news reporting. All major international news agencies are Western (French, British and American) and this is mirrored at least to some extent in the reports.

Finally, there are specialized news organizations that provide useful complements to the news resources discussed above. There are security- and intelligence-oriented periodicals that provide conflict information on aspects rarely covered elsewhere (for example *Jane's Defense Weekly* and *Jane's Intelligence Review*). Similarly, there are specialized international news sources that focus on particular regions or countries. The *Africa Research Bulletin* and *Africa Confidential* are two examples of well-regarded sources with a regional focus.

Types of information found in news reports

The information gathered from news resources primarily concerns events, actors and issues, so-called 'hard facts'. It is generally easier to find reliable information on big events than small events, and on extraordinary events than ordinary events. News reporting also provides evidence from which inferences can sometimes be made regarding people's beliefs, interests, expectations and emotions, commonly referred to as 'soft issues'. In fact, news media often make these inferences and report on such issues directly. Researchers using news reports should be aware that such reports are interpretations and not necessarily facts, and as with any inference from observation there is always a possibility that the inference is mistaken. 'Hard facts' are typically easier to ascertain than 'soft issues'. The former can be observed directly while the latter are inferences from observations. In either case, it is always important to consider how the source gained knowledge about what it reports. As we discuss further below, news reports describing what people feel, believe or want in a conflict situation are often based on very loose foundations. There are several examples of situations where media have attributed goals to a rebel group that are incorrect. The rebellion in southern Sudan, led by the Sudanese People's Liberation Movement (SPLM) between 1983 and 2005, is one example. Throughout the conflict most media reports referred to the rebellion as being secessionist and described the SPLM as a secessionist organization. However, looking at statements from the SPLM themselves reveals that the SPLM, although based in the south and recruiting from the south, was formed as an explicitly *non*-secessionist organization fighting for a federal state and remained so throughout the rebellion. Inferences that a group fights for goals that are consistent with one of the group's main characteristics or identities (for example 'Kurdish', 'Communist', 'Islamist', 'Democratic', or 'Popular') may often be true, but the Sudanese example shows that this is not always the case. Therefore, and since information about the parties and their goals and beliefs is generally available from the conflict parties, the best source for that kind of information is the parties themselves.

In sum, news resources provide information relevant to the dynamics of conflicts. Information about structural conditions is more often found in other types of sources such as statistical yearbooks, encyclopedias and data collections from the UN, the World Bank and university researchers. Information about a particular party's goals and beliefs is found in statements from the party itself. Most rebel organizations maintain fairly sophisticated websites with current as well as historical information on the struggle from their point of view. Interviews, surveys and focus groups are also suitable for ascertaining soft issues (see Chapters 7–10), but these tools are not nearly as widely available to researchers. As the Sudan example shows, researchers should be careful and avoid basing their description of soft issues on news media alone.

Complementary sources of information

Reports published by IGOs and NGOs are other valuable sources of information. IGOs and NGOs operate under different conditions than news media and are oftentimes able to operate in areas where media is either not present or severely restricted. However, they often have their own agendas and restrictions that might influence their reporting. IGOs and NGOs may sometimes be partisan, or semi-partisan. Even being perceived as taking sides by the warring parties might influence the reporting adversely because it affects what information the organization can obtain from the parties.

In our experience some of the most useful NGO reports on armed conflicts are produced by the International Crisis Group (www.crisisgroup.org), Human Rights Watch (www.hrw.org) and Amnesty International (www.amnesty.org). In addition to NGOs with an international focus, there are numerous NGOs working in specific countries or regions that provide useful information on conflicts, for example, the Informal Sector Service Center in Nepal (www.inseconline.org), the Ethiopian Human Rights Council (www.ehrco.org) and Southasia Terrorism Portal (www.satp.org) to name but a few. IGOs also provide valuable information for conflict researchers. One example is IRIN (Integrated Regional Information Networks) of the UN Office for the Coordination of Humanitarian Affairs, a rich resource for humanitarian news from most conflict countries in the world (www.irinnews.org).

In general, encyclopedias, reference works and scholarly case studies are useful for background information. An excellent place to start is the Uppsala Conflict Database, which provides information on all armed conflicts since 1975, as well as information on one-sided violence, non-state violence, peace agreements, conflict prevention and so on since 1989 (www.ucdp.uu.se). The Economist Intelligence Unit's country reports provide useful summaries on the political and economic situation that tend to be more up-to-date than encyclopedias and reference works. Note that the resources just mentioned are but a few examples and the landscape is constantly changing. While we have found these resources useful, there is no substitute for researchers doing their own searches for sources of information and it is always a good idea to consult a research librarian and/or area specialists.

Finally, as already mentioned above, partisan sources such as media controlled by the conflict parties is a useful resource for establishing their views of themselves and of their adversaries, as well as their goals and strategies. Partisan sources, governmental as well as non-governmental, are often found on the internet. A special problem concerning internet material is to establish the authenticity of the source; for example there may be false flag operations set up by an opponent. To circumvent this problem, one can try to locate official, authorized pages through websites of specialized academic institutions to see what resources area experts use. In general, established link collections are resources for handling the authenticity problem on the internet. Link collections at major universities and academic centers of excellence for the geographical area of interest are good places to start. Needless to say, partisan sources offer partisan views and any such information should be taken for what it is and treated with caution.

From the field to the news consumer

Of all the events taking place in the world on a given day only a tiny fraction ever become news items and of all the news items only a tiny fraction end up in a newspaper or news broadcast. The decisions journalists make in processing the news (discarding most of the material, choosing what to include and how to present it) have a strong influence on public perceptions of the state of the world. As shall be seen, it also has implications for how one should go about collecting conflict information.

News items are filtered and selected in several stages before they reach the news consumers. This is schematically illustrated in Figure 4.1. In the real world there are sometimes fewer but often more selection stages than is allowed for in this simple figure. Nevertheless, it illustrates the point that what reaches the news consumer is only a small fraction of all the news items, which in turn are only a fraction of the events that could potentially have become news items. First, the reporter or stringer selects what stories and events to write about and submit them to the news agency. Note here that the reporter selects not from the set of all events but from the much more limited set of events which the reporter has gained knowledge about. Second, from the set of all news reports filed by reporters and stringers the news agency makes a selection of what to publish and what not to publish. Finally, the news desk at the news organization selects and publishes some small fraction of all the news items published by the news agencies. At each stage of the process the potential news items are selected on the basis of their perceived news value. This means that not all events are equally likely to become news items; some news items are more likely to make it through the selection process and reach the news consumer. This selection process introduces bias in the overall picture even when each news item in itself is accurate and unbiased.

Matters related to armed conflict are typically considered newsworthy and are therefore likely to become news items if they are observed and if conditions in the field allow for their reporting. Whether or not conflict-related news items are selected by news organizations and passed on to the news consumer is a different issue and will depend heavily on a number of circumstances described in more detail below and in Box 4.1. Whether or not an event becomes a news item will also depend on where in the world or in a country it takes place. The extent to which the news sources are affected by selection bias will depend on where in the news food chain the news source is located, and also on the particular news source utilized.

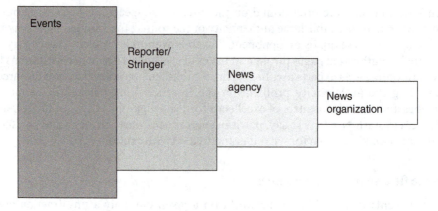

Figure 4.1: The filtering of news through the news chain

Presence or absence of observers

How much information is obtained depends on the extent to which someone is observing what is happening and reporting it to the world. Reporting, by journalists, NGOs and scholars alike, is uneven. Some conflicts receive a lot of independent coverage, while others do not. For example, Europe is much better covered than Africa, and North America is much better covered than South America. In most conflicts there is independent reporting by journalists and NGOs, and sometimes by scholars, but in some cases little or no independent reporting is available. Current examples include Eritrea, China, Iran, Myanmar and the Angolan province of Cabinda.

News media presence follows a general pattern of center versus periphery. Almost by definition, being peripheral implies less media presence. This pattern applies within countries as much as between countries. All else being equal – and it is not always equal – major powers have more media presence than minor powers, economically important and developed countries have more media presence than less economically important and developed countries, and so on. Capital cities and economic centers in countries have more media presence than small towns and rural areas. The presence of other types of observers often follows the same pattern – although scholars and NGOs sometimes deviate. Conflicts, on the other hand, tend to follow the opposite pattern, occurring mostly in the periphery at least in the initial stages of conflict. This means that the early stages of conflicts in peripheral regions of peripheral countries may go unreported at the time. One example is the Maoist insurgency in Nepal, which began early 1996 but where reporting on the conflict was virtually non-existent during the first year or two.

Battlefields, war zones and war-torn countries more generally can be dangerous places for journalists. Reporting on violence is a high-risk job and journalists are sometimes deliberately targeted or threatened. One may think that this would have profound effects on coverage and the presence of reporters in the conflict zone, but recent studies suggest that neither levels of violence nor the targeting of journalists significantly affect the news flow except in the most extreme cases (for example in Chechnya after 1999, see Urlacher, 2009). Poor infrastructure, harsh terrain and physical barriers to areas where battles are fought seem to have a larger effect on the presence of journalists and the levels of reporting (for example in Afghanistan, the

Democratic Republic of Congo and Sudan). War reporters, it seems, are less inclined to camp out in remote and inaccessible areas where poor communications and other obstacles may prevent or retard their work. Thus, the center-periphery division may have a greater impact on what areas are covered by war reporters than levels of violence and threats to journalists.

Censorship and media restrictions

How much information is available about a conflict also depends on the press freedom and openness of the country where the conflict is taking place. It is, for example, extremely difficult to establish what is going on between the Chinese government and the Uighur in Xinjiang, or between the Eritrean government and various Eritrean rebel groups. There have been and still are many reports of violence in both places, but it is very difficult to ascertain the details of what is going on. In contrast, the high levels of press freedom and openness of the countries in Western Europe make it relatively easy to know in great detail what has transpired between Euskadi ta azkatasuna (ETA) and the Spanish government, or the Irish Republican Army (IRA) and the British government. However, even in the most free and open countries, conflict information is often restricted in some ways and conflict itself often brings with it additional restrictions (see, for instance, Vultee, 2009). The nature and extent of such restrictions and limitations is important knowledge for the conflict analyst. Questions that need to be asked are what sources are allowed to have a presence in the area of interest, and, if it is a select few, why are those selected and how might that affect their reporting?

An important aspect of media restrictions is the existence of censorship, formally imposed by one of the parties – most commonly the government – or informally where the warring party will counteract reporting on certain events. When using news media as a source, it is helpful to be aware of the existence of censorship, which type of information is censored and how this might affect the reporting. The yearly Freedom of the Press Index provided by Freedom House (www.freedomhouse.org) can serve as a useful first indication of the severity of the problem in the country of interest. For recent years, Reporters without Borders (en.rsf.org) provides even more useful information, including a Press Freedom Index and specific country information. It is not uncommon for governments even in countries with relatively high levels of press freedom to impose censorship on particular types of reports, for instance on military operations, or to ban journalists from areas of combat. One example is Sri Lanka during long periods of the war with the Liberation Tigers of Tamil Eelam (LTTE). Most likely, such censorship is there to avoid disclosing military strategies or because the governments want full freedom in how they portray events. Even in the freest countries where there is no censorship of the news media, governments and military authorities still attempt to control or influence the flow of information. They do this for example by arranging press conferences, providing video material or privileged access, or embedding reporters with their own troops.

Filtering and selection bias

Selection bias is a subtle form of bias found in all news media to a greater or lesser extent. Whether it is a problem or not depends on the question being asked, but one does well to reflect on how selection bias affects the perception and understanding of events in a country or a region. Basically, selection bias occurs when some things are systematically reported while other things are systematically unreported, or under-reported. Selection bias yields a distorted picture of the situation as a whole even if the parts that are reported are reliable and truthful. To see how this works and some of the problems it entails for the conflict analyst, consider the following problems and examples.

Information published in the news is selected on a number of often unstated criteria. Selection occurs in a number of places along the way from the field to the news consumer. The first and the last filters involve the most severe selection. The first selection takes place in the field where the reporter or stringer decides what information will be collected and forwarded up the food chain, either via a news agency or directly to a news organization. The last selection is made by the news organization deciding what information to pass on to the news consumer. News organizations like newspapers, news programming on radio and television networks, are severely restricted in the number of items and the amount of news they can carry in any given day. The format simply does not allow even the 24-hour news networks to carry more than a small fraction of all the news items available to them from reporters and news agencies.

News consumers and conflict analysts need to consider what information is published and what is not published, who made the selection, and on what criteria. Often the selection criteria may not be entirely clear even to the news media itself, but culture, political and national interests and the like often play a role. Box 4.1 presents a list of 12 conditions affecting the news value of an event, and thus the likelihood that it will be selected and passed on up the news food-chain. Conflict-related events typically score high on several factors (including negativity, personification, frequency and threshold) and thus have a high inherent news value. In short, if conflict events are observed by or otherwise come to the knowledge of journalists, they are likely to become news items. However, to locate relevant information and to minimize the risk of bias, it is necessary to consider a few of the other factors as well.

The most important factor to consider is towards which audience the news resource is geared. The intended audience will be reflected in the news resource's selection of information to publish, because news resources depend on viewers, listeners or readers to (directly or indirectly) generate the revenues that keep them in operation. Even non-commercial and publicly funded news resources have an intended audience for which they will want to be relevant – whether or not their funding is directly dependent on ratings or subscriptions. What is considered newsworthy thus depends on the relevance to the intended audience. Consequently, to identify and understand selection bias the researcher needs to consider what the audience's interests are, what issues are salient to the audience for cultural, political, or economic reasons. Compare for instance, CNNs American edition to its international, Asian and European editions with respect to the views and emphases conveyed, the topics covered, and so on.

In general, the big international news agencies are much less selective than news organizations, whether international or national. This is because they cater to a wide variety of news organizations and news agencies in different parts of the world with different audiences. News agencies are also less selective because they do not have the same restrictions on how many items they can carry on any given day. News organizations and agencies based in the conflict area have smaller and different primary audiences than the international news agencies, but may have more comprehensive coverage and make different selections of what to publish, because their primary audience is different

Box 4.1: Making the News: Newsworthy or not?

The conditions listed below affect both the likelihood that an event or occurrence becomes a news item in the first place and the likelihood that it will be considered sufficiently newsworthy to be published (pass through the news filters). The criteria are drawn from the seminal work of Galtung and Ruge (1965). Additional factors have been put forth in later works but they are either combinations of the 12 factors identified by Galtung and Ruge (for example, conflict), or not relevant to our purposes (for example, sex and nudity). The effects of the conditions listed below are additive, so scoring high on more than one criterion increases the news value of the event:

- **Frequency:** Events that are sudden and fit the news resource's time format are more likely to become news items. Events and processes that unfold over very long time-spans will not be recorded as news unless they reach some dramatic turning point or culmination that does fit the time format.
- **Threshold:** There is some threshold that an event has to pass before it becomes a news item. Thus, events of a greater magnitude are more likely to become news items than events of a smaller magnitude.
- **Unambiguity:** Events that are unambiguous and which require less background knowledge to comprehend are more likely to become news items.
- **Relevance:** Events that are relevant or meaningful to the intended audience are more likely to be recorded as news. Among other things this implies some measure of ethnocentrism; news from culturally proximate nations is more likely to pass the filter.
- **Consonance:** Events that fit the news media resource's and its audience's expectations are more likely to become news items than events that defy expectations.
- **Unexpectedness:** Events that are out of the ordinary are more likely to become news items than events that are everyday occurrences.
- **Continuity:** There is inertia in news reporting. Events and stories that have already been reported are often followed up in subsequent reports. Thus related events in the same overall story are more likely to become news items than they would otherwise have been.
- **Composition:** News items compete for space. Hence, the likelihood that a story is published depends not only on its inherent news value, but also on the news value of competing stories and on concerns with composition. This principle primarily affects news organizations since they have much more restrictive formats than news agencies. News broadcasts and newspapers have limited space and typically strive for a balanced composition of different types of news.
- **Reference to elite nations:** Events that concern more powerful nations are more likely to become news items than events that concern minor powers.
- **Reference to elite persons:** Events that involve powerful, rich, famous, or otherwise influential actors (individuals or organizations) are more likely to become news items.
- **Personification:** Events that are perceived as being caused by, involving, or affecting identifiable subjects (an individual, a collective, or an organization) are more likely to be reported.
- **Negativity:** The more negative an event is in terms of its consequences the more likely it becomes a news item.

and usually more concerned with what is going on in the conflict. As a general rule, the closeness and/or salience of the conflict to the news organization's audience has a strong influence on the amount and detail of the coverage, as well as on what issues and events are reported and what is left out.

Things that are unsettling, provoking, or somehow consequential for the audience and how they feel about themselves and others influence the selection of information included in the reporting (relevance, consonance and negativity in Box 4.1). If it is interesting to the audience it is reported whether or not it is of any major importance to the locals where the conflict is taking place. One example is the Taliban dynamiting 1,500-year old Buddha statues in the Bamiyan valley in Afghanistan in March 2001. The dynamiting of the Buddhas of Bamiyan received plenty of coverage in Western media, in stark contrast to the relative lack of attention given to the fighting in Afghanistan in the fall of 2000 when the Taliban conquered the UIFSA (United Islamic Front for the Salvation of Afghanistan) stronghold Taloqan in the Takhar province – events that were arguably of much greater significance to the Afghan population.

Another example of selection bias is the television images of jubilant Palestinians in the West Bank following the attacks on the World Trade Center and the Pentagon on September 11 2001. It illustrates how consonance may distort reporting. The interesting point here is what was reported and what was not reported. On September 11, journalists on the West Bank and in Gaza set out to document the popular Palestinian reaction to the attacks. Reuters and AP reported on Palestinian celebrations of the attacks, showing pictures of a dancing and chanting Palestinian woman along with some friends making the V-sign. In spite of many journalists in the West Bank and Gaza actively seeking Palestinian reactions, only a few celebrating Palestinians were found. But this was not what was reported to news consumers. Instead, pictures of a few Palestinians dancing in the street, taken by Reuters and AP, were broadcast across the world along with claims of large numbers of Palestinians celebrating in the streets. A more accurate description of the popular Palestinian reaction would have been that they generally did not take to the streets to celebrate. Yet news organizations around the world elected to report celebrations.[6]

Selection bias does not necessarily imply that what is reported is incorrect. What it does imply, however, is that what is reported is only part of the picture. This means that the picture is not representative of what is occurring and being felt locally. If this is what the researchers want to know, they need to take into account that the picture painted by the news organizations outside the conflict location may be lopsided or unrepresentative. Things that are important locally, to the conflict actors, their constituents and others present in the conflict zone may not always be reported by news media outside the conflict country/region, and what is reported may be important to an outside audience but not to the conflict actors. This presents a potential problem when trying to analyze a conflict to understand its dynamics. Local and regional news resources are often useful for this purpose because their threshold for what is relevant to their audience is often lower, and their coverage of everyday life is more comprehensive.

Another and perhaps more subtle form of selection bias, which is applicable to all news media, is that contrasts and changes are reported, while the status quo is not. The status quo typically scores lower on several news values. In the news, information will be found about major escalations and the highest level of fighting, but not always lulls in the fighting or de-escalations, unless these are accompanied by some peace initiative, initiation of negotiations, or some similarly newsworthy matter. This means that the fluctuations covered in the news reports are somewhat lopsided so that escalations, worsening of situations and extraordinarily bad or shocking events are over-represented in the reporting. Negativity is a news value. There is also an asymmetry between negative and positive developments that tend to give negative developments higher news value on the frequency criterion as well. Positive developments are more often gradual and long-term processes that do not fit well with the news cycle. The gradual normalization of relations between two former conflict parties may go unreported, as may the rebuilding of destroyed infrastructure and many other important but slow-moving positive developments. This should be kept in mind since it implies that positive developments risk being missed simply because they are slower and less dramatic even if they have a very significant long-term impact.

News organizations also seem to develop what might be called 'news fatigue', especially concerning conflicts that do not have immediate relevance to their audience. While the onset and escalation of a conflict may be extensively covered, the continuation of the same conflict can go largely unreported, even at relatively high levels of violence, until something dramatically new happens. Meanwhile, new conflicts, or for other reasons more newsworthy conflicts, may dominate the news although they are small and insignificant conflicts compared to some ongoing but unchanging conflicts that are hardly covered at all by news organizations outside the conflict country. The continuation of the same patterns is old news, even if the conflict remains very intense and bloody. Unchanging conflicts, especially in far away places – from the perspective of the news organization's audience – soon lose interest. The news organizations move on to cover something new or more salient, even if that is a lesser conflict by any standard, and even if that too is far away. An example of this is the reporting of such wars as those in Afghanistan, Angola, Somalia, Sri Lanka and Sudan in much of the 1990s. These were long running, very bloody, and to a large extent unchanging conflicts that received comparatively little coverage in Western media. These can be compared to the coverage of, for example, the conflict in Macedonia in the late 1990s, which in most respects was a much smaller conflict but which was new and close to Western media audiences. Changes from attention to oblivion can occur rather quickly. For example, the conflict in Chechnya received major media attention throughout the first war in 1994–1996 and also when it re-erupted in 1999. However, soon after the outbreak in 1999, reports became scarce although the war was still active on a comparatively high level. It can even be that similar and simultaneous events receive very different degrees of attention. Cases in mind are the refugee crises of Angola, Sierra Leone and Kosovo, which were all highly acute in the first half of 1999. The Angolan and Sierra Leonean crises received a small fraction of the attention given to Kosovo in Western media. The reasons are obvious. Put in the words of a high ranking UNHCR officer later in 1999:

> You look at Kosovo: Not only can you relate to it as European, there was also a concern for a major refugee outflow. It's a hell of a long way from Africa to Europe, a great distance till you actually get people landing on your shores.
>
> (Vick, 1999)

Contrasts and changes dominate news media reporting, while the business as usual and the status quo are considered less newsworthy. Not much information about the ordinary everyday life lived by the vast majority of people will be found. Major dislocations in everyday life may be reported when they occur and occasionally thereafter, but for the most part what life looks like for the average person in a war-torn country will not be reported on the evening news, or even in the news wires.

Finally, the availability of still and moving pictures is important. For television news it is obvious that the availability of pictures is of great importance for their news evaluation, but it also matters for print media (but presumably not for radio news). The fact that pictures are important for many news organizations implies that they are of some importance also to the news agencies. This is not to say that a news item has to be accompanied by moving (or still) pictures to be included in television news casts (or newspapers), only that it increases the likelihood that it will be included.

Re-circulation

Using news reports requires being aware of potential re-circulation of information in various media. It is quite common and it sometimes gives the impression that something is a verified fact, while it really is not. Researchers may be led to believe that since something is reported in several places, this somehow indicates several original sources or some other measure of verification. A pertinent example is the reporting of Bosnian war casualties. If any journalist or policy maker is asked about how many people were killed in the Bosnian war, 1992–1995, the most likely answer is about 200,000. This figure has been repeated so many times by so many different journalists, analysts and policy makers that it simply 'has to be' the correct figure. What most people do not know is that this figure originally came from one source and one source only. This source is not just any source; the figure was given in the summer of 1993 by the Bosnian government, that is, one of the parties in the war.[7] In addition, the statement was made at a critical point of the war when the Bosnian government was appealing to the rest of the world for support. At the time nobody questioned if the Bosnian government might have political motives for inflating facts about the war. The number of war-related deaths has since been established as being closer to 100,000 (RDC, 2007; Tabeau and Bijak, 2005). Despite being refuted, the 200,000 figure is still commonly cited in news media as well as in research.

The Bosnian example points to three different problems. The first problem is the re-circulation of information from a single original source into numerous second-hand reports, which gives the impression that the number was a verified fact. Second, many second-hand reports did not clearly identify the original source for the number, making it difficult to see that they were all referring to the same original source. Thus, it was easy to get the erroneous impression that the figure had been confirmed by several independent sources. Third, the figure came from a party to the conflict (a source with a clear bias), at a time when it was beneficial for the source to inflate the casualty figures. These facts about the original source were also obscured in most second-hand reports, making assessment of the reliability and validity of the 200,000 figure very difficult. Finally, this example also serves as a reminder that it takes quite a bit of time before corrections sink in.

Conflict actors using news media

Media are a part of the battlefield and news media are often used by conflict actors and interested parties as a means to disseminate their views to constituents, opponents as well as to the outside world. If they can thereby create a favorable view of their cause in the outside world, and a hostile view of their opponent, they may gain substantive advantages versus their opponent. The Bosnian casualty figures discussed in the previous section is one example of this. But not only verbal or written statements may be directed at the outside world. The conflict analyst needs to be aware that some of the actions and events being reported may be directed primarily to an outside audience, rather than at the adversary or the apparent target. This way they may indirectly hurt their opponent or affect the outcome of the conflict by sending messages to outside parties. At least part of the stone-throwing in the Israeli occupied areas in the West Bank and Gaza during the Intifadas can be seen in this light. The primary purpose of the stone-throwing may in some cases have been to hurt Israel's standing in the world community and gain sympathies for the Palestinian cause, rather than to hurt Israeli soldiers by pelting them with stones. The lesson from this is that researchers need to consider if what is observed are actions between the conflict actors or between a conflict actor and the news consumers.

Conflict actors often intentionally try to influence reporting in more subtle and manipulative ways than outright censorship or information blackouts. Moreover, they do so not only verbally but also through various types of actions designed to entice outsiders to actively support their cause and oppose their opponent's cause, or to deter outsiders from intervening. In sum, researchers need to be aware of the fact that conflict actors sometimes play to an audience, using the news media for their own purposes, because it may affect how their actions are interpreted.

Description and interpretation in news reports

When collecting information about conflict situations it is important to have an understanding of how the words in the source material relate to the real world. There are several issues here that in our experience are useful to be aware of. First, the language and terminology used in news reports tend be inconsistent across cases, over time, and between different news sources. Second, there is a distinction to be made between description and interpretation. Many things reported are not directly observable. Third, is the problem with diction (the choice of words) and labeling in reporting on conflict situations. Labels and labeling are particularly difficult in conflict situations because words often have normative connotations. Finally, news reports sometimes contain poorly supported generalizations and reifications.

Before discussing each of these issues, it is useful to establish a simple baseline, an idea of how words and concepts ideally relate to the real world. This will make it easier to see where the problems lie.

On the need for clear definitions

When collecting information on armed conflicts researchers are typically trying to categorize some event, to establish whether a particular phenomenon is present or absent, or to determine its extent or degree. In other words, they are measuring. To do this a yardstick is needed, something to measure against, and it cannot be assumed that sources apply that yardstick or even that they are consistent in applying the same yardstick across cases and over time. Thus, before even beginning to collect information, the key concepts in the study need to be defined so that they become measurable, thereby making clear how the words relate to the real world.

First, the term used in the study must be given a meaning or connotation. The word attached to some phenomenon is a label, the meaning given to it is the concept. The concept needs to be clearly defined, or else it will not be clear what is meant by the word. For example, if the label 'war' is to be put on some phenomenon in the real world, 'war' first has to be conceptualized by giving it a clear meaning. Once this is done, the concept also needs to be defined operationally. To define a concept operationally is to delineate its empirical referent, that is, to specify exactly what the concept refers to in the real world. For example, to operationalize the concept of war is to list the observational criteria that need to be met before something observed in the real world can be called a war (see Chapter 6 for a more detailed discussion on operationalization). Thus, ideally words have a clear meaning and a clear empirical referent. In news reporting, simple descriptive terms and words with well-established meanings may come close to this ideal. But as soon as the reporting moves away from simple descriptive terms like 'bomb' and 'aircraft carrier' to more complex, ambiguous, or value laden terms like 'war', 'ethnic group' or 'terrorist', meanings and referents become unclear and terms are often inconsistently applied.

Inconsistencies in terminology

The words and labels used to describe phenomena in the real world are often not consistently applied over time, nor are they consistently applied across sources or cases. The meaning and empirical referent of the term will vary across sources and contexts, even if the same term is used in the source materials. In other words, just because sources use the same word it does not mean they are referring to the same phenomenon in the real world. Likewise, different terms may be used to describe the same phenomenon in different sources and contexts. What in one context is described as sectarian violence may in another context be described as ethnic violence, and in yet another context be described as tribal fighting or clan fighting.

Descriptions and interpretations

There is a difference between description and interpretation – a matter of degree no doubt – but still consequential. To grasp the distinction, consider the events in New York on September 11 2001. A simple description would be that 'two airliners crash into the World Trade Center (WTC). Fuel starts fire, people die, the buildings collapse, people observing this event report that they feel terror ...'. Those are words corresponding directly to observable facts. An interpretation of these facts might sound something like this: 'Two airliners are deliberately crashed into the WTC. The planes were full of fuel in order to cause maximum damage and make the buildings collapse.' The interpretation that the planes were crashed intentionally is inferred from the observable facts. Similarly, the interpretation that the amount of fuel was chosen to maximize damage is made for the same reason. But no one actually has access to the hijackers' intentions; their intentions are inferred from their actions. Therefore the interpretation is already one step removed from simply describing observable facts; a layer of interpretation has been added to the facts. Alternative interpretations of the facts are excluded by demonstrating that some alternatives are either impossible or at least highly unlikely given the known facts. This is why it may be concluded that the September 11 events were intentional. The likelihood of the crashes being unintentional (accidental or random) is so remote that it may safely be concluded that they were intentional. But was the intention of the hijackers to make the buildings collapse, or was that an unexpected consequence? With fewer facts, or less clear-cut facts, inferences become more uncertain.

In short, intentions and other unobservables reported in news media are interpretations of the observable facts, and not direct observations. It is therefore worth reflecting on claims made in news reports about intentions and other unobservable matters, and to keep in mind that they are inherently more uncertain than observable facts because they rely on inferences that may be wrong. Researchers should always ask themselves how the journalist or reporter knows the intentions, and on what observable facts these claims might rest.

Labels and diction

Continuing the example from above, many news sources would label the WTC episode an act of 'terrorism'. But different sources may refer to different things when they use the word 'terrorism'. This means that terminology or labels in the sources cannot be taken at face value. An event is not necessarily an act of 'terrorism' just because a source says so. It is not necessarily an act of 'terrorism' even if two or more independent sources say so. Whether or not the event should be classified an act of 'terrorism' depends on how the analyst has defined 'terrorism' and whether or not the event the source(s) refers to conforms to the definition of an act of terrorism.

Moreover, the word 'terrorism', like many labels used to describe actors and events in conflict situations, has normative connotations. The choice of a label with strong normative connotations over a more neutral synonym is a form of bias and it is sometimes an indication of the news resource's bias or a quoted source's bias. Thus, the use of language or labels with negative or positive connotations such as 'terrorists' or 'freedom fighters' rather than more neutral synonyms like 'insurgents' or 'armed opposition' should alert the reader to potential bias.

The choice of labels to describe actors and events is important because it affects perceptions of the conflict. Labeling in conflict situations is similar to labeling in other adversarial settings. In a court of law for example, the two sides often argue about what label best fits the evidence. The prosecutor may argue that it is first degree murder while the defense may argue that it is involuntary manslaughter. The judge and/or the jurors ultimately decide which label should be applied and the legal consequences depend on the choice of label. In conflict situations labels also have consequences, mainly political consequences but sometimes legal consequences. For example, some states avoided labeling the genocide in Rwanda genocide at the time, at least in part because they were signatories to the 1948 Convention on the Prevention and Punishment of the Crime of Genocide which commits the signatories to prevent and punish the crime of genocide.

More generally, diction affects how an event is interpreted or understood by the reader or listener. For example, the word 'murdered' has strong negative connotations, whereas the word 'killed' is more neutral. Serious news agencies and news organizations therefore have elaborate policies on the use of language, trying to keep it as neutral as possible and as close to the observable events as possible. Reuters, for example, has such a policy (see further reading, below), and among other things it bans the use of the word 'terrorism' other than in quotes (direct or indirect speech). This is a good thing, but it should be kept in mind when constructing search strings. A key word search on 'terrorism' in a news database would miss many Reuters reports on events that may be defined as terrorism. Thus, key-word searches should be designed so that they also capture the empirical referent of the concept in focus.

Generalizations

Like many other types of source materials, news reports often contain generalizations and reifications – many of which rest on rather loose foundations. News reporting labors under time and space constraints and so cannot describe every nuance and detail. Hence, simplifications and generalizations are commonplace. This is not necessarily a bad thing; it is helpful to sort the important from the peripheral and it is useful to know what is true on average. The average, typical, or normal is a baseline against which the not so typical and the extreme can be compared and understood. For example, it may be very useful to know if an organization claiming to represent a group really is representative of the people in the group. To actually know that, one needs to know what people in the group think on average. But – short of conducting a survey – it is often impossible to ascertain what people in a particular group think, or what people in general think. Generalizations of this kind are often unwarranted, because news resources rarely have solid information about what more than a handful of people think, feel, expect, want, or believe – the generalization is mere guesswork. It might be an educated and insightful guess, but there is usually no systematic evidence to back up claims about what people belonging to an ethnic group want, or even what the average or typical person in this group wants. Observed behaviors and events like riots and demonstrations may provide some grounds for making inferences, but it is easy to slip into generalizations that lead to unwarranted reifications of the actors or the people they claim to represent. Continuing the example with ethnic groups: ethnic groups themselves are not agents and do not have the capacity to think or believe. The individuals subsumed under the label may or may not share the same identities, beliefs and wants, and may or may not think in the same way. Talking to a few people in the group does not provide reliable information about what they all think, or what they think on average. Thus, when generalizations in news reports are encountered, caution is advisable and one should always ask on what evidence generalizations are based.

Simplifications may help sort the important from the unimportant, but sometimes salient distinctions and details are lost in reporting in order to make the news more unambiguous and easier to understand for the intended audience. For example, in complex conflict situations like Somalia, Afghanistan and Burundi, news reports have commonly lumped together conflict actors under aggregate labels although these actors are in reality separate. These simplifications typically become more severe the more complex the conflict and the lower the relevance of the conflict for the intended audience.

Searching for information

A good strategy for obtaining information on a particular conflict is to draw on a variety of types of sources. In the end, the possibility to do so depends on how much resources are available, not least in terms of time and language skills. Our general advice is to always devote some time at the initial stage to make a quick inventory of available resources for the country (or countries) of interest, apply source critical criteria and then make a well-informed selection of sources. This will save time in the long run. One way to assess the quality of different news media resources is to consult the area studies literature to see what resources area experts use. In some cases this will mean ending up mainly with local or regional sources, in others mostly international news sources. And, in the end, the choice of sources also always depends on the question the researcher seeks to answer.

The importance of knowing the sources and their potential biases cannot be overstated in this context. No source should ever be consulted without first having evaluated it according to basic criteria for source criticism described in detail in Chapter 3. Note also that initial evaluation of the source and its potential bias is especially important in regard to local news resources in the conflict country. Outside scholars are rarely as familiar with such sources as they are with international sources, and it usually requires more local knowledge to identify the degree of independence of a particular source. It should be noted that bias is not necessarily a bad thing, but may instead be an advantage if the focus of the study is on how a particular party perceives the conflict. However, if the goal is impartial description, bias may be a very real and serious problem. The main lesson here is to always strive to detect bias so that the source can be evaluated and used accordingly.

If it is important for the research question to have comparable source material across cases, then comparable source material should be used for the comparison to avoid biasing the results. This means that the researcher will not use all the available information in every case for the comparison, but the surplus information can be used to learn something about the range of uncertainty in the information used in the comparison. If, on the other hand, knowing exactly what happened is the priority, then making use of all the available information is a more appropriate strategy. It should always be kept in mind that differences across cases may be due more to differences in news coverage than real differences on the ground.

Searchable news databases

Many news agencies as well as news organizations provide searchable news databases. There are also much larger information databases such as Factiva and LexisNexis which have some real advantages over most other resources. LexisNexis contains around 10,000 sources, of which just over 3,000 are general news sources (www.lexisnexis.com). The even larger Factiva database contains more than 28,000 news sources, reporting in 23 languages from more than 157 countries (www.factiva.com). Thus, LexisNexis and Factiva contain unsurpassed amounts of searchable information from large numbers of news sources, including the major news agencies as well as regional and national news sources. They also provide global and continuous coverage over time. The coverage is more comprehensive in its scope than are any scholarly work. Scholarly works contain structured and selected information, which is good for overview and understanding, but may leave out a lot of information that may be of interest for the particular purposes of a study. There are also downsides to using the large information databases. They are quite costly and unless the researcher has a clear idea of what he or she is looking for, the sheer volume of information can be quite overwhelming.

Given limited time and resources there are basically two ways to reduce the workload. The most obvious way is to narrow the search by making the search string more restrictive, for example, by adding more key words. This will produce the desired effect of reducing the workload but it also means that there will be less variation in the information returned by the search. In a sense, the researcher will be looking at the world through a straw. For some purposes this is perfectly okay – only a particular slice of information may be of interest. For other purposes, however, a better way to reduce the amount of work while minimizing the information loss is to limit the search to a select set of sources. To avoid selection bias, a variety of different sources should still be used. For example, only one or two major Western wire services that best cover the area of interest can be chosen, along with the relevant regional and national news sources. This may significantly reduce the amount of material the search returns without severely restricting or biasing the information retrieved. There are no hard and fast rules here, but with experience knowledge will be gained as to what sources are best for different countries or regions of the world. To make an informed decision when restricting a search to particular sources we recommend experimenting. First, a complete search for a limited time period is made. Then – step by step – searches are made more restrictive for the same limited time period. The information from the full search is then compared to the searches restricted to fewer sources to determine at what point the cost of lost information outweighs the gain in reduced workload. Later, it is always possible to go back and make more specific searches on a more inclusive set of sources to make sure information on some key event, actor or issue that is of particular interest was not missed.

For research tasks with more limited ambitions, like a course paper, searches can be restricted to only one or a few sources. However, limiting sources to only a few requires serious consideration of whether this restriction may affect the results of the investigation.

Prepare well and save time

It is important to become familiar with the conflict. A good way to begin is to create a preliminary overview of the conflict, which would include a background description and a basic timeline. This is useful for gaining a basic understanding of actors and issues and, to identify major events, turning points and relevant political, social and economic background conditions. This information is often best gleaned from scholarly case studies, articles and reference literature. The Uppsala Conflict Database is a useful starting point for armed conflicts from 1975. Another good way to find sources and starting points for building the first overview is to consult a research librarian (or an area specialist). A basic understanding of the conflict is necessary for an effective search and utilization of news databases. Being familiar with a case is useful for writing clever search strings. A search in a large information database like Factiva or LexisNexis may return many thousands of news wires. News wires are short updates of what has happened since the last news wire. They do not repeat all of the history and context that has gone before, so it makes sense to read them chronologically. Moreover, to make sense of news wires, it is extremely helpful to have a good understanding of the context and history of the conflict. Without a good understanding of the conflict it may take some time to figure out what a particular news wire is all about, and with thousands of news wires this can be quite costly.

Two strategies for constructing search strings

There are some pitfalls in searching news resources for information that may unintentionally create selection bias – in addition to that inherent in news reporting. Relying on a single type of news resource is one such pitfall. As argued throughout the text, using a variety of different types of news resources is one way of minimizing the risk of simply copying the selection bias inherent in the news media.

Another problem, especially in computerized searches, lies in the construction of a search string. The search string systematically determines the information retrieved, so if the search string systematically picks up some information but not others, it will induce selection bias. In general, subject and key word searches may be problematic, because they run a risk of systematically missing something important. For example, a search where only conflict terms are included may exclude cooperative and conciliatory events of great importance, biasing the result to the more conflictual. If conflict is what you search for, conflict is what you get, even if in reality conflict does not dominate the interaction between the parties.

Similarly, if the search concerns a particular group or organization, all names for that group must be used. It is not uncommon for groups to go under one name when described by the government, another name when referred to by the group itself, and yet another name in international news media. This could even concern which language a name is given in. For example, Chechnya is the Russian name for a region in the North Caucasus, the local name being Ichkeria; Sendero Luminoso is the local name for a leftist guerilla in Peru, and Shining Path is the English or international name for the same guerilla. If only Chechnya and not Ichkeria are used in the key word search, the search will return a sample of information biased towards the Russian and international sources and views of that region. It might not always make a big difference, but sometimes it is crucial. In this context it is also worth pointing out that names have different spellings in different sources. This is particularly problematic in regard to the spelling of names in Arabic and Persian which are transliterated differently in different sources. For example, the Shiite group Hezbollah may be transliterated Hizbollah, Hezbollah, or Hizb'allah. There is also the possibility of misspelling of names, which is actually not all that uncommon. Since this is the case, it may be a good idea to consider search words that are not name-specific but that render a search result that includes the information of interest.

As noted above, the terminology used in reporting is not consistent across news sources and cases or over time. The same empirical phenomenon may be called many different things in different sources. This implies two things. First, the key words should not be restricted to what the researcher has chosen to call the phenomenon of interest. All the words that others may use to describe the phenomenon of interest should be included. Second, make use of the operationalization, the yardstick as it were, including language that is close to the empirical referent. This is imperative because large news agencies like Reuters have explicit policies of using descriptive, neutral language that is close to the empirics. For 'terrorism' this may be words like 'bombing', 'hijacking', or 'kidnapping.' In short, if key word searches are conducted, key words need to be carefully chosen so that the search string does not produce a biased selection of information.

Alternatives to key word searches are spatial and temporal searches – duly noticing alternative names for the spatial domains like, for instance, Chechnya and Ichkeria. A fruitful way to go about this kind of search is to begin with finding the turning points in the conflict from the case study and historical literature. This information can be used to delineate the initial search temporally, and then systematically move gradually backwards and forwards in time (and perhaps extend outwards geographically) following leads and tracing processes over time until the endings and beginnings of the process of interest are found. But one should not stop just yet. Extending backwards in time may result in the researcher stumbling on some previously unnoticed prelude to the period of interest. Extending forward in time also helps pick up corrections and clarifications of news reports that were issued at the time. News media, and news agencies in particular, have the nice quality of sometimes correcting mistakes in reporting, but it may take some time. Many news agencies have elaborate policies for correcting erroneous information. They also send out alerts when they suspect that some previous news item may contain incorrect information, or when a source has changed its story or retracted some previous statement. Moreover, new information often becomes available over time. For these reasons, it is often rewarding to follow the reporting even a couple of years after the end of the period of interest. This is also useful to keep in mind when studying an ongoing conflict.

Spatial and temporal search strings are not as discriminating and therefore not as efficient as key word searches. This may not sound like a major drawback, but spatial and temporal searches can be prohibitively time-consuming. The reduced risk of inducing selection bias through a spatio-temporal search has to be weighed against alternative uses of limited time and resources. Depending on the scope and purpose of the investigation a carefully designed key word search, or a combination of key word and spatio-temporal search is often preferable (for example, combining a verb or type of event and the name of a geographic location).

It is important to always document the search string and the sources used. Without documentation the results of the study cannot be replicated and replicability is a core scientific principle. Moreover, in our experience, documentation is invaluable for the researcher in order to avoid a host of problems, including duplicate searches and being unable to relocate sources. One may assume that the details of the research process will be remembered, but memory is surprisingly short and unreliable.

Going back in time

When moving back in time the available sample of news resources becomes much more restricted than it is today. The time span for which the large news databases are currently useful is limited to about the mid-1980s. Before the 1980s options are much more limited and usually not available in electronic format.[8] One exception is Keesing's Record of World Events/World News Archive, which is an important source with a global coverage that is available electronically from 1931 to the present (www.keesings.com). But Keesing's has higher news thresholds and contains less information compared to the large news databases. This means it will have to be complemented with news resources on paper and micro-fiche, which are much more time-consuming to search. Moreover, unless the researcher is in the conflict country, he or she may have trouble finding in-country news organizations or news agencies further back in history. *BBC Summary of World Broadcasts,* the paper predecessor to BBC Monitoring Service, is available back to the 1940s and so is the similar Foreign Broadcast Information Service (FBIS) produced by the US Central Intelligence Agency (CIA).[9] It should also be noted that a few regionally focused news resources are available for earlier periods, for example *Africa Confidential,* which is available from 1960, and *Africa Research Bulletin* from 1964. In general, the further back in time the fewer the news resources. Furthermore, as the world has developed news coverage has become more even, whereas previously the difference between center and periphery was much larger. This implies that if a researcher relies only on news resources, the present will appear much more eventful than the past.

Information shortages

How should information shortages be interpreted? Is nothing happening, or is no one reporting what is happening? The lack of news reports may indicate that nothing newsworthy is occurring, but it may sometimes simply indicate either that reporters are not present or that there are severe restrictions on their reporting. Complete absence of information about armed conflicts is uncommon, but not unheard of. As mentioned above, the Maoist insurgency in Nepal went on for some time before there were any news reports that reached outside Nepal, but eventually it was picked up. In this situation there is little one can do except search for information from other types of sources, and investigate whether there are journalists present and under what conditions they operate. The more common situation is one where there is little or no independent coverage.

What can be done if there is little or no independent coverage and all information is more or less controlled by the conflict parties? This is a difficult problem, and it severely limits the possibilities for doing serious conflict analysis. Yet, there are some possibilities. Even in cases where there is no presence of independent observers in the conflict zone the actors themselves usually make at least some information available. But such information is partisan and liable to be skewed in ways that can only be guessed. The conflict actors, moreover, often contradict each other and researchers may not have access to any independent confirmation that allows them to assess the veracity of the claims. Nevertheless, the conflict parties, unwittingly or otherwise, sometimes corroborate each other on at least some issues. When they do, the information is probably reasonably accurate. For example, the parties may both say that a battle has taken place. However, they might have completely different accounts of who did what in this battle, and what the outcome of it was. In this case, it is probably safe to assume that a battle did take place, but not much else. This type of situation – with little or no independent observers present in the conflict zone and contradictory partisan reports – often occurred during the clashes between India and Pakistan along the Line of Control in Kashmir in the 1980s and 1990s. It is also currently the situation in Ethiopia in regard to the Ogadeni conflict.

Unfortunately the conflict actors seldom corroborate each other on pieces of information that interest researchers the most when doing conflict analysis. Researchers are then left to their own good judgment – not a very satisfactory situation. However, judgments can be significantly improved by the use of external information and criteria for assessing the reasonableness of the reported facts. It is often possible to draw on existing knowledge of similar situations in the past, and this knowledge can be used to determine the outer bounds of what can possibly be true, and to guide critical common sense.

For example, professional military literature can be consulted for figures concerning average casualty levels per day for various kinds of fighting, between various types of military units, using various types of equipment, in various types of terrain, as well as the distribution of casualties between attacker and defender. With this kind of historical information and statistics it may be possible to determine the range of reasonable casualty figures, resulting in a ballpark figure. Though the actual casualty rates in the specific case would still be unknown, the researcher would get an idea about what kinds of claims by the parties might be true and what claims are highly likely to be untrue.

As always, the level of uncertainty and the possible sources of error should be stated up front in the analysis. Weaknesses in the available material are not weaknesses of the analyst, and it does not reflect negatively upon the analyst to be clear about problems and uncertainties in the source material. On the contrary, identifying shortcomings in the source material reflects favorably on the analyst, because it shows that the analyst is aware of the problems and is not misleading the reader into believing that the facts are clear-cut.

Conclusions

News resources are invaluable for gathering information about conflicts around the globe. No other type of source provides comparable amounts of information. But, as should be clear by now it comes with a number of problems and limitations. Bias and error are always potential problems in the information provided by news resources. However, while the possibility of getting the facts wrong can never be completely eliminated, there are ways to reduce problems with reliability and bias, thereby improving chances of getting it right. It takes practice, knowledge and a critical mindset to make the best use of news resources.

To begin with, researchers should always use source criticism to help identify potential problems so that these can be taken into account and dealt with appropriately. The principles of source criticism are explained at length in Chapter 3, so here some aspects that specifically concern their application to news reporting are highlighted. News reports are typically secondary sources, but identifying the original source on which the news report depends is important, albeit sometimes difficult. As the examples above show, identifying the original source greatly enhances the ability to assess the reliability and bias of the information, since it will depend on the reliability and bias of the original source. This can not be evaluated unless the original source is known. Ideally, each event or fact should also be corroborated by different original sources, preferably both by the parties themselves and by independent sources. Recall that a source is not the same as a news article; there may be numerous news articles from different news media on a particular event, but still only one original source underlying all those articles, for example one of the parties involved in the event.

Once the original source of the information in the news report has been identified, partisan bias is often relatively easy to detect. Researchers should also ask themselves whether the news resource itself is independent and if it might have some partisan bias in its selection or presentation of news items. Researchers should always try to avoid relying only on what is selected for one or a few similar audiences, and avoid as many levels of filtering and selection as possible by going directly to the original producer of the news item. In most cases this means going to the news agencies and the in-country or in-region news organizations, complementary NGO reports, specialized news organizations and scholarly works. It is often a good idea to look at both partisan and independent resources, because they too are liable to have different emphases in what they report. Local media in the conflict country will typically have a lower threshold for what is newsworthy but may instead be partisan or suffer from more censorship and self-censorship. Media in neighboring countries and regional media also have lower thresholds than international media, but may suffer less from partisan bias and censorship or self-censorship than media in the conflict country. Turning directly to the international news agencies is a good way to get non-partisan reporting that is not censored, while avoiding the worst selection effects. Combining different types of news resources in this way by no means eliminates the problem of selection bias. It does, however, avoid some of the most severe selection effects while at the same time giving the analyst an idea of how severe the problem with partisan bias, selection bias, censorship and self-censorship might be in the different types of news resources.

While the suggestions above and the tools offered by source criticism are valuable in gathering and assessing information, they cannot substitute for common sense, experience and a substantive knowledge of the problem at hand. Researchers have to exercise their critical faculties. Critical questions to the information obtained include: Is the information provided reasonable? Are the facts related even possible? The ability to accurately assess the plausibility of a piece of information is contingent on knowledge of the context and of the phenomena at hand. Knowing the phenomena of interest well, having an idea of what the outer bounds may be and what is typical, or average, in similar situations is very helpful when assessing the plausibility of a piece of information. Aggregate casualty figures, for example, have a tendency to be overstated in early assessments and then to be adjusted downward over time as missing people and refugees are accounted for and more accurate records can be established. The Bosnian casualty figures discussed above follow this pattern.

Finally, as suggested in the introduction to this chapter, news reports are only 'a first rough draft of history'. The details even of major events may sometimes be missed or misunderstood when relying exclusively on news resources. In some cases what actually transpired will never be learnt or only long after the facts when historians have had time to go through the archives and set the record straight. Furthermore, in most cases useful complementary information can be found in other types of source materials like scholarly works, and NGO and IGO reports. For many types of research questions archival materials, various types of statistical materials, interviews and/or surveys are necessary to complement information found in news materials.

Summary

News resources

- News reports provide detailed accounts of what happened, who did what to whom, when and where in conflicts around the world. For current or recent conflicts, news resources provide unrivalled coverage and amounts of information. Not everything is covered well in news reports however; therefore it is always a good idea to combine news reports with other types of sources.
- News media presence follows a general pattern of center versus periphery, within countries as well as between countries. Being peripheral implies less media presence leading to less available information. How much information there is also depends on the press freedom and openness of the country where the conflict is taking place.
- News items are filtered and selected in several stages based on their news value, before they reach the news consumers. Most events never become news items and the news that reach the news consumer is only a tiny fraction of all the news items that are produced every day. This selection process introduces bias in the overall picture even when each news item in itself is accurate and unbiased.

- To minimize selection bias researchers should always try to avoid relying only on what is selected for one or a few similar audiences, and avoid as many levels of filtering and selection as possible by going directly to the original producer of the news item.
- To identify and assess bias it is useful to compare what is reported in different types of media.

Searching for information

- For any research project, it is important to formulate a clear question, purpose or focus to guide the information gathering. It is also essential to become familiar with the conflict. Without focus and preparation it is easy to get lost or become overwhelmed by vast amounts of information.
- Carefully think through where the relevant information might be found and make an inventory of possible sources. Apply source critical criteria to make a well-informed selection.
- The key words used in searches should be carefully chosen so that the search string does not produce a biased selection of information. Try to be exhaustive in the use of language and synonyms, remembering that terminology and spelling vary greatly between sources.
- Spatial and temporal search strings reduce the risk of inducing selection bias but are not as discriminating and therefore not as efficient as key word searches.
- Always document the search string and the sources used.

Being an informed news consumer

- Apply source criticism; do it always and it will become second nature.
- Triangulate. Gather information on the same event from multiple independent sources. If they do not agree, try to assess what is most reasonable and remember that the majority is not always correct, nor is the truth always somewhere in between.
- Ground your critical common sense in the appropriate frames of reference. The more general knowledge about how things normally work and the more knowledge about the specific context, the easier it is to evaluate separate pieces of information.
- Remember that information is part of warfare and news media is a part of the battlefield.

Further reading

Galtung, J. and Ruge, M. (1965) 'The Structure of Foreign News: The Presentation of the Congo, Cuba and Cyprus Crises in Four Norwegian News Papers', *Journal of Peace Research*, 2 (1): 64–91.

Harcup, T. and O'Neill, D. (2001) 'What is News? Galtung and Ruge revisited', *Journalism Studies*, 2 (2): 261–80.

Harvey, C. (2010) 'The Web as a Reporting and Research Tool'. Online at: <www.newsline.umd.edu/italy/reportingtool.htm> (last update 3 February 2010).

Leth, G. and Thurén, T. (2000) 'Source Analysis for the Internet: Summary', in G. Leth and T. Thurén (eds) *Källkritik för Internet*, Stockholm. Styrelsen för Psykologiskt Försvar: 142–8.

Reuters (2008) *Handbook of Journalism* (http://handbook.reuters.com/index.php/Main_Page).

Sartori, G. (ed.) (1984) *Social Science Concepts: A systematic analysis*, Beverly Hills, CA: Sage Publications.

Vultee, F. (2009) 'The Second Casualty: Effects of interstate conflict and civil conflict on press freedom', *Media, War & Conflict*, 2 (2): 111–27.

Notes

1. Parts of this chapter build on Öberg and Sollenberg (2003).
2. The quote is commonly attributed to Philip Graham who uttered these words to the foreign correspondents of *News Week* magazine in London in 1963. Philip Graham was publisher of the *Washington Post* as well as President and Chairman of the Board of the Washington Post Company, owner of *News Week*.
3. We have restricted ourselves mainly to traditional news resources in this chapter and do not touch upon relatively new and emerging phenomena like interactive media and citizen journalism. While it seems likely that these new forms of news resources will become more important in the future they are, for the time being, of subsidiary importance. There are situations when such media resources may be a complement to the traditional news media, such as during the demonstrations in Iran in the summer of 2009 when little other information was available. But, establishing authenticity is often a serious problem, and the identity of the source of the information is often unknown. For helpful general tips on evaluating websites see Harvey (2010) and Leth and Thurén (2000), listed in 'Further reading'.
4. There are large differences between news organizations, some having high journalistic standards while others do not. As a general rule however, the large international news agencies are stricter in their adherence to objectivity and neutrality. They both can and have to be stricter because they cater to a global audience of professional journalists. News organizations on the other hand often are not similarly strict because of their audiences or their governments. Competition for audiences often drive news organizations to use stronger or more sensational language to attract viewers/readers, and when conflict events directly affect their primary audiences they often use less than neutral language. Even the most reputable news organizations do on occasion abandon principles of neutral language in reporting when their primary audiences are affected. An example is when the BBC, in its online news, labeled the perpetrators of the subway and bus bombings in London on July 7 2005, 'terrorists'. This was in contradiction of BBC policy and the language was subsequently changed replacing the word 'terrorists' with 'bombers'.
5. For example All News Papers (www.allnewspapers.com); Mondo Times World Wide News Media Directory (www.mondotimes.com); 4International Media and News Papers (www.4imn.com).
6. This example is taken from a documentary program broadcast by Media Magasinet, Swedish Public Service Broadcasting, October 11 2001.
7. The same figure was given in 1994 by Cherif Bassiouni, United Nations special rapporteur on Bosnia.
8. Useful link collections to online news archives on the web are provided by the Special Libraries Association News Division and hosted by ibiblio.org, a virtual library maintained by the University of North Carolina, Chapel Hill (www.ibiblio.org/slanews/internet/archivesindex.html).
9. The FBIS successor, Open Source Center (www.opensource.gov) is available in electronic form from the middle of the 1990s to the present.

5 News Reports versus Written Narratives

Collecting information using different types of empirical sources

Frida Möller

Introduction

Gathering information about events, actors, behavior and issues is a key aspect of empirical peace research. For most research projects, news reports and narratives are the two key sources of information and sometimes they are the only sources of information available to the researcher. Even in projects involving field research such as interviews and surveys, news reports and written narratives play an important role. In order to select the appropriate source material for a particular project, it is valuable to understand the strengths and limitations of different types of sources.

Empirical sources are generated for different purposes, directed at different audiences, and have different ambitions. Therefore sources vary in terms of their focus, comprehensiveness, level of detail and so forth. Some sources may provide detailed factual information on a whole set of events but miss putting them in a context. Other sources may offer rich descriptions of particular events and their context and background, while leaving out other events entirely.

Thus, different types of empirical sources may provide different pictures of the same reality. The choice of empirical material is therefore an important step in the research process. This chapter looks at the strengths and limitations of the two most commonly used types of empirical sources, and sets out to investigate how they differ.

Understanding differences between various types of source materials may also be valuable for users of existing datasets. Datasets often rely heavily on news reports because they provide easily available and up-to-date information. However, in recent times there has been a discussion of whether systematically collected information based on news reports actually captures the events that diplomats and people on the ground, such as mediators and belligerents, would define as significant. Some would even question if data based on news reports can generate an accurate and unbiased account of the phenomena it tries to quantify. Therefore, understanding the source materials underlying datasets is useful also for users of such large datasets.

This chapter evaluates and compares two different types of material – news reports and written narratives – to explore whether they paint a similar picture or if they differ in some important aspects. Written narratives include memoirs, historic accounts, reports and so on. 'Narrative' is here used in its original literal meaning: a story of events, experiences and the like, whether true of fictitious. The chapter also looks at what details can be extracted from the two different types of sources and if they capture the same types of events. If narratives cover events that are not in included in news coverage, why might they have been left out? If news reports capture situations that are not mentioned in the narrative presentations, which are they, and how can that be explained? Finally, are some sources more suitable for certain research purposes?

The peace process in Burundi 1994–2004 is used as a case study to evaluate the two different types of empirical sources. The Burundi case makes for an interesting comparison of sources as the news media covered the situation as it unfolded and it has also been the topic of several books with diplomatic, scholarly and journalistic accounts of the many shifts and turns in the efforts to prevent Burundi from becoming another large-scale civil war and genocide in Central Africa.

Evaluating the information found in different empirical sources will help us understand their strengths and limitations. This in turn will provide a better foundation for interpreting and analyzing data and will put researchers on a more secure footing when discussing the choice of empirical sources and will serve to stimulate thinking on the study of peace and conflict.

The chapter is outlined as follows: starting out, narratives and news media reports as empirical sources will be presented respectively. This is followed by a presentation of the information located using the two types of material, applied to the Burundi case. Thereafter, the empirical sources will be analyzed and compared. Finally, in concluding the chapter a few recommendations will be made.

Narratives

Narratives are stories of events, experiences and the like told by participants, observers or scholars. Typically published as books, book chapters, booklets and/or reports, narratives tend to focus on a single event or a set of events, or on a particular actor or set of actors and their role and experiences in the events of interest. Many narratives are primary sources written by key actors themselves or by first-hand observers, recording their own experiences. Other accounts are secondary sources based on reports, news or interviews with people who have taken part in an event or have insights into the topic (see Chapter 3 for details on primary and secondary sources). Narratives are selected and structured presentations, focusing on what the authors view as the most important or interesting aspects. Such descriptions can be rich in reflections on the issues, actors and actions in the case – including personal reactions, the atmosphere at meetings, tactics and strategies of opponents and third parties. These descriptions do not necessarily strive for a complete collection of information, but rather emphasize what the author and publicist consider to be significant and salient. The factors, events and processes deemed most important for understanding the outcome of a process or the occurrence of some event are selected for inclusion. Thus, the information is selected at least in part based on hindsight and therefore on the dependent variable. Descriptions of the context and background are usually well developed in narratives, whereas day-to-day activities tend to be much less prominently reported. Narratives as an empirical source are well illustrated by Howard Wolpe, US Special Envoy to the Great Lakes Region of Africa:

> The scope of this paper does not permit a detailed story. My purpose, rather, is to identify the most significant events, decisions and factors that have helped shape the process and are most directly responsible for both its achievements and its shortcomings.
>
> (Wolpe, 2003: 8)

News reports

News media cover events more or less instantly as the events unfold. In doing this, they often provide the reader with easily observable facts about an event such as information on what type of event it is, where it occurred and who was involved. This is the core of news reports. Information that describes the background, the atmosphere, motives or intentions is often left out as that requires either space or private information that reporters do not always have in the midst of events. News can be both a primary and a secondary source. News reports that describe events that the journalist has not taken part in or experienced him/herself are considered secondary sources. This type of source is more common than primary news sources where the journalist has first-hand experience of the event in question. But even first-hand accounts are filtered through the eyes of the journalist and must be looked at critically.

Information based on news reports is relatively easily available and is sometimes the only continuously available data source. Today, researchers have access to both local and international news but the amount of attention a country or an event receives varies dramatically and depends on an array of conditions, described in Chapter 4 in this book. The news media supply the readers with reports on what they believes readers are interested in, which means that a Western-based news organization might cover New York City more intensively than the whole African continent. It is important to keep in mind that the picture of the world presented by news media is not the full picture – it is merely a small sample of all the events taking place. Even so, conflict-related events are typically better covered than most other types of events because they tend to have high news value. However, it is important and valuable to include a variety of different news sources, both local and international, to reduce the risk of potential bias (see Chapter 4).

The case of Burundi portrayed in narratives

The peace efforts taken in Burundi to avert a major war and a possible new genocide are well documented in various written narratives. A brief description of the Burundi conflict and the peace process until 2004 is outlined in Box 5.1.

What kind of information do the narrative sources on Burundi's peace process contain and what turns of events do they consider as central? There are both first- and second-hand accounts describing the Burundi peace process, published in books, book chapters and various analyses and reports. The first-hand accounts are written by participants in the peace process such as peace envoys and are based to a large extent on their personal observations and experiences. The second-hand accounts, often written by academics specializing in the region or Burundi in particular are usually based on interviews, UN documents, reviews of previous literature and various reports (including news reports). Many narrative accounts focus on a particular theme or a period such as the mediation by South Africa and former President Nelson Mandela. Most of the narratives covering the peace process with the exception of the reports and briefs by the International Crisis Group (ICG), were published from 1998 up to the first years of the 2000s, the period when the peace efforts intensified. Most accounts were published a few years after the events took place. The reports and briefs by the ICG were often thematic in nature covering current affairs and topics and were all written and published more or less at the time of the events.

There are a number of narratives written by individuals who took part in the peace efforts. One example is the account by Howard Wolpe, former US special envoy to the

Box 5.1: The Case of Burundi: A short summary

Background

The population of Burundi is made up of Hutus (majority) and Tutsis (minority). Ever since independence in 1962, the Tutsi minority has controlled all societal powers. The Hutus have been victims of brutal repression by the Tutsi army and as a result, extremism has flourished among Hutus. In the early 1990s, Hutu rebels launched an armed struggle. The most basic way of viewing the parties to the conflict is as a Tutsi government fighting Hutu rebels. In reality, both sides in the conflict are more complex. In 1993 and 1994, several attempts at democratically governing the country were made. When, in late 1993, Burundi's first democratically elected president, Melchior Ndadaye, a Hutu, was assassinated together with a number of his ministers, extremism increased in the country and the violence escalated.

Parties to the conflict

The resistance side in the conflict consists of a number of Hutu rebel groups. The Hutu groups have a history of factionalism and as a result, a majority and possibly all of the rebel groups stem from two movements – Palipehutu and CNDD. Initially, the conflict in Burundi was a purely internal affair. However, this changed drastically in the mid-1990s when Burundi became part of a regional conflict complex with its neighbors.

Conflict behavior

The conflict is characterized by a large amount of inter-group killings, with victims often being civilians. Massacres of both Hutu and Tutsi civilians have taken place on a number of occasions, carried out by both the government forces and the Hutu rebels. In fighting between the armed rebels and the government army, most Hutu rebel groups have utilized guerrilla strategies, fighting the government from rear bases in neighboring states.

Third-party involvement 1994–2004

Numerous outside parties have actively participated in the conflict since the mid-1990s; some have taken sides and become secondary warring parties to the conflicts. Others have tried to initiate dialogue between the parties and negotiate an end to the conflict. In 1996, multiparty talks were initiated by former Tanzanian President Julius Nyerere as mediator. Not all parties were present in the early years of the peace talks as the government objected to the participation of the active rebel movements, who for their part set up pre-conditions for taking part in negotiations. In late 1999, former South African President Nelson Mandela took over the role as mediator. For the first time, all active rebel groups were invited to participate in negotiations. The negotiation finally led to the signing of the Arusha peace and reconciliation agreement on August 28 2000. It provided for army reform and a transition to democracy. However, two of the main rebel groups – the CNDD-FDD and Palipehutu-FNL – did not sign the accord.

In 2003, negotiations between the government and CNND-FDD continued and resulted in a number of agreements. Then, in 2004 the first face-to-face negotiations between the government and Palipehutu-FNL took place but soon broke down. However, later the same year (on September 7 2004), a ceasefire agreement was signed between the government and the Palipehutu-FNL.

Great Lakes Region, who describes, portrays and analyzes his participation in the international efforts to prevent another large-scale war. Another central mediator whose narrative of the events has been published is the former special representative of the UN Secretary-General for Burundi, Ahmedou Ould-Abdallah, who details his experiences of mediation in the mid-1990s. Wolpe and Ould-Abdallah provide first-hand accounts of the peace initiatives and offer valuable details about their perceptions of the situation. Not only are the perceptions and planning process of the intermediaries portrayed; many narratives also illustrate the strategic deliberations that took place among the conflicting parties in Burundi: how they calculated the future turn of events and how they could adjust their strategies accordingly. For example, there are numerous detailed accounts of meetings where Ould-Abdallah shares his recollection of conversations with political parties in Burundi as well as with other third parties. Likewise, Wolpe focuses on 'behind-the-scenes-diplomacy': the intentions, setting, strategies and thought process of the third parties. Many other narratives describe the motives, strategies and actions of the many parties engaged in Burundi. Also, much of the material describes the context in great detail in order to give the reader a deeper understanding of the situation. In sum, the accounts provide an interesting description of the political moves and games playing out behind the scenes, as well as the reasoning, interests and motives of various actors in the process.

Although key figures like UN special representative Ould-Abdallah and US Special Envoy Wolpe provide fascinating and detailed portraits of the intense periods in which they participated, they do not provide detailed answers to the questions 'when, who, where and what?' When did they meet with the parties, what did they discuss? Instead, narratives tend to focus on the question 'why?' Why, for example, did the summit in September 2003 fail, or why was civil society largely excluded from the peace process?

Narrative accounts often do not explicitly describe the extent of the efforts of the third parties. It is sometimes very clear that the international community was intensely engaged in the peace process, but is not obvious how this engagement was manifested – how often did the mediators meet with the warring parties? Did they talk once a month or several times a week? However, it has to be noted that in general, reports by the International Crisis Group (ICG) stand out in this regard as they are very detailed and often give answers to when, who, where and what as well as the why and how. ICG reports are often very thorough and offer in-depth reporting that is very informative and useful.

In sum, the range of available narratives focuses on somewhat different phases and themes. They cover the direct attempts by third parties to prevent full-scale war but also include and elaborate on key political events and processes. The following pivotal events and developments are outlined as particularly significant in the narrative accounts:

- The attempts to save democracy, stabilize the political situation and prevent political parties rebelling after the coups in 1993 and 1996.
- The mediation efforts in 1995–99 by Julius Nyerere, former President of Tanzania.
- The mediation by the Catholic community of Sant'Egidio in 1996–97.
- The mediation efforts led by former President of South Africa, Nelson Mandela, following the death of Julius Nyerere in October 1999.
- The intense negotiation period leading up to the signing of the Arusha accords on August 28 2000.

- The period following the Arusha accord (2000–2004) with attempts to consolidate the agreement.
- The surroundings of the implementation of key aspects of the Arusha agreement, such as the presidential changeover on April 30 2003.
- Attempts to include the more extreme rebel groups, CNDD-FDD and to some extent Palipehutu-FNL, in the negotiations in the early 2000s.
- The negotiation leading up to the signing of the Global Ceasefire agreement with the CNDD-FDD on November 16 2003.

In conclusion, some general points can be made. First, narratives describe the larger context and the broad approach of the international community but also give insights into the interests, motives and reasoning of some of the third parties. Second, the narrative accounts detect a macro-level shift in the approach of the third parties such as including all parties to the conflict in the negotiations rather than just a few; and Mandela's threat to resign as mediator. Third, narratives generally do not allow for the detailed documentation of the who, what, where and when of individual preventive measures.

The case of Burundi portrayed in the news

Let us now look at the dynamics of the peace efforts made in Burundi in 1994–2004 based on the information found in news reports. The news articles were retrieved using a news and information service database produced by Dow Jones International called Factiva. Factiva includes more than 28,000 leading sources from 157 countries in 23 languages. Using the Factiva search engine, over 2,200 articles and news telegrams that matched a search string were retrieved from a number of different local, regional and international sources including BBC Monitoring Services (with translated local news and radio broadcasts), Reuters, Xinhua (Chinese agency), All Africa (a news agency that distributes African news and information) and Associated Press. By selecting a variety of news sources with different audiences, the risk of bias is reduced. The differences between local and international news resources and their strengths and weaknesses are covered in more detail in Chapter 4.

The information found in the news articles illustrates that the peace efforts by the international community were characterized by a step-wise escalation in the number of talks and activities from the mid-1990s to 2004. Using media reports it is possible to follow the developments in the international peace efforts and get quite a clear picture of the general takes and turns:

- The first years of third-party mediated talks (1994–96) were mainly concerned with the violence in general and the huge flows of refugees stemming from the fighting. The news reports describe several meetings between mediators and the government of Burundi, but no talks with any of the rebel groups.
- New strategy: Former Tanzanian president Nyerere was appointed mediator in March 1996, which seem to change the overall peace-making strategy as they now included rebels in the talks. The news reports describe a number of peace talks in Rome with the CNDD rebels, mediated by the Sant'Egidio Community, on issues such as a ceasefire and reform of the armed forces. A continuous peace process was held in late 1996 to May 1997. The material illustrates how, in 1998, Nyerere

attempted to restart the talks and consequently met separately with the government and the rebel groups CNDD and Frolina as well as taking part in a number of face-to-face meetings with some of the parties.

- Nelson Mandela replaces Nyerere in 1999 when Nyerere dies. Under Mandela's direction the Arusha multiparty peace talks continued into 2000 and finally led to a peace agreement. Media covered the intense shuttle diplomacy and talks with rebels by South African politician Jacob Zuma and mediator Mandela in a series of attempts to persuade the rebels to come to the negotiating table and to agree to a ceasefire. In the following years the mediators finally managed to get government representatives and the rebels who were previously left out – the CNDD-FDD and the Palipehutu-FNL – to the negotiation table.

In sum, using news reports as a source gives an illustration of the events and developments that took place during the peace process based on easily observable facts. The general shifts in the mediation tactic can be registered as shown but the material does not give information on the motives or reasoning behind the strategies and tactics of the many parties in Burundi.

Comparing news reports and written narratives

There are a number of aspects that need to be looked at when comparing and evaluating the two types of empirical sources: do news reports paint the same picture as narratives and how do the two types of sources describe the peace efforts in Burundi in 1994–2004 in terms of frequency, depth and substance of information?

Locating events

The quality and detail of a source can mean many things – it can represent the separate number of events found in the material or the scope, depth and variety of the information. Let us start by looking at how many separate events can be located using the two sources. In order to disaggregate a set of events or a process into separate events, an event must be operationalized, meaning that a number of predefined conditions need to be met for an occurrence to be labeled an 'event'. An event is here seen as an initiative by a third party where it is possible to determine where the event took place (geographical location), when it took place (time), who participated in the event (identity of third-party and Burundi actors), etc. When applying these conditions to the material it is clear that news articles locate more events than narratives do, as illustrated in Figure 5.1. About one third of the events found in news reports are found also in the narratives: 130 compared to 357.

Even though news articles do generate a larger number of separate events, Figure 5.1 illustrates that the two types of material overall capture the same general trend and thus describe the same flow of events. News reports capture a wider set of events than narratives do. As suggested earlier in this chapter, one would expect fewer events using narratives as they concentrate on a few events and situations deemed to be of particular significance. But as key events are preceded and/or followed by a number of less high profile events, the trend over time should therefore be the same. The results illustrated in Figure 5.1 point in this direction. Some studies argue that media sources to a higher degree cover large events than smaller ones, resulting in an underreporting of events

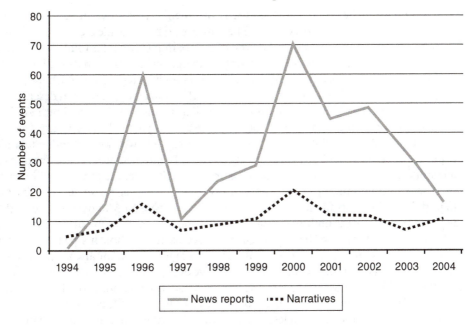

Figure 5.1: Number of events located using news reports and narratives

(McCarthy *et al,* 2008). However, as Figure 5.1 shows, media reports tend to include more separate events than narratives do.

The fact that news reports do locate a wider set of events is a significant result and begs the question: why? A first explanation is that narrative accounts may miss some events as they tend to focus on the events and issues deemed most significant and leave out large numbers of what – at least in retrospect – are deemed less significant incidents. By using news reports it is possible to locate a large number of these less prominent events such as meetings between heads of states where issues such as the refugee crisis or ethnic violence in Burundi were discussed. These might be regarded as day-to-day activities and are not considered significant in narratives unless they had some important affect on the peace efforts. The fact that these events are reported in the news media suggests that they were considered significant enough to be newsworthy at the time they took place. This means that determining which events are significant can only be done with hindsight. As narratives are typically written long after the events have occurred, what in retrospect turned out to be minor and less significant events are screened out. As time passes only a few events will be viewed as important enough to be labeled noteworthy and, as a consequence, make it to a narrative account such as a book or a memoir. It is likely that the selection here will mean that fewer events are covered, and that this builds on an understanding of what turned out to be 'important'. As a result, many incidents are left out and not recorded in the narratives. This biased picture presents a problem for anyone interested in analyzing, for instance, the effects of different types of conflict prevention measures.

The fact that narratives cover a more narrow set of events and actors than news reports may also result from a certain bias among the authors. As the contributors to these publications were often involved in the peace efforts that they portray, they are possibly biased in the sense that they focus on 'their' experiences in terms of which actors were involved and efforts taken. The authors do not provide a complete picture. The statistics speak to this underreporting of actors in narratives: a total of 41 unique third parties were located in Burundi using media coverage compared to 33 with the narratives. This in turn leads to a similar discussion on bias regarding which narratives get covered – what cases and actors get published? It is much more likely that descriptions and biographies that focus on high-profile mediators such as former South African President Nelson Mandela or former special representative of the UN Secretary-General for Burundi, Ould-Abdallah, get published than some less well known individual like the president of Gabon. If only certain conflicts, events and mediators are allowed to tell their story, there will be a selection bias that in turn will affect the outcome of research based on narrative sources. A final observation is that even narrative accounts by and biographies of high-profile mediators can be omitted. Nelson Mandela was central to the peace process in Burundi from 2000. Despite the fact that a number of biographies and accounts of him have been written, none seems to mention his peace efforts in Burundi. Consequently, even the memoirs of a prominent mediator are not a guarantee that information on all the peace efforts they have ever participated in are included, not even the ones that made it to the news headlines. There is probably also selection bias in which conflicts are covered by published narratives – high-profile conflicts or crises are more likely to get published than less well known ones as they are viewed to be significant and important. Also, as narratives are written with hindsight the outcome is already known, which may mean that successful events and actors are more likely to be included, leaving out less successful third parties and occurrences as they are not viewed as significant for the outcome. Again, this bias in what is and what is not reported in narrative accounts may undermine valid inference. If the bias is related to what is to be explained in the study, then relying exclusively on narrative sources will weaken the validity of any inference made. Thus, for example, analyzing the success of peace efforts based on narratives alone is problematic because the information contained in the narratives is likely to be selected because it is believed to be related to the outcome of the peace effort.

There is a similar but much less severe bias in news reports. News media are not neutral unselective recorders of events. Rather, the news media are part of a political and economic setting, which results in a selection process where some events are selected and others are left unreported (see Chapter 4 for details). Factors such as the size of an event, the proximity to the news organization and the timing of the event all affect the likelihood of it being reported. Other conditions that may affect which events are selected are geographical and cultural closeness to the intended audience, financial aspects etc. (Oliver and Maney, 2000). As a result, large and intense events close to the major news agencies and their audiences are more likely to be reported. Similarly, events where significant and prominent people involved are considered to have high news value. It is also possible that media coverage may be intense in the beginning of a series of events when the incident is new, but decrease over time as interest fades, unless there is some new development. This selection bias may have consequences for what is reported and the content of news articles. The Burundi example points to this: the number of articles published covering the peace efforts sharply increased in the beginning of the period but faded as times went by. Then in 1999 and 2000 when a high-profile person like Nelson Mandela took over as mediator and negotiation intensified with the Arusha multiparty peace talks, the number of news articles increased again.

Content and detail

Written narratives often summarize series of events and present a more analytical and interpretive picture that gives insights into what takes place behind the curtains, the reasons and motivations behind the acts of the actors involved and so on. Narratives are selected and structured accounts designed to provide an understanding of the situation. Narratives also reveal information on how different levels and/or actors interact such as how one set of events within the UN affects the local level, and vice versa. Information on this type of interaction is more difficult to identify in media-based material. News reports on the other hand portray everyday activities with a high level of detail when it comes to facts like dates, locations and people involved but leave out much information about the context. Neither do they usually provide the reader with an in-depth analysis and interpretation of the events.

Basic and observable information, such as dates, location, type of event and actors involved, affect the number of events being registered if they are the conditions for an event to be recorded. As narratives tend to focus more on summarizing, explaining the setting and analyzing the situation, much of the basic information is left out, resulting in fewer events being covered. A simple case in point is what narratives report as *one* mediation event covering three days – Monday through Wednesday – where ceasefire conditions are discussed. This event is reported as *two* separate events in the news reports: one mediated meeting on Monday and another on Wednesday, but no meetings on Tuesday. The news also reports that different topics were discussed on the two days of reported mediation. On Tuesday, there was a recess in the mediation as each party had to confer with its own members. A similar example taken from the Burundi case demonstrates this point: the information found in narratives often simply states that the mediator made several visits from October to December but does not provide information on when these visits took place, how many meetings there were or who participated. This example points in part to the lack of basic information in narratives but it also points to how news and narratives focus on different aspects of explaining and describing an event.

Trying to locate basic information in the case of Burundi, the general picture is that news locates more events for each year between 1994 and 2004, but looking more closely, news material records *fewer* events than narratives do for 1994. Even though 1994 saw little preventive activity, some attempts by the international community were made to control the deteriorating situation. News reports only include one meeting in 1994; one between the Presidents of Rwanda and Burundi on how to stop the border violence between the Hutus and the Tutsis. This event was not captured in the narratives, probably because it was viewed as an everyday occurrence even though it was a high-level meeting between two Presidents. The media on the other hand did not include a meeting between the UN Special Representative and the CNDD that is captured in one of the narratives. This is an event that seems to be important enough to be covered in the news but that probably was not common knowledge at the time or was not considered as newsworthy based on other criteria. In 1995, news reports located more events in general and also picked up more low-key episodes. The trend continues in 1996 as news media report almost four times as many events. The following year, mediation by Sant'Egidio, a Christian community in Rome, is picked up in both types of material. However, the information found in the narratives is more extensive and detailed, probably because these talks were supposed to be secret and thus not all information

Table 5.1 Points of comparison

	Written narratives	*News reports*
Number of events	Restricted number of events – focus on the important ones	Large number of events – include both low and high profile
Content and detail	Summarize and often aggregate sets of events and processes	Focus on basic, disaggregated information
	Present the context and analysis	Cover day-to-day activities
	Provide 'secret' and 'politically sensitive information'	Answer 'what, when, where, who?'
	Answer 'why?'	
Bias	Focus on significant and high-profile persons, events and cases	High interest in the beginning of a process but coverage fades when nothing 'new' is happening
	Select information based on what, in hindsight, is considered important	Focus on international and/or domestic level, not local level
General information	Qualitative information	Quantitative information

reached the media at the time of the talks. More details are covered in the narratives as some of the participants in the talks are the authors of the narratives and thus have private information they can make public after the fact. Secrecy is often only necessary at the time of the event when certain information may be politically sensitive. After the fact, it is more likely to become public knowledge. For 1998, the empirical sources cover similar numbers of events and processes but in 1999, news media locate twice as many events as narratives do. The intense mediation process under the leadership of Nelson Mandela that took place in Arusha, Tanzania in 2000 is covered in both types of material but the information found in the news media is much more extensive and detailed. In total, 71 events are registered this year, of which 22 are where Mandela participated. In contrast, narratives capture a total of 20 events for the same period, only seven including Mandela. For 2001–2004, news reports again record more events than the narratives do (see Table 5.1).

It is apparent that information contained in narratives has difficulty meeting the strict definitions and operationalizations necessary when systematically collecting events data. Despite being very detailed on certain aspects, narratives often do not provide enough information on separate events to pass the inclusion criteria, thus answering questions such as 'Who participated?', 'When did the event occur?', 'What kind of activities took place?', etc.

Conclusions

This chapter has pointed to the similarities and differences, strengths and limitations of using different types of empirical sources. This is not a definite review of how news media and narratives cover events at all times and in all places. Rather, it serves as an example of the different characteristics typical of the two types of sources. The

Burundi case illustrates the importance of source criticism and of taking the various characteristics of different types of material into consideration when designing a research project.

A few findings are worth highlighting. First, it turns out that the news reports do locate the events that diplomats, mediators and other actors define as significant. The news material in large news databases generally also picks up events that one might think would not end up in any news reports, such as mediated talks by the president of Gabon, a small African country. Thus, news reports capture the important events and processes outlined in narrative accounts as well as locating many low-key actors and events that are not found in the narratives. What seem to be less well covered in news sources are efforts by local actors such as civil society and non-governmental organizations. Despite this, it is possible to obtain a good picture of the dynamics of the peace efforts using media reports. Overall strategies and turning points in the process are well covered. This can be seen in the coverage of how the international response shifted from excluding extremist rebels to including all parties to the conflict; how UN mediator Ould-Abdallah seemed to use a strategy that focused on governmental and political actors, whereas former President of Tanzania Nyerere also included some of the armed factions; and how Mandela dealt with all parties. This is not to say that news reports provide a complete picture of everything that actually transpired, but we can conclude that compared to narrative accounts, news reports include a larger number of events and do not seem to leave out any key aspects. Thus, the fear that events are systematically underreported in news reports seems to have been overstated. In fact, underreporting of events is much less of a problem in large news databases like Factiva and LexisNexis than it is in narrative accounts.

Despite the many benefits of using news reports, there are some challenges. The search string used when retrieving news articles in a news database such as Factiva or LexisNexis affects which articles are retrieved. Consequently, it is important that some effort is put into constructing the search string so one is fairly confident it covers the articles of interest. On the other hand, the up-side with search strings is that they can be kept constant across cases, to generate comparable material. Another challenge that news reports face is that public information is limited regarding some aspects, especially when it comes to secret or private information or even politically sensitive information. It may only be possible to publish politically sensitive information a number of years after the event has taken place, as illustrated by the example of the mediation led by Sant'Egidio, a Christian community in Rome. But this example also illustrates that it may be difficult to keep information from leaking into media reports. Information on the secret mediation efforts led by Sant'Egidio was located in both news reports and written narratives but the information in the news was less comprehensive and detailed than the one found in the narratives. If one looks for information on these types of secret or behind-the-scenes events and processes, narratives are to be preferred. Also, if one wish to get a deeper understanding of the motivations and interests of the parties in a conflict at some critical juncture, narratives by first-hand observers such as the ones by US and UN envoys Wolpe and Ould-Abdallah are better.

A second important conclusion is that narrative accounts encounter many of the same problems that were expected using news reports. Clearly, published memoirs or diplomatic accounts are selective in the information they provide. They focus on the more spectacular and dramatic and that which, with hindsight, is deemed particularly important by the narrator. Unsuccessful third parties and peace processes are less likely be included in narratives as they are not viewed as significant. Moreover, some mediators' stories are published while others' are not. Less prominent and less successful third parties are less likely to publish narratives of their own, or have their story told by someone else.

Despite these limitations, narratives provide the researcher with valuable information that is not captured using news reports. Narratives provide insights into the motivations and reasoning of various actors and give the reader a deeper understanding of the situation. In this sense, narratives present a more detailed portrait of the peace efforts and the setting, while putting the actions and developments into a larger perspective.

Ultimately, the question of which type of source material should be used depends on the research question. The two types of empirical material reviewed here suit slightly different purposes. If the main purpose is to collect information on who did what to whom, when and where, news reports are often better and provide a more comprehensive picture. However, if the main objective is to gather information on variables such as the actors' motivations and objectives, or to obtain information about intra-party dynamics, context, atmosphere and strategies employed in particular events and processes, narratives are usually better as they provide more detail and nuance. Furthermore, if one intends to focus on specific, intense and high-profile diplomatic interactions such as the Arusha peace process and less on the day-to-day activities proceeding and/or following the intense periods, narratives provide a more detailed picture. However, one does well to remember that many of these intense periods are often preceded and followed by low-key events that may be significant in understanding outcomes even if they are not well covered in narrative accounts. In a peace process, for example, the low-key everyday events that often precede a more intense period leading up to a break-through in negotiations might not have led to the breakthrough in the short term but may have been vital in preparing the ground for the intense, high-profile period that did. Thus, the low-key everyday events may be what connect the dots and may in the long run be just as important as the high-profile meetings in producing the final outcome.

In sum, news reports and narrative accounts provide somewhat different types of information and have different strengths and weaknesses (see Table 5.2). In many ways they complement each other, so combining them is often a fruitful strategy. Media coverage can be used to pick up the general dynamics and provide a relatively detailed picture of the 'who, what, when and where' while narratives would complement this picture with information about behind-the-scenes events, intra-party dynamics, actor motivations and the like.

Recommendations

As demonstrated, the two types of material each have strengths and limitations. One needs to be aware of these in order to make an informed choice of source material. The potential selection bias that both sources suffer from requires the researcher to take steps to try to minimize the associated risks. How then should one go about trying to limit the restrictions of the empirical sources? As proposed, a key step is to select the type of material based on the purpose of the intended research project. If the aim is to gather basic information and general trends, news reports might be preferred, but if the purpose is to focus and analyze certain key events and developments, narratives are probably better.

The most fruitful option is often to combine the two types of empirical sources in an effort to maximize the information and get different aspects of a case or phenomenon.

Table 5.2 Strengths and limitations of narratives and news reports

	Written narratives	News reports
Strengths	• Provide 'secret' and 'politically sensitive' information • Supply information on atmosphere, intentions, motives • Put the events in a context, which results in a greater understanding • Explain how different levels and actors interact, including intra-actor dynamics	• Easily available • Provide large number of events, are less selective • Include information on low-profile events and actors • Supply detailed quantifiable data • Cover day-to-day events and processes • Comparable across cases
Limitations	• Focus only on what is deemed significant and important (in hindsight) • Little or no attention to low-profile cases, events and actors • Lack detailed documentation of the 'who, what, where and when' • Significant underreporting of events	• Do not include 'behind the scenes information' or secret events • Fail to provide the larger context • Few events on local level, for example, by civil society actors • Difficult to discern intra-actor dynamics

News reports would then be used to capture the 'who, where and what' and narratives to answer 'why' and 'how'. Piecing different types of information together may create a more comprehensive picture than simply using one type of source material. Finally, it bears repeating that the choice of news sources is vital. Using only one Western-based news source like the *New York Times* when analyzing an African conflict will not result in the best quality information. Instead, combining different news sources, as described in Chapter 4, provides a much richer and less biased pool of information.

Summary

- Narratives describe the larger context and the broad approach of the international community but also give insights into the interests and motives of some of the third parties.
- News reports give an illustration of the events and developments based on easily observable facts such as date, location and actors involved.
- Narratives and news reports capture the same trend of events.
- News reports locate the events diplomats, mediators and other actors define as significant.
- Narratives cover fewer events and actors.
- Narratives provide better coverage of behind-the-scenes activities and politically sensitive information.
- When using news reports retrieved from a database, it is important to take time constructing the search string.
- Combining news reports with narratives is often fruitful. News reports provide more extensive coverage of the general dynamics and key events in conflicts. Narratives complement this picture, providing more contextual information as well as more information on soft issues like motives and interests.

Sources used for the Burundi study

News reports used

Approximately 2,200 news articles from AFP, Reuters, All Africa, Xinhua, BBC and Dow Jones.

Written narratives used

Bentley, K.A. and Southall, R. (2005) *An African Peace Process. Mandela, South Africa and Burundi*, Nelson Mandela Foundation, Cape Town: HSRC Press.

Buyoya, P. (1998) *Mission: Possible. Building peace in Burundi*, Paris: L'Harmattan.

Havermans, J. (1999) 'Burundi', in M. Mekenkamp *et al* (eds) *Searching for Peace in Africa. An overview of conflict prevention and management activities,* Utrecht: International Books.

International Crisis Group (1998) 'Burundi Under Siege. Lift the sanctions; re-launch the peace-process', *ICG Burundi Report No. 1,* 27 April.

International Crisis Group (2000) 'Burundi: Neither War nor Peace', *ICG Africa Report No. 25,* 1 December.

International Crisis Group (2000) 'The Mandela Effect: Prospects for peace in Burundi', *ICG Central Africa Report No. 13*, 18 April.

International Crisis Group (2001) 'Burundi: Breaking the Deadlock. The urgent need for a new negotiating framework', *ICG Africa Report No. 29*, 14 May.

International Crisis Group (2002) 'Burundi after Six Months of Transition: Continuing the war or winning the peace?', *ICG Africa Report No. 46*, 24 May.

International Crisis Group (2002) 'The Burundi Rebellion and the Ceasefire Negotiation', *ICG Africa Briefing Paper*, 6 August.

International Crisis Group (2004) 'End of Transition in Burundi: The home stretch', *ICG Africa Report No. 81*, 5 July.

International Crisis Group (2004) 'Elections in Burundi: The peace wager', *Crisis Group Africa Briefing*, 9 December.

McCarthy, J.D., Titarenko, L., McPhail, C., Rafail, P.S. and Augustyn, B. (2008) 'Assessing Stability in the Patterns of Selection Bias in Newspaper Coverage of Protest during the Transition from Communism in Belarus', *Mobilization: The International Quarterly* 13 (2): 127–46.

Maundi, M.O., Zartman, I.W., Khadiagala, G. and Nuamah, K. (2006) *Getting In. Mediator's entry into settlement of African conflicts*, Washington DC: United States Institute of Peace Press: 57–84.

Ould-Abdallah, A. (2000) *Burundi on the Brink 1993–95. A UN Special Envoy reflects on preventive diplomacy*, Washington DC: United States Institute of Peace Press Platform for Conflict Prevention and Transformation: 197–208.

Renda, E. (2000) 'Mediation efforts in Burundi', in *Conflict Trends 2000/3*, The African Centre for the Constructive Resolution of Disputes, online at: <http://www.accord.org.za/publications/conflict-trends/downloads/438-conflict-trends-20003.html> (accessed 26 May 2010).

Weissman, S.R. (1998) *Preventing Genocide in Burundi*, Peaceworks No. 22, Washington DC: United States Institute of Peace.

Wolpe, H. (1998) 'Negotiating in Burundi', in Francis, D. (ed.) *Mediating Deadly Conflicts. Lessons from Afghanistan, Burundi, Cyprus, Ethiopia, Haiti, Israel/Palestine, Liberia, Sierra Leone & Sri Lanka,* World Peace Foundation Reports Number 19, Cambridge, MA: World Peace Foundation.

Wolpe, H. (2003) 'Burundi: Facilitation in a regionally sponsored peace process', unpublished manuscript, The Africa Program, Woodrow Wilson International Center for Scholars: 38–44; 48–9.

Part III

The Practice of
Information Gathering

6 Systematic Data Collection
Experiences from the Uppsala Conflict Data Program

Ralph Sundberg and Lotta Harbom

Introduction

Researchers aspiring to say something about a large number of cases, that is, those who want to be able to generalize from their findings, need good quality data that is comparable over time and space. There are many concepts and phenomena that researchers believe to be existent worldwide and which they feel should be studied on the global level so as to discover how certain phenomena play out under specific – spatial, temporal or other – circumstances. Collecting data that covers the entire globe in its vast diversity of contexts and societies is a daunting task for any researcher or research group, and also one that contains many pitfalls and difficult choices. The rewards to be gained in the form of possibilities for generalization and hypothesis testing are, however, considerable.

Apart from being aware of the general challenges associated with global data collection, those researchers or students interested in questions of peace and conflict also need to be aware of the pitfalls and difficulties that these specific topics present. Collecting global data on armed conflicts is arguably more problematic than on many other phenomena, simply because of the nature of the topic. Information emanating from conflict settings tends to be both uneven and sketchy, with problems such as biased news reports and information black-outs being the usual order of the day. There is also some disagreement in the literature on exactly what constitutes an armed conflict and how it should be measured. Being aware of these problems, researchers can take steps to minimize their impact.

This chapter is based on the experiences of the Uppsala Conflict Data Program (UCDP) and the lessons learnt during its approximately 30 years of activity in the field of global data collection. We draw on these experiences to provide suggestions and guidelines for readers interested in launching their own data-collection efforts, be it large-scale, well-funded enterprises or small-scale data gathering by a single student for a Master's thesis.

The chapter begins by discussing the relationship between theoretical concepts and operational definitions and variables: how can a theoretical abstraction be translated into an empirically measurable variable? It then proceeds to give some hands-on advice regarding the construction of variables, discussing issues of validity and reliability as well as outlining the pros and cons of, for instance, different variable scales. The third part of the chapter outlines the actual process of data collection, discussing among other things the advantages and disadvantages of different types of sources. The chapter's fourth part speaks both to hands-on advice regarding the creation of large datasets, but also to issues of format and structure. Finally, the chapter ends with some concluding remarks. Throughout the chapter, different problems and their solutions will be illustrated by using examples from UCDP's creation of its wide range of datasets. Special attention will be given to the process of defining the key concept in the program – armed conflict – and how this has been made measurable and quantifiable.

Box 6.1: The Uppsala Conflict Data Program (UCDP)

Based at the Department of Peace and Conflict Research, Uppsala University, UCDP is a world-leading provider of data on organized violence and peace efforts, offering a range of different outputs pertaining to these issues. Apart from providing datasets on armed conflicts, one-sided violence and non-state conflicts (these concepts will be discussed further on in the chapter), the program also maintains a freely available online database (www.ucdp.uu.se/database). The database includes information on a range of variables such as negotiations, third-party action and peace agreements, as well as on the characteristics of the different groups recorded in the data. For a detailed history of the development of the program, see Wallensteen (2003).

From theoretical concept to operational definition

Starting out with the intention of creating a dataset, regardless of whether it is a large-scale data program or a single university student launching a new project, it is important to devote time to pinpointing exactly what the phenomenon of interest is. The first task is to define the meaning of the theoretical concept – its connotation. At this initial stage in the process it is advisable to turn to the scholarly literature to see what is written about the phenomenon in focus, and how it has been conceptualized. Doing so will not only provide general guidance but will also facilitate the crafting of a definition that is theoretically relevant. The idea is thus to both build on what has already been done in the field and to construct a definition that can be used to further a theoretical understanding of the concept in focus (Sartori, 1970).

Having defined the meaning of the concept, thereby establishing the theoretical 'core' of the phenomenon of interest, the next step is to define the empirical referent – or denotation – of the concept. What does the concept refer to in the empirical world? Defining the empirical referent of the concept is the first step in creating an operational definition. An operational definition is a specification of how the empirical referent of the concept can be measured and thus delineates the phenomenon of interest in observational terms. An operational definition should be precise enough to ensure that it captures the phenomenon of interest and nothing else, and strict enough so that that *the same* phenomenon is captured across different cases. To be applicable across cases and contexts, as well as over time, the operational definition also needs to be sufficiently general.

There is sometimes a tension between being strict and precise on the one hand, and being general on the other. Making the operational definition vague or wide to make it more general risks resulting in data that includes entries too disparate for comparisons to be meaningful. Subsequently, it makes sense to argue against basing a definition of a concept on a specific case or on a small number of cases. This could easily result in a definition that needs to be stretched as the spatial and temporal scope of the data collection is expanded. At the same time, it is important to be aware of the dangers inherent in wanting to create a definition that captures too wide a phenomenon. Using data that is too inclusive, researchers run the risk of comparing apples and oranges, ending up with dubious or even misleading results. The danger of so-called 'conceptual stretching' will be discussed further, later in this chapter.

Operationalizing armed conflict

Turning to the experiences of the UCDP, the original concept of interest was armed conflict, including both interstate and intrastate armed conflict.[1] Attempting to translate this concept into an empirically measurable definition that was strict and precise, yet general enough to be applicable across countries and over time, was a time-consuming task. Working from the perspective of conflict theory, from previous data-collection efforts, and from empirical observations, the program attempted to create a definition that could be applied globally.

Armed conflict is closely related to and sometimes used as a synonym for war, so war was one natural starting point for conceptualizing armed conflict. War is commonly conceived of as meaning large-scale organized violence for political purposes. The range of different situations that would fit this definition is large and rather diverse, including not only what we traditionally think of as wars like World War II (an interstate war) or the American Civil War (an intrastate war), but also genocides and communal conflict. It was therefore necessary to become more specific.

Another natural starting point in defining armed conflict is in conflict theory. Armed conflict is a sub-set of all conflicts. In conflict theory, conflict is often understood as incompatible interests. Johan Galtung's work from the early 1960s elaborates this understanding of conflict and was used to further specify the meaning of armed conflict (Galtung, 1969). Galtung describes a conflict as the interplay between 1) an incompatibility (the issue of contention), 2) attitudes, and 3) behavior (the actions undertaken by the parties). Working from these components, UCDP focused on incompatibilities and behavior, as these correspond to armed (behavior) and conflict (incompatibility) while being relatively easily observable – unlike attitudes. From the common understanding of war and empirical observations it was clear also that organized actors were a prerequisite for any type of sustained large-scale combat towards a political end. Thus, in specifying the concept of armed conflict, focus was on incompatibilities, behavior and actors. These are the three core components that underlie UCDP's definition of armed conflict.

In order to develop a definition of 'armed conflict' that would be useful for data collection the empirical referents of the three core components needed to be defined and operationalized.

While all three concepts are integral parts of the UCDP definition, it soon became evident that it was incompatibilities more than anything else that would set the program apart from other conflict data enterprises. From the data collection launch, there had been an idea of what the phenomenon of study would look like, based on both empirical knowledge and conflict theory. However, deciding how to structure the data and how to separate between different conflicts was not an easy task. For UCDP much attention was placed on what issues the parties were fighting over and to see if these could, in fact, be aggregated to more general types of overarching incompatibilities. Studying the data already collected and the world around them, the Uppsala team realized that the type of phenomenon that they had set out to record fell quite neatly into two broad types of incompatibilities: those fought over governmental power and those fought over territorial issues. These two types of incompatibilities appeared to be contextually and temporally neutral, which made them suitable for global data collection. It is important to emphasize here that the incompatibility and the underlying reason for the conflict are two completely different things. When studying incompatibilities, what is captured is the stated goal of the struggle and not the reasons given for it. In a vast majority of cases, the goal of the group's struggle would be formulated as seizing power or at least fundamentally changing the system of government, or to gain a larger amount of autonomy for its region or even to opt for secession. Incompatibilities were, thus, specified to be 'stated manifestations of possible underlying incompatibilities or goals' (Heldt, 1993: 34). For the benefit of capturing this globally, the 'stated' part of the definition was and still is of key importance. To avoid codings based on the coder's own judgment, which would introduce an element of arbitrariness in the data, cases where the parties do not make any statements at all are excluded from the main dataset and instead recorded in a dataset of unclear cases.

For the second core component, *behavior*, the type of behavior relevant for UCDP's definition was the use of armed force. Some may argue that it is important to have a wide definition of armed conflict, including behavioral aspects such as hostile statements and other kinds of provocations. UCDP chose to confine the analysis to the use of armed force resulting in battle-related deaths, that is those deaths incurred in fighting between two conflicting parties. One reason for this is that preventing and solving deadly conflicts has traditionally been a major concern of peace research and it was primarily to this discipline that the program aimed to make a contribution. Another reason for this focus was that the use of deadly armed force is a behavior that is relatively easily observable. It is also typically deemed newsworthy and is therefore reported in the news media – a prerequisite for creating a dataset based on open sources.

Lastly, the third core component, *actors*, had to be specified so that the data would not come to include unwanted disparate entries. It was decided to focus on state-based conflicts since most of the deadliest armed conflicts were fought between states or between governments of states and organized opposition groups. For theoretical reasons it was also felt that a distinction should be made between different types of armed conflicts involving different types of actors (for instance interstate, intrastate, and communal conflict) and different behavioral patterns (for instance one-sided violence versus reciprocated violence) as they may have different causation and dynamics. Moreover, at the time the program was not equipped to deal with the vast amount of material that would have been needed for coding all types of situations.[2]

The decision to focus on conflicts that included governments was also driven by the fact that the program aimed to capture political conflicts over governmental power and/ or territorial claims. Included were opposition organizations, operationalized as any non-governmental organization that had announced a name for itself, had stated political goals, and used armed force to achieve them. This definition fits, for example, rebel groups. The data was subsequently able to include both conflicts between governments (interstate conflict) and conflicts between a government and a non-governmental organization (intrastate conflict). The definition was constructed wide enough to be able to include both these phenomena. Yet it was narrow enough to avoid including events such as communal violence; situations such as those where pastoralists and agriculturalists fight one another in the Horn of Africa or when the cattle-raiding activities of the different sub-groups of the agropastoral Karimojong group turn deadly in eastern Uganda. Constructing the definition of actors in this way was also in line with the demand for observability. As Birger Heldt argued in a 1993 article on UCDP's definition, '[v]iolent events connected to the incompatibilities of government and territory between organizations and governments of states or between governments of states, are reported in the media and manageable in number' (1993: 32).

The process of translating the theoretical concept *armed conflict* into an empirically observable definition came to result in the following definition:

> An armed conflict is a contested incompatibility that concerns government or territory or both, where the use of armed force results in at least 25 battle-related deaths in a year. Of these two parties at least one has to be the government of a state.

Building on this very specific yet contextually and temporally neutral (in the sense that it is applicable to the present, but also to recent history) definition, UCDP has been able to create a range of datasets that are widely used by both the academic community and policy makers.

Broadening the scope without jeopardizing quality

Having undergone the above process, some researchers may find that that the definition misses something of importance. Maybe the definition arrived at only captures part of the intended phenomenon, or maybe studies of the data collected point to a need to expand the empirical scope of the data collection. In our experience, trying to expand the original data would inevitably run the risk of conceptual stretching, and the new data may therefore become too disparate and unsystematic to allow for comparisons over time or across countries. As a general rule, therefore, we recommend starting the process anew, working from a new theoretical concept towards another empirically observable definition, rather than trying to stretch the existing definition to include more.

Box 6.2: Conceptual Stretching

Conceptual stretching occurs when the original concept is distorted so as to broaden its meaning and make it applicable to a different situation or context. When conceptual stretching occurs, concepts run the risk of being rendered meaningless and, in the words of Giovanni Sartori (1970: 1035), we appear to cover more by saying less, 'and by saying less in a far less precise manner'. The problems that this phenomenon can cause researchers can be illustrated by the debate concerning fatalities in the armed conflict in the Democratic Republic of Congo (DRC). It is commonly argued that more than 5 million people have died in this conflict. However, this figure is based on an understanding of 'armed conflict' that not only focuses on battle-related deaths, but also on indirect violence such as deaths due to starvation and disease. If this type of violence is included in the concept of armed conflict it can pose problems for peace research. For example, if a researcher is interested in investigating the durability of peace agreements, the 2001 accord in DRC would be considered a failure due to this concept stretch, since thousands of people died after it was signed, albeit not in direct violence between the conflict parties, but due to other forms of violence, starvation and disease.

If the new concept is closely related to the original one, it is a great advantage if the new definition is crafted so the two are mutually exclusive. If this is achieved, users of the data can themselves decide if they want to study the two phenomena separately or if they want to merge them. Many times there are different theoretical foundations for two theoretical concepts, wherefore researchers would generally prefer to study them separately, testing different hypotheses by using different datasets. Apart from enhancing the quality of the data, providing different datasets for closely related phenomena and making these mutually exclusive and therefore possible to combine is, thus, also a service to the users.

For any research program there is often an ambition to expand. This was also the case for UCDP. Criticized for being too narrow in its definition of armed conflict, the program decided to expand its scope. In 2002, the work to construct two new categories of organized violence commenced. After more than 20 years of experience of collecting data on armed conflict, the UCDP team had a fairly good idea of what types of organized violence had *not* been coded in the original data; there was a consensus that the main gaps were violence against civilians and conflicts between rebel groups or ethnic groups, not involving the state. The two new categories, one-sided violence and non-state conflict, were subsequently developed in much the same way as armed conflict had been in the late 1970s and through the 1980s. By consulting the theoretical literature and getting a distinct sense of what the phenomena actually entailed, and by evaluating it against the empirics, the program eventually arrived at two operational definitions. It doesn't serve the purpose of this chapter to go into this process in detail but for an overview of the process of creating the two new categories of organized violence, see Eck *et al* (2004).

However, it is important to point out that the definitions were formulated so as to guarantee that there would be no overlap between any of UCDP's three categories of organized violence. Armed conflict events can never be coded as one-sided violence since the definition of the former prescribes two organized actors, and neither can it be coded as non-state conflict since this category explicitly excludes all state actors. Similarly, one-sided violence events cannot be mistaken for non-state conflict since the definition of the latter type stipulates two organized parties.[3] As a result, researchers interested specifically in one of the three categories can simply use the dataset relevant for their study. At the same time, researchers interested in observing the presence or absence of organized violence in different countries can merge the three datasets without double-counting. Yet another advantage of broadening the scope of the data by adding separate and mutually exclusive categories is that research can be done on how these different types of organized violence relate to one another. Note also that if all types of organized violence had been included in the same category from the start (or by stretching the concept), it would not have been possible to separate different categories of violence and ask questions such as how one type of organized violence relates to another. In other words, it is often desirable to have narrower definitions, or separating between sub-categories of a phenomenon: first, because it increases the resolution of the picture of reality provided by the data, and second, because it makes more fine-grained analysis possible. There is also an asymmetry here: data with a finer resolution can (if properly constructed) be aggregated to give the bigger picture, but aggregated data cannot be disaggregated.

Constructing useful variables and indicators

Having constructed a definition to capture the meaning of a theoretical concept and subsequently having operationalized the definition, the next step in any data collection is to create variables and/or indicators that may in turn capture the operationalization's measureable criteria.

The primary goal of any data-collection effort is to construct variables and indicators that are valid and reliable measures of the theoretical concept of interest. Validity has to do with how well the measurements capture the empirical referent of a theoretical concept. Reliability has to do with measurements being replicable and consistent across cases. In addition to the primary concerns of validity and reliability, there are several issues of a more practical nature that need to be considered. To generate global data, variables and indicators need to be case insensitive to ensure global applicability across time and space. Finally, in the construction of measurements the advantages and disadvantages of different variable scales, especially with regards to quantitative data collections, should be considered.

Validity

Validity concerns the degree to which a variable captures the theoretical concept of interest. If a measure systematically includes more or less than the empirical referent of the theoretical concept there is a problem with validity. The measure is not picking up what it is supposed to pick up. In practice, the most common problems with validity stem from having an operational definition that is either too broad or too narrow. In the first case such a variable will capture phenomenon that are somewhat unrelated to the theoretical concept, and in the second case the variable will capture only parts of the phenomena and exclude cases that would, theoretically, be of interest.

In terms of the UCDP operationalization of armed conflict as 'a contested incompatibility that concerns government and/or territory where the use of armed force between two parties, of which at least one is the government of a state, results in at least 25 battle-related deaths in one calendar year', there are several parts of the operational definition that require measurement, such as 'government', 'parties' and 'battle-related deaths'.

To exemplify a scenario in which validity is lost due to using a too broad operationalization, one can consider what happens when battle-related deaths are excluded from the above definition and instead organized violence, whether or not it is a battle (reciprocated violence), is measured. Applying such an operationalization across cases could force us to include, in the list of armed conflicts, a long list of massacres of civilians, such as the Rwandan genocide, in which governments or rebels kill civilians. One would then have to revisit the theoretical foundations and ask if massacres and genocides really are valid cases of 'armed conflict'.

Constructing a variable that is too narrow in scope will exclude cases that are theoretically of interest and thus reduce validity. This scenario can be exemplified by considering the UCDP criterion of 25 battle-related deaths. This cut-off point for deaths caused by combat was selected because it was believed that the threshold of the Correlates of War (COW) project (1,000 battle-related deaths) excluded a number of cases that were conceptually part of what is generally thought of as armed conflict (albeit perhaps not war) (Singer and Small, 1972). For instance, India's long-running

Maoist insurgency has rarely passed the 1,000 deaths per year threshold but is, in the minds of many people, a classic example of insurgency and fits into the theoretical definition of an armed conflict.

It is important to be aware that the perfect measure does not exist, and that operationalizations will almost always include or exclude cases that would intuitively be of theoretical interest. This has also been the case in UCDP's coding exercises. For instance, in 2007 the armed group Fatah al-Islam fought a prolonged battle against the Lebanese government in a Palestinian refugee camp, in which at least 400 people were killed. In most people's minds such a long battle was surely an armed conflict. The fighting was, however, not included as an armed conflict by the UCDP since the rebel group lacked a stated incompatibility. The real world does not always fall into neat categories and the great variations in the human condition ensure that there will always be borderline cases and some cases are inevitably lost when applying strict criteria. It may be tempting to make exceptions for cases that intuitively fit but which do not conform to the operational definition. Doing so may increase face validity, but it undermines the reliability of the data and the integrity of the operational definition. It makes the data unsystematic, because the same definition is not applied to all cases, and unsystematic data undermine comparisons across cases. Modifying the operational definition to improve its validity is a better strategy, but it is not always possible and only really advisable if it is discovered that the operational definition is clearly too narrow (or too broad). Changing the criteria to allow a borderline case to be included and then applying this new operationalization systematically typically means including numerous new cases that were correctly excluded by the original operationalization. Thus it may reduce rather than increase validity.

Validity and comparability across time and space

In large datasets validity may also become an issue if the theoretical concept does not have the same meaning across time and space; that is across the set of cases (Collier and Mahon, 1993). Likewise, operational definitions may be context sensitive. If care is not taken to ensure that an operational definition is neutral across time and space there is a risk of systematic error. It is therefore important to make sure that the theoretical concept and the operational definition travel well, picking up the same phenomena without systematic differences between time periods or, for instance, countries.

Problems with operational definitions that are context sensitive are surprisingly common. One example is identified by Joakim Kreutz (2006), in a critique of definitions of terrorism. While studying definitions of violence against civilians and terrorism, Kreutz closely scrutinized the US Department of State's definition of terrorism and discovered that due to the operationalization, attacks in industrialized and urbanized countries were more likely to be counted as terrorism compared to attacks in poor and developing nations. This was due to the fact that attacks in industrialized countries were much more likely to cross the threshold of 'major property damage' exceeding the US$10,000 mark since their infrastructure is much more valuable than infrastructure in poor countries. In practice, a single bomb in Paris is thus much more likely to be recorded as terrorism than a bomb in a slum in Bombay. This validity problem causes a bias in the data so that any inferences based on this data concerning terrorism in the form of bombings of urban areas are likely to be systematically flawed.

Because large datasets are used to say something about general conditions in the world one should take care to avoid context-sensitive measurements unrelated to the theoretical concept since that may introduce significant bias in the data. A hands-on tip to those wishing to construct data comparable on a global scale is to focus on a measure, like intensity in terms of battle-deaths, that disregards local contexts and which can instead be related to the context at a later stage. For instance, 1,000 fatalities is a completely different situation in a country with 10,000 inhabitants than one that has 1,000,000 inhabitants. This is, however, an assumption that should be made separately from the intensity variable itself. Any theoretically motivated case-sensitive modifications can usually be left to a later stage.

A good way to avoid context-sensitive measurements is to run pilot studies of the coding rules for several different countries and time periods, so as to identify at an early stage if the operationalization suffers from any unwanted biases.

Reliability

Reliability concerns to what degree the use of an operationalization yields the same results every time it is applied to the same cases. It does not, as does validity, say anything about whether or not the right phenomenon is captured, but instead if the same phenomenon is recorded across cases. Thus, reliability is about how many random or unsystematic errors a method or variable produces in the data.[4]

The choice in terms of reliability in a data collection exercise is not one between too broad or too narrow. It is instead a function of the complexity of the coding scheme and the measurability or observability of the phenomenon. The simpler the variable is to code the more reliable it will be. The more complex the process of identifying a variable's value, the higher the risk of random errors. The second scenario is caused by the fact that complex coding schemes and difficult to observe phenomena introduce subjectivity into the coding process. However, there is often a tension between reliability and validity, since using variables that are very simple to identify may reduce validity.

A comparison between the coding schemes of the Conflict Barometer of the Heidelberg Institute for Conflict Research (HIIK) and UCDP sheds some light on problems one might encounter in the sphere of reliability when coding conflict data. Whilst the UCDP separates the intensity and the existence of armed conflicts into two different variables, the HIIK project definition of war does not separate between existence and intensity. This is in itself perhaps not much of a problem, but it highlights how reliability may be adversely affected when many different dimensions and coding decisions are forced into one variable.

HIIK defines 'war' as:

> a type of violent conflict in which violent force is used with a certain continuity in an organized and systematic way. The conflict parties exercise extensive measures, depending on the situation. The extent of destruction is massive and of long duration.
>
> (HIIK, 2009: 84)

Compared to the UCDP's simple way of measuring the number of battle-related deaths to set an intensity score, HIIK's variable is composed of several dimensions that need to be coded based on judgment. Formulations such as 'a certain continuity' and 'the extent of destruction is massive and of a long duration' are, in general, more difficult to measure consistently for the individual coder. The difficulties, compared to the UCDP's approach, appear as the sub-concepts mentioned above cannot be ranked according to an easily applicable scale, but instead require a subjective assessment by the coder. Coding procedures requiring subjective assessments are often introduced to increase face validity, but the process of subjective assessment runs the risk of lowering reliability as assessments may vary across coders, and even across the source material analyzed.

Simplicity in the application of an operationalization is, thus, a key to reliable data collection. While such simplicity is not exceedingly difficult to use in data collections that aim to capture simple concepts, it is not as easily done when attempting to represent more complex phenomenon. This is due to the fact that too simple operationalizations might cause validity problems instead. For example, a simple operationalization of democracy could be that elections are held; something that would be very easy to code. Such an operationalization is, however, not very valid, since elections in some countries might be systematically fraudulent or not have any real power over government change. The variable is then not likely to capture actual democracy. This tension between reliability and validity is something that each person attempting to collect data must consider at some length at the initiation of the process. One way to deal with the problem is to break down the theoretical concept along its constituent dimensions, and measure each sub-concept separately and then create an aggregate measure based on these simpler codings. This is the strategy employed by the Polity project (Marshall and Jaggers, 2009) in measuring democracy, and also in the UCDP in measuring organized violence.

Finally, and on a more practical note, good documentation of coding rules and how they are applied is essential for reliability and replicability. Coding rules and practices are documented in special codebooks that may also document individual coding decisions. The importance of codebooks and how they are created is detailed further on in the chapter.

Box 6.3: Validity and Reliability

Validity and reliability relate to each other like accuracy and precision. Valid data captures the correct data, meaning that it is accurate. In terms of a dart board this means hitting the bulls-eye, if that is what you are aiming for. Reliability means that the method or measurement used is precise, in that it captures the same thing every time it is applied. Relating this also to a dart board means hitting the same score every time, even if it is not the bulls-eye.

Choosing scales

Scales are tools for measurement that either record quantitative attributes (ratio and interval scales) or order values according to existence or hierarchy (nominal and ordinal scales). The scales used are an intricate part of any data collection, since the choice of scales has consequences not only for reliability and validity, but also for the way data can be used in analyses.

The choice of scale for a variable is heavily dependent on, a) the phenomenon one wishes to measure; b) the quality and detail of information available to code the data;

Table 6.1: Scales

	Nominal	Ordinal	Interval	Ratio
Ranked hierarchy	No	Yes	Yes	Yes
Equidistance	No	No	Yes	Yes
Absolute zero	No	No	No	Yes

and c) the type of analysis one wishes to use the data for. The starting point in choosing a scale for measurement should always be the theoretical concept, but the availability of sufficiently detailed and nuanced information is usually the limiting condition. It is almost never a good idea to throw away information, so in principle one should always use the highest scale suggested by the theoretical concept, and if this is not possible, then the highest level allowed for by the available information. This will maximize the information content in the data, and higher order scales can always be collapsed into lower order scales (but not the reverse) if need be. A well-planned pilot study will be able to show what type of data it is possible to collect.

The information problem can be illustrated with the measurement of conflict intensity using battle-related deaths. The theoretical concept to be measured has a natural scale. The number of battle-deaths is also a natural ratio scale, so using a ratio scale would in principle be the optimal choice. However, if sources do not allow coders to count the exact number of battle-deaths – perhaps because the sources use vague language like 'scores killed' or 'hundreds of dead and wounded' – a less demanding scale may have to be used. It would still be possible to determine whether or not battle deaths occurred (nominal) and perhaps rank-order the intensity of battles (ordinal) (see Table 6.1). In fact, the latter is what the UCDP does when it ranks conflicts according to their intensity: a minor armed conflict having more than 25 and less than 1,000 battle-related deaths per year and a war having more than 1,000 battle-related deaths per year.

In practice, there is often also a trade-off between information content (which may affect validity) and reliability. Continuing the example from above, if the available sources only contain vague information like 'scores killed' or 'hundreds of dead and wounded', then coding the data on an ordinal scale will involve more subjective judgment on the part of the coder than coding it on a nominal scale. Simply determining whether there were battle-deaths reported requires little or no subjective assessment, while ranking cases according to whether they had more or less battle deaths would require more subjective assessment.

Data collection

The above section touched briefly upon issues pertaining to the actual data-collection exercise. The following will more closely discuss the promises and pitfalls of delving into the empirics. This section will elaborate upon the pros and cons of global versus country-specific sources, building on other data collections, issues of comparability of data, the use of pilot studies and the importance of codebooks. First, however, we will discuss efficiency, that is how to make the most of limited resources. Efficient coding practices are important because they allow the data-collection project to invest scarce resources in raising the quality of the data – for instance by gathering additional information instead of wasting resources on cumbersome scoring cards, unnecessarily complicated variable constructions, or unclear coding rules.

Efficient coding practices

Collecting data on global phenomenon, often also across a vast expanse of time, can be a daunting task in terms of the man-hours required to accomplish the task. For example, the UCDP at the current time (2010) employs three project managers, seven full-time coders and several part-time coders in order to update and develop its data collection.[5] No matter what one wishes to study, collection of global data is time-consuming. Even if the coding exercise is not global in scope, being efficient is important.

It is, thus, of great value if speed and efficiency can be ensured in the coding procedure. A first step here is to ensure that the definitions and operationalizations are simple to apply. Second, to the extent possible the source material to be used should be defined in advance. Third, the actual coding process (entering variable values into Excel, Access or other software) should not be overly complex.

Steps to ensure the simplicity of operationalizations have been discussed above, and focused on minimizing the need for coders to make difficult decisions based on qualitative assessments. Simple, straightforward and directly observable operationalizations save large amounts of time while improving reliability. It bears repeating here that simplicity and observability sometimes have a cost in terms of validity. Thus, there is often a trade-off that the data collector must face when coding more complex phenomena.

Having simple coding rules that do not require a lot of subjective assessment of the source material is also key to ensuring inter-coder reliability. Inter-coder reliability is the ratio with which individual coders agree on setting variable scores when confronted with the exact same material. Reliability is high when all coders agree on the same outcome, and low when few or no coders agree. This is important if the coding exercise is a collective one since low inter-coder reliability causes data to be unacceptably affected by decisions made by individuals, producing inconsistent codings across cases (unsystematic error). Having a clearly written codebook to which coders can refer when faced with uncertainties saves a lot of time and trouble. Some hands-on tips on codebooks can be found below.

In terms of source material it is important to decide in advance where the locus of the information gathering will lie. This is not to say that flexibility should not exist, only that scampering wildly about in the empirical domain is likely not only to be a waste of precious time but also to introduce varying quality into the data. The UCDP has a clearly defined structure for data collection in regards to its annual updates, namely to first conduct searches for news articles (using specific keywords) in Factiva,[6] second to turn to similar data collections such as terrorism monitors and think tanks, third to go through NGO reports such as Human Rights Watch, OCHA and Amnesty, and fourth to validate unclear cases through contacting a network of regional and country experts. Even though this extensive procedure presumably only fits the budget of large-scale projects it shows how a predefined structure not only can save time through minimizing search needs, but also ensure comparability across time and space since the same sources are always consulted.

In terms of entering data into a format/sheet that can later be analyzed, efficiency is gained through not having these being overly complex. Using dummy variables (that can only attain the values of 0 or 1) can be one strategy for simplifying the process of entering the data into the coding sheet. Using dummies minimizes the need for coders to constantly refer to the codebook. Note that all nominal level and ordinal level variables can easily be transformed into a set of dummy variables without loss of information. Simply create one dummy variable for each category/value on the original variable (less one, which will be the reference category). Using dummies necessarily yields many variables and few values, something which in the UCDP's experience is more efficient than having few variables and many values.

Using dummies is, however, not exceedingly important. What is important is to not force too many aspects or dimensions into the same variable. Doing so increases the number of values a variable can take, in the end confusing the coder and often decreasing the ease with which one can create future variables from the existing ones. The UCDP's Peace Agreement Dataset is a case in point. Instead of having a small number of variables with many values in order to measure the type of concessions a peace agreement yields, each possible type of concession (selected from the empirical universe) has a variable of its own, which can only attain the value of 0 or 1. The data becomes easy to code, easy to aggregate and disaggregate, and the coding process is efficient.

Sources for global data

In collecting data on the global level it is important to have access to sources that have global coverage or at least a number of regional sources that together cover the entirety of the globe. In its daily work the UCDP makes use of both sources with global coverage and sources with regional coverage in order to produce the best data possible under existing economic and temporal constraints.

The foremost advantage with sources with global coverage is that key words and search strings can be kept constant and produce the same type of 'hits' throughout an entire database system (or the like), producing comparable source material. The downside is that global coverage nearly always is less detailed than, say, regional or country-based sources (see Chapter 4 for details). The choice of sources depends on a number of factors, including what concept or phenomenon is to be measured, how much detail is needed to code the data, the intended spatial and temporal coverage, and so on. It also depends in part on the resource constraints of the project because these force trade-offs and compromises to be made.

When conducting the annual updates to the lists of armed conflicts, perpetrators of one-sided violence and non-state conflicts around the globe, the UCDP's primary tool is the Factiva database, produced by Dow Jones International. Factiva is a news database that collects news articles of different types from approximately 20,000 sources from 159 countries in around 22 languages. In addition to global news organizations such as Reuters and Associated Press, Factiva also provides television transcripts and transcripts from BBC Monitoring: a source which translates local radio, TV and newspapers into English. Factiva contains a relatively advanced search engine, where subscribers can enter keywords, search for specific types of news, specify what countries are of relevance, which news agencies should be included and much more. Coverage is extremely good from the mid-1990s and onwards, but is poor or non-existent before approximately 1987. Articles can be downloaded by the tens of thousands and subsequently be analyzed by coders. LexisNexis is a similar database which is more focused on law, business and public records.

Another global source, which was widely used by the UCDP in the creation (together with PRIO, the International Peace Research Institute of Oslo) of the UCDP/PRIO Armed Conflict Dataset, 1946–2001, was Keesing's World News Archive. This archive, which is also searchable albeit not with such finesse as is Factiva, contains records of world events since 1931. Its editorial team is based in Cambridge, UK, where analysts process raw data from a variety of sources to create monthly reports of the world's most important social, political and economic events. Although the records have a distinct leaning towards providing much more detailed information on events in the Western world than on other regions, its archives are an invaluable source for those wishing to collect data far back in time. It is one of very few electronic sources that extends past the last 20–30 years and still maintains global coverage.

After going through the material provided by such global sources (for the annual updates, the UCDP goes through approximately 40,000–60,000 news articles) attention is turned to sources that provide either regional data or global data within specified fields of interest. The UCDP consults a number of regional sources, so the examples below are only a few of many.

The South Asian Terrorism Portal (SATP) provides impressive coverage of terrorist-related incidents and information in South Asian countries such as India, Bhutan, Nepal and Pakistan. The web page and its research are run by the Institute for Conflict Management, a non-profit, non-governmental organization in New Delhi. Even though its data and analyses are written with a relatively pronounced pro-government leaning, the amount and quality of the information available are impressive and free for anyone to view and download. Amongst other things the portal provides detailed portraits of rebel outfits, incidents of violence, background documents and research notes.

Human Rights Watch (HRW), one of the world's leading organizations dedicated to protecting human rights, publishes reports on the situation in a wide selection of countries, all with the common denominator of experiencing human rights violations. These high-quality reports give important in-depth information that is most commonly relevant for the one-sided violence category, but at times they also provide significant details about armed conflicts and non-state conflicts, even though the latter two tend not to be the main focus. The major perks of HRW reports are, arguably, their in-depth coverage and the organization's unassailable reliability.

For organized violence in Africa, *Africa Confidential* and the *Africa Research Bulletin* are useful sources of information. Providing comprehensive coverage of political and military developments, these publications utilize a network of local correspondents across the region. Apart from generally tracking political and military developments, entries in *Africa Confidential* and the *Africa Research Bulletin* can give information about issues ranging from international linkages between different conflicts to the who's who of obscure rebel groups.

In its annual updates the UCDP uses these types of sources to supplement the reading and coding of news articles, which – for some countries – only supply the basis of discovering whether or not there is any notable armed activity. In the end, the information contained in the UCDP Database and UCDP datasets is distilled from these tens of thousands of documents and reports that are scrutinized by a team of professional coders each year.

Biases in global data collection

Without a doubt the availability of sources, both global and country-based, affects the final product. In the case of conflict data, isolationist and oppressive regimes are much more difficult to obtain data on. This inevitably means that coverage of organized violence, perhaps especially one-sided violence, becomes somewhat biased. This is simply due to the fact that open countries and countries within which many organizations such as NGOs function will have better coverage. However, not even the most oppressive regimes can completely control information and any large-scale disturbances such as armed conflicts are likely to be reported on in the end. Reporting bias is likely to be more severe for most other types of information, including lower level conflict behavior such as strikes or riots.

Reporting bias is likely to be encountered by anyone who wishes to gather data from countries where specific types of information are sensitive. Country-specific sources can be a way to get around this problem if, for instance, NGOs still manage to operate despite an oppressive regime. This is, however, not likely to be the case across all countries one wishes to collect data on.

Other problems when gathering data on the global level are language and media/other interests in specific countries and regions. The English-speaking world and countries within its sphere of interest inevitably have better coverage in this modern-day lingua franca. In terms of English-speaking media, this problem is mitigated but not resolved through gathering translated news articles from BBC Monitoring. BBC Monitoring service simply cannot capture everything that might be of interest. Without proper language skills in at least a few of the world languages, for instance English, French, Spanish, Arabic, Russian and Chinese, data collection risks being uneven across countries. The scale of this problem really depends on what type of data collection one wishes to carry out and the type of comparisons it will be used for. Uneven reporting across countries affects comparisons across countries and regions, but not comparisons over time. For the UCDP's part, comparability across time is a very important issue and something that is not affected since systematic under-reporting of deaths over time still ensures comparability. The problem is a larger one concerning comparability of, for example, fatality tolls across cases, as the UCDP inevitably acquires more precise data on highly publicized conflicts within the Anglo-Saxon world's sphere of interest (like, for instance, the Israel-Palestine conflict). Whilst the project admits to this issue of comparability there is no easy way around it; the data collection should be guided by the best sources available. It is not a viable alternative to consciously under-report fatalities from a country that is covered by an extensive number of sources for the sake of making it comparable with less well-covered cases. First steps towards resolving such issues of comparability are instead to admit that the problems exist, ensure transparency in the work, and perhaps also be wary of drawing conclusions based on the data too hastily or with too much vigor.

Building on other data collections

When embarking on a large-scale data collection it can be very tempting to simply merge what others have done into your own data to create a more comprehensive coverage of a phenomenon. The obvious drawback is that in such cases one often cannot get to the actual raw data that underlies the final coding (which lessens control of the product). But there are also other issues to pay heed to.

First of all, there can be enormous problems of both theoretical and operational mismatches. Second, even though coding procedures in two separate projects may appear to be almost completely similar, coding practice may differ and there may very well be several issues in the coding processes that produce biases or create poor inter-coder reliability when different data are merged.

For instance, in regard to terrorism it might be tempting to merge two of the world's largest databases on terrorism, namely the RAND Corporation's Database of Worldwide Terrorism Incidents database and the START Global Terrorism Database (at the University of Maryland), to create a much larger selection of cases.[7] The work that needs to be put into such an exercise to ensure compatibility between data, however, severely outweighs the benefit of the larger selection of cases that will become available, since the definitions used by these two projects fail to overlap completely.

Both projects' definitions of terrorism are very similar, but contain several coding criteria that need to be examined by individual coders and decided upon according to qualitative assessments. In line with the advice given in the section on definitions and operationalizations, such coding decisions inevitably invite problems not only for coding, but specifically for comparability across projects. Without a doubt both projects have skilled teams of analysts, something which, however, does not mean that their modus operandi in coding overlaps. Running comparability tests between these two databases to acquire knowledge regarding the overlapping of cases (for example by comparing a few hundred or a few thousands events of terrorism) is a very time-consuming exercise. It might, moreover, not produce the desired result.

The UCDP is never content to include any data collections into its own unless the actual source data can be acquired, analyzed and subsequently recoded. This is a secure way of ensuring the reliability and validity of the coding and something we recommend should be practiced when creating new data.

As an example, when creating the UCDP/PRIO Armed Conflict Dataset 1946–2001 (Gleditsch *et al*, 2002), the UCDP relied on previous data collections only as a starting point for analysis, not for integration into the dataset directly. Work proceeded first through creating a candidate list for armed conflicts, based on a selection of datasets that all dealt with some form of organized violence. Approximately 13 datasets were selected for analysis out of a much larger universe of possible cases, with the observations within each dataset entering a joint 'master list' of possible armed conflicts.[8] In terms of country-years this master list yielded more than 1,500 possible years of armed conflict. Each possible conflict year was then scrutinized using the UCDP's coding criteria and employing the methodology of sources described earlier in this section.[9]

The alternative, which undeniably would have been much less time-consuming, was to merge the existing datasets either into a 'meta dataset' that would contain the entirety of information of all datasets, or only include those cases on which there was agreement according to UCDP criteria. Although the exact results of this alternative are hard to gauge, the UCDP method should be classified as both more valid and reliable since actual source data could be analyzed and not simply accepted at face value. Through using other data collections as a guideline in the work, but supplementing the data with full control over the information sources that finally created the dataset, ensured complete control of the final product; and control over validity and reliability.

As always, the path taken by data collectors or large projects should be chosen on the basis of the resources available for coding, the difficulties identified in mapping a concept and the source material available. It almost always becomes a trade-off between different strengths and weaknesses; a natural fork in the road in a world of limited time and resources. The 'perfect' data collection does not exist and individual researchers must instead engage in the types of choices and trade-offs described above.

Writing a codebook

The codebook is the core of the project in any data-collection venture. It should contain detailed information on all the variables, values and coding decisions that are relevant for the coding process itself and for the final product. The ideal codebook allows not only users to use it as a reference point for understanding the data in front of them, but should also clearly delineate to any coder exactly how and why a variable should be coded.

A codebook commonly begins with a short introduction to the dataset at hand, explaining who created it, what the unit of analysis is and what research gaps the data aims to fill. In short, what the purpose of the data is.

Second, codebooks briefly discuss the theoretical definition of interest, followed by the operational definition that the data collection attempts to record. Thereafter any separate parts of the operational definition are specified.

Third, a codebook briefly explains the coding rules used for every separate variable. Often these coding rules are accompanied by examples of coding decisions or documentation of each coded case (depending on the size of the dataset). Sometimes such detailed documentation or coding examples can be found in an appendix.

Fourth, the codebook should detail what source material has been used, how it has been collected and if any specific key words or search terms have been used in its extraction.

Last, the codebook should list all variables available in the dataset and list their full names, abbreviations in the data, a short description of what they entail, the type of values they can attain (text, 0–1, 0–10, etc) and the scale used, if applicable.

It is a good idea to make two different versions of the codebook, where one is meant for public consumption and has somewhat more brevity and one that is for internal coding use. The latter version of the codebook should be a continuous working document, with very specific details on important coding decisions made and intricate descriptions of coding rules. It is not necessary to include these in the final and public version of the codebook since this would make that document too long, but it is very important to keep this type of documentation for purposes of transparency and stringency.

Separate coding decisions and coding rules that are difficult to apply must be recorded to ensure inter-coder reliability and because it is impossible to remember each separate rule and decision as time passes. This will be especially important if one wishes to expand on an existing dataset: if one cannot recall the coding scheme there will inevitably be all manner of problems and inconsistencies. If temporary staff or research assistants are used it is important to keep good records of coding rules and decisions as well as sources used for each data-point since specific staff members may not be around to answer questions in the future. Without good records it will be impossible to reconstruct the coding process and it will be much harder to replicate. But even if you have done the coding yourself, the importance of keeping good and detailed records cannot be overstated. You may remember what you did a week later, but a year later you will not remember the details of hundreds or thousands of separate coding decisions.

In short, the importance of a solidly written codebook cannot be stressed enough. The codebook is the key not only to interpreting the data and bestowing it with transparency – which is good for users and the data's scientific value – but also to ensuring replicability and inter-coder reliability, which is good for those who work with the actual coding. Rewriting and modifying the codebook should be a work in progress throughout the entire data-collection process.

One should have a more or less complete codebook by the time the big data collection push begins, but after that point it should be updated with any difficult choices or modifications to variables that are made. A great way of testing if a codebook is up to scratch is to put it to the test in a pilot study.

Using pilot studies

Since a large-scale data collection enterprise is time-consuming and not something one wishes to redo over and over again due to errors, it is a good idea to initiate the project, be it an individual or collective one, with a pilot study. A pilot study is a data-collection project in miniature format, where the definition, operationalization, coding rules and data collection are tested on a small sub-set of cases to gauge their workability.

The pilot study should function much in the same way as the actual data collection itself, but pay more heed to the way the operationalizations and rules interact with the studied empirics. The coder should note, while applying the rules given, if the operationalization is difficult to apply, if it discriminates between the phenomenon at hand between cases (in the spatial or temporal domain), if the chosen source material is of sufficient quality, and if the scales chosen provide enough detail for the project's final output, to mention but a few of the things that need to be checked.

Having completed the data collection in the pilot study, the data recorded should be scrutinized closely so as to determine if that which was captured corresponds to the theoretical definition used and the concept in general. If not, parts of the process need to be modified before yet another pilot study is launched. In this way the coding endeavor's final form will not only be honed towards the empirics and theory one wishes to record, but one will also save time in comparison to redoing a whole coding exercise.

There are numerous problems that can be encountered when attempting to collect global data, no matter how much time has been spent on an initial version of a codebook. It is better to identify these problems at an early stage through a pilot study since these issues can then be resolved before the final version of the coding begins. Not only does this save time, but it also ensures a higher quality of data.

When doing a pilot study one should design it so that it includes cases in different contexts, different countries and different time periods in order to cover as much variation as possible. The pilot study should make clear any problems with operationalizations and source material, and also the match between the two. Can the variables of interest be found in the empirical material? Is the empirical material sufficiently detailed? Is the operationalization sufficiently clear? Does it discriminate between empirical cases? To make maximum use of a pilot study its designers should note not only problems with the operationalizations and the source material, but stand ready to modify any part of the process that is too time-consuming, difficult, or even outright detrimental to the data's quality.

Pilot studies do not always identify negative problems, but can instead be enlightening. Delving into the empirics might, instead of uncovering difficult choices to be made, shed light on new ideas for the data collection and give any definition or operationalization a more solid empirical ground.

Building useful datasets

After having identified the theoretical concept of interest, defined its meaning and empirical referent, constructed variables and indicators, and located the empirical material to be used, only the construction of the dataset remains. Key in creating a dataset that can be utilized effectively by the individual researcher and the scholarly community alike is the structure one chooses to create for the input data. Structure relates both to the actual format for the data file and to simple measures to increase the possibilities for users to gain an overview of the data, to merge it with other data, and to revise it with minimal effort.

In terms of data format the computerized world is advanced enough to convert almost any format into any other available one. Still, it is advisable to have the final product in formats that are lingua franca, such as the Excel format or CSV (Comma-Separated Variable), to decrease the risks of the conversion process.

The actual formats for data collection have a much wider range of possibilities in terms of computer code, from using Excel sheets and Access databases, to web browser-based user interfaces. Smaller data collections can make do with just using Excel or similar software for simple calculus, whilst a database program is more appropriate for collections where the number of cases (units of analyses) reach into the tens of thousands. For instance, at the time of writing the UCDP is taking steps to completely abandon Excel-based coding procedures in favor of a network-based database, since the evolution towards more disaggregated conflict data has pushed the number of included observations above 200,000 in some spheres of the data. Only a custom-built and searchable database is capable of giving a satisfactory level of structure and overview of such vast amounts of information. The database in question is capable of thereafter exporting all of the data into almost all available computer formats, aggregated to whatever level of analysis required. For smaller data collections, up to a few thousand observations, Excel or Access is sufficient.

In terms of structuring an actual dataset to increase its user-friendliness and the general ease with which one can work with it, a few pointers are also in order.

A dataset is comprised of a number of rows and columns, where the rows are normally the observation (that is, unit of analysis) and the columns are variables. Each cell contains a value representing the value of the variable in that column for the observation or unit of analysis in that row. Civil war datasets for example, typically have a country-year as the unit of analysis and civil war as one of the variables. Thus, each row has a unique country and year, for example Sierra Leone 1991, and in the civil war column has a value of 0 or 1 depending on whether there was a civil war or not in that particular country that particular year. Thus, each row would be one case of whatever one wishes to observe, and each column would list a separate variable/indicator. Each cell then contains the value for a given observation on a specific variable/indicator.

As simple as this might sound there is always the risk that a dataset becomes very difficult or almost impossible to use to gain an overview as the number of cases increases. It is thus a good idea to, from the start, include a variable in the dataset that is a pure identifier (an ID code). Constructing a unique ID code allows users and administrators to much more effectively revise possible errors, makes communication regarding a dataset easier, and – if constructed in a smart manner – makes sorting, case selection and merging with other data much easier.

In more complicated data structures identifiers become even more important. In converting its data from an aggregated to a disaggregated format, the UCDP has made use of identifier codes, termed RelID (Relationship ID), to set out how one set of data relates to another.[10] The RelID code contains information on individual events of combat, and to what country, conflict, time period, type of violence and dyad an individual event belongs. The code allows for identification of disaggregated data's relationship with aggregated cases, and provides an overview that would otherwise be very difficult to attain. Even in less complicated data structures an ID code that can identify individual cases and also contain valuable information for sorting, selecting and merging data is a particularly useful addition to a dataset.

In most cases it is also valuable to create a dataset that is compatible with other data collections, usually in terms of the unit of analysis. The unit of analysis is dependent on the level of aggregation of the dataset, that is, the dataset's temporal and spatial specifications. The most common form of dataset today is probably the 'country-year' format, where a concept is measured at one point in time (year) in one place (country). More fine-grained disaggregated data might map a concept per month, per region, or as in the case of ACLED (Armed Conflict Location and Event Data) (Raleigh *et al*, 2010) per specific geographic point and single day. The choice of structure in this case is dependent on what uses the data is intended for. The bulk of global data that might be of interest to scholars within the peace and conflict sphere is most often only available with any accuracy in the country-year format, such as UN data on population and development, etc, World Bank data on economic factors, and the indicators of regime type contained in the Polity IV data. Maximum compatibility is thus reached by constructing datasets at the country-year level.

Disaggregated studies of various phenomena – such as armed conflicts – are, however, on the increase in the scholarly community. Disaggregated data on organized violence is compatible with an ever increasing amount of other disaggregated data, including information on, for instance, land degradation, ethnic composition, road coverage and other factors. Disaggregated data has the added benefit that it can answer research questions that aggregated data cannot, and it can at the same time also be aggregated to the country-year format in simple ways. For smaller data collections the gathering of global data on a disaggregated level is, however, not really an option due to the enormous increase it yields in the possible universe of cases. For example, a spatial disaggregation from the national level to the district level of Afghanistan increases the number of cases from 1 to 398 per studied year. On a global scale the universe of cases is thus enormous, especially if the data is also in a time series format.

To further maximize compatibility with other data it is also recommended to follow the available lists of independent countries, such as the Correlates of War-list (Correlates of War Project, 2008) or the Gleditsch and Ward list (Gleditsch and Ward, 1999), when constructing a country-year dataset. Identifying an independent state is more difficult than it might intuitively appear, and simply building on lists created through certain coding rules not only removes the risk of mistakes but also increases compatibility and possibilities for the direct merging of datasets. In general it is always a sound idea to conform to lists of this type, as the possibilities of compatibility are large. For instance, the UCDP follows the Gleditsch and Ward country codes for assigning locations of armed conflicts, after which one can follow the UCDP's list of conflicts to assign dyads, etc. With a well thought-through method of organization this process can continue down to the lowest level of data points available.

In sum, compatibility and user-friendliness should guide the process of creating a dataset, for the sake of both the creator and the future dissemination and use of the data.

Conclusions

Global data for quantitative analyses is of importance to frontline research, especially since more advanced methods of analysis are constantly making their way into the social sciences and require more fine-grained input. On top of the impact a single dataset may have on research, a sound data-collection effort also opens up for future expansions of the project and may thus spawn more and even improved datasets, much as has been the case with the UCDP's original lists of armed conflicts. The gains of producing global data can thus often be twofold: serving the individual projects and the larger whole of cumulative research.

But, as this chapter has shown, the problems and pitfalls are plentiful, throughout all the stages of production. Since the world commonly presents such an enormous universe of cases it is of utmost importance to think the entire process through, from theoretical abstraction to the final numbers entered into an Excel spreadsheet. Although the separate pieces of a project might look robust on their own it is not until the parts are forged into a solid whole that one is really capable of visualizing the entire process, from start to finish. Paying heed to all of the parts of the process is what, in the end, yields data of the highest quality. Time, attention to detail and creativity are other important ingredients needed to successfully create high-quality datasets.

Collecting global data is as much a daunting task as it is a rewarding one. A well-conceived project that is rigorously executed has a good chance of producing unique data for the greater benefit of the research community.

Summary

- Devote time to the concept of interest; figure out what it is – exactly – that the research seeks to capture.
- Turn to the scholarly literature for guidance and to make the definition theoretically relevant.
- Create a definition with the need for comparability, generalizability and observability in mind.
- Construct variables that capture the theoretical basis of the operational definition. Make sure that the variables will measure what they are intended to measure (validity) and capture the same thing across many cases (reliability).
- Make an inventory of sources that can be used to collect the data.
- Write a codebook that includes detailed information on all the variables and values, and that comments on coding decisions that have implications for the data. Work on the codebook should be an ongoing process throughout the data-collection exercise.
- Do a 'test drive' by carrying out a pilot study. Adjust definitions, variables or sources if problems are encountered.

Further reading

Eck, K. (2005) 'A Beginner's Guide to Conflict Data: Finding the Right Dataset', *UCDP Paper No.1*. Online at: < www.pcr.uu.se/publications/ UCDP_pub/ UCDP_paper1.pdf> (accessed 26 July 2010).

King, G., Robert O.K. and Verba, S. (1994) *Designing Social Inquiry: Scientific inference in qualitative research*, Princeton, NJ: Princeton University Press.

Sambanis, N. (2004) 'What is Civil War? Conceptual and Empirical Complexities of an Operational Definition', *Journal of Conflict Resolution*, 48 (6): 814–58.

Sartori, G. (1970) 'Concept Misformation in Comparative Politics', *American Political Science Review*, 6 (4): 1033–53.

Small, M. and Singer, J.D. (1982) *Resort to Arms: International and civil wars 1816–1980*, Beverly Hills, CA: Sage.

Wallensteen, P. (2003) 'The Uppsala Conflict Data Program 1978–2003: How it all began, how it matured and where it is today', in M. Eriksson (ed.) *States in Armed Conflict 2002*, Uppsala: Uppsala Publishing House.

Notes

1. While the scope of study has widened since the early 2000s, this section will look explicitly at armed conflict.
2. In 2002, UCDP expanded its data-collection exercise to also include non-state conflicts, which to some extent overlaps with the concept 'communal conflict'. The non-state conflict category is broader, though, also including conflicts between rebel groups or between militias. Note, though, that UCDP still views these conflicts as different from the category of 'armed conflicts' and that the definition of the latter hasn't changed. Instead, a new category has simply been added in the coding exercise. This is expanded upon later in this chapter.
3. Note that the level of organization required for non-state conflicts is looser than for armed conflicts and one-sided violence, as both formally (for instance rebel groups and/or militias) and informally (for instance ethnic groups and/or religious communities) organized groups are accepted. Even given this, there is a distinct difference compared to one-sided violence, since no matter the level of organization, there have to be two similarly organized actors involved in non-state conflicts, whereas one-sided violence by definition can only include cases with one organized actor.
4. If an operational definition causes not random errors of measurement but systematic errors, there exists instead a problem of validity, since the definition used captures the wrong thing.
5. Note, however, that the program runs several parallel coding exercises.
6. Factiva is an online news database, whose uses are expanded upon further on in this section.
7. RAND Corporation's Database of Worldwide Terrorism Incidents is available at www.rand. org/ise/projects/terrorismdatabase/, and the START Global Terrorism Database at www. start.umd.edu/gtd/.
8. These datasets were: COW Interstate Wars, COW Civil and Extrasystemic Wars, COW Militarized Interstate Disputes v.2.10, International Crisis Behaviour, KOSIMO, Licklider's Civil War Termination Dataset, Polity98, State Failure Project, Minorities at Risk, Polyarchy, Overt Military Interventions Dataset, Intrastate Conflicts with Third-Party Interventions dataset and the Jacob Bercovitch & Gerald Schneider conflict dataset. At a later stage several other sources were also consulted to consolidate the list. For details on these datasets and how they were used, see Gleditsch *et al* (2001).
9. Some exceptions did exist; for instance, the coding team did not deem it relevant to further analyze if there had been a war in Korea between 1950 and 1953. Other clear-cut cases were also not analyzed further.
10. The UCDP embarked on such an enterprise in order to construct its UCDP Geo-referenced Event Dataset (UCDP GED); a disaggregated dataset on organized violence with global coverage. In short, the exercise entailed disaggregating all of the data that underlies the

datasets on state-based conflicts, non-state conflicts and one-sided violence in order to create a dataset consisting of hundreds of thousands of individual events of the use of deadly force. Each event is complete with a geo-referenced location and exact time and participants, to mention a few of the variables available.

7   Comparative Field Research in War-torn Societies[1]

Kristine Höglund

Introduction

This chapter addresses methodological and ethical questions that arise from field research in countries that are experiencing or have recently undergone a violent conflict or civil war. The chapter focuses on the particular challenges of pursuing comparative research in such contexts. By now there is a significant methodological literature, including some of the chapters in this volume, which describes the challenges involved in field research and which provides practical advice for scholars involved in such research. These include, for instance, suggestions on how to record and organize the empirical material, time-management and budgeting, and interview and survey techniques.[2] However, hardly any of these studies review these issues from the point of view of comparative research and few of these examine issues related to research design.[3]

The main challenge confronting the researcher using a comparative method is that there may be differences in the cases of study concerning how insecure the research environment is, and how sensitive the research topic is considered to be by those participating in the study, or by the power holders of the country in which the research is carried out. In peace research, unlike many other disciplines which may find themselves doing research in volatile contexts, the insecure research context is not by accident, but by design. The very focal point of peace research regards matters related to war and peace, life and death. This is the case for most studies on research themes that are at the core of peace research, for instance studies on political violence, on reconciliation processes, and on armed groups such as paramilitaries, rebels or guerrillas. The insecurity of the research setting is determined by the type of conflict that is studied, and when in a conflict's trajectory the research is carried out. The research context will change as the conflict develops in new directions: an escalation in the conflict will make matters worse and de-escalation will generally improve the research context. Yet in a post-war context the legacy of violence, changing power relations and continued repression of regimes can also hamper or influence the research process in important ways. Other challenges are results of the sensitivity of the research focus. In many instances, it is a combination of both an insecure research environment and a sensitive research topic that causes problems in the research process.

Concerns about the research topic and the research context have implications for practically every part of the research process and for the research on each of the cases under study. This chapter analyzes the research challenges relating to: 1) the crafting of the research design, 2) the data-gathering process (the field research), and 3) analysis of the data and publication of the study. It includes reflections on the experience of doing research on peace processes and political violence in various parts of the world and makes use of existing scholarly literature on comparative research and field research in sensitive, insecure and demanding environments. While some of the issues reviewed in this chapter are specific to or compounded for peace research, others overlap with research in other social science disciplines. The challenges are particularly severe when a scholar is new to a research context. But improving research skills, careful preparation for field research, and concerns about ethics are equally important for the more experienced research scholars.

The chapter should be read as a complement to several of the other chapters in this book dealing with specific data-gathering techniques that can be used both in comparative and single-case studies; see especially the chapters on in-depth interviews (Chapter 8), focus groups (Chapter 9) and surveys (Chapter 10). The purpose is not to cover all methodological and ethical questions of field research in conflict-ridden societies, but to address those challenges that are intrinsic to comparative research. Comparative research is not only fraught with challenges, but also has several advantages compared to other research approaches, and the chapter highlights the potential of comparative research in overcoming some of the difficulties inherent in research in conflict-torn societies. Finally, it is important to make clear that this chapter is written from a Westerner's point of view and that issues related to insider-outsider perspectives on conflict-related issues will be discussed briefly later on in this chapter.

The chapter is divided into five parts. The next section provides a brief introduction to comparative field research and then moves on to discuss issues related to important elements of the research design. In particular, questions concerning case selection and concepts/measurements are discussed. In the third section, the challenges of the fieldwork itself are raised and issues such as access to informants, research procedures and risk assessment are analyzed. The third part outlines some of the key practical and ethical issues in relation to the analysis of the empirical material and in publishing the findings of the research. The final concluding section summarizes the main challenges emerging from comparative research in conflict-ridden societies.

Research design in comparative field research

Comparative qualitative research can be developed in different ways, but entails contrasting two or more entities. It is based on the careful analysis of the cases selected for analysis. For this reason, the conclusions in this chapter pertaining to field research are also applicable for in-depth analysis of one case only. Comparison is often cross-national, but can also include comparison within a state, be it between different rebel groups, administrative units (such as provinces or municipalities), or social, ethnic or religious groups. Since field research requires substantial resources and knowledge about the local context, it is often a wise research strategy to do comparisons within one or two countries, at least for an individual researcher, rather than to include too many countries within a specific research project. Time can also be an important factor. Comparisons can be made, for instance, between different regimes over time, in a state. The examples presented here are predominantly drawn from cross-national studies, but the challenges are often present in comparisons within countries as well. This chapter complements existing literature on qualitative methods, and a basic knowledge of the different comparative research techniques is assumed.[4]

The perspective in this book is that research aspires to cumulate knowledge based both on theoretical/conceptual development and theory-driven empirical research. In terms of qualitative, comparative research methods, a multitude of techniques can be used including structured focused comparison, and within-case analytical methods such as process tracing or analytical narratives. Field visits serve two purposes: 1) the collection of both primary and secondary data through various research techniques, such as interviews, surveys, focus groups or participant observation, and 2) an improved understanding of the case and the context, which will facilitate the analysis of the data.

Research designs for comparative research in conflict and post-conflict environments need to be carefully crafted. A research design determines the structure of the research: the elements that jointly integrate the research question, theory, method and data. Two issues will be examined in relation to the overall research design: 1) case selection, and 2) concepts and measurements.

Case selection

The selection of cases is critical to any research design, not least comparative, qualitative research. Case selection has to be guided by the objectives of the study and with only a few cases, a random selection of cases is usually inappropriate. A number of important points have been made about case selection and related problems. Different consideration can drive the selection of cases: for instance, cases can be studied because they are typical or most-likely cases, or because they are deviant or extreme cases (see for instance George and Bennet, 2005; Gerring, 2007). For comparative research, the essential issue is case selection, which provides for an 'appropriate frame of comparison' (Collier and Mahoney, 1996: 66–69). This involves, first, an identification of the variation in the outcome that is to be explained.[5] Outcomes can, for instance, relate to the level of violence in post-war societies or variations in the achievements of a reconciliation process. Second, it involves the identification of cases that in fact are comparable and where it is expected that similar causal processes are taking place. In other words, an assumption about *unit homogeneity* is made, to ensure that comparison is made between phenomena that are in fact comparable. What is considered comparable is highly dependent on the research question. The most common approach in comparative case study research has been to select cases that are as similar as possible, in order to make the assumption that the conditions that the cases share do not influence what is to be explained. This research strategy may make it easier to distinguish the influence of the specific factor or conditions under study. An alternative approach is to make comparisons between cases from dissimilar situations, such as different social, cultural and geographical contexts. The basic idea is that cases should be selected from as different social systems as possible and if common causes or social processes can be found in spite of these contrasts, the research design provides strong arguments for building a theory on the findings (Przeworski and Teune, 1970: 34–9).

Besides these general guidelines, practical issues come into consideration. Is there comparable information about the cases? If I plan on carrying out field visits and gather information on-site, what countries and regions within those countries are accessible? The research environment in which the research will be carried out will have implications for several aspects of the data-gathering process.

Because of the need to take into consideration practical issues relating to data availability and accessibility, there is a risk that a certain type of selection bias is introduced in comparative research. Researchers may prefer to study cases where they expect data not to be too difficult to gather or where they will not place themselves or others in unnecessary danger. The result may be that certain cases become overrepresented, in particular those in which peace has taken hold or at least where there is not a full-fledged war.[6] Peace research has a tendency to use fairly simplified terms such as 'success' versus 'failure' or 'peace' versus 'war'. But if research is to improve understanding about the driving forces for peace, the cases in which peace has not been achieved also need to be analyzed.[7]

Another type of bias – partly related to the stage a conflict is in – is a result of international involvement in a conflict. Countries where international involvement is extensive – in terms of preventive and conflict resolution efforts such as a UN peacekeeping mission or donor commitments – usually have more documentation on the conflict and better access for outside researchers who can use contacts with the international organizations to reach the research participants needed for the study. But the information emerging from international organizations should be assessed with the same criteria as any other source. The pros and cons of partnering with local or international organizations to gain access and protection, but also the risk for research fatigue, will be discussed later in this chapter and are also discussed in Chapters 8, 9 and 10.

How can it be ensured that a case selection is made that is both theoretically and methodologically relevant and in which data can be gathered without major risks for the researcher and the informants? First, there are a number of misperceptions about the data availability and accessibility of war-torn countries. It is interesting to note that, contrary to common perceptions, news coverage of a civil war does not appear to decrease when violence escalates (Urlacher, 2009; see also Chapter 4 in this book). This finding points to the accessibility of different types of data. Conflicts that include high levels of violence, such as the Darfur conflict in Sudan, have attracted attention from scholars and reporters, and secondary data is ample. But pursuing fieldwork in Sudan to obtain primary data may involve considerable challenges. While it is easier to travel to and collect primary data in areas with less conflict and violence, there are generally fewer studies, reports and news reports that provide secondary information about the area. Consider the difference between comparing communal violence in Darfur and eastern Sudan in 2010. While eastern Sudan will be easier to travel to than Darfur, because the east is relatively peaceful (especially in comparison to Darfur), there are fewer secondary sources to support and contextualize findings. As in most types of research, these are important trade-offs in terms of information access, which need to be considered.

Second, there are steps that can be taken to increase awareness of how the selection of cases is made and how it is affected by the availability and accessibility of information. First, as in all comparative research, the criteria for case selection should be guided by the research objectives – and thus there should be clear criteria and transparency in terms of the type or class of cases that are of interest. In other words, it should be possible – at least theoretically – to identify the universe of cases. While it may not be possible to identify all relevant cases, a clear delineation of the criteria for the selection of cases helps to extend focus beyond those events that have received most media and scholarly attention so far. While there is nothing wrong with studying already well-researched cases, it is important to consider why such cases have received attention and how including such cases in a study may or may not bias the findings.

Once a set of cases has been identified that fits the criteria for inclusion, it is possible to probe into how accessible the cases are. Preliminary research is required to survey the type of sources available. In order to assess how research can be conducted within a specific country and region, area experts may be consulted. What is the climate of doing research in the country in question? What events may influence the political situation in the countries in which the study is carried out? Raising such questions at the stage of the case selection process will assist the researcher in making an informed decision about the pros and cons of a specific case sample. If there is uncertainty about how accessible information is on particular cases, it is useful to keep a list of alternative cases for a plan B.

It can never be known with certainty to what extent a case will be difficult to research and how accessible it will be at the time the field research is pursued. Changes in the conditions can happen fairly rapidly. For instance, I began my field research on the failed 1994–95 peace process in Sri Lanka in 2002 when a ceasefire made travelling to the war-torn areas in Sri Lanka possible. By late 2005, travelling to the same areas had become precarious due to an escalation of violence. What are the options for comparative research in such a situation? Should the case be dropped? In many instances, there are alternative ways in which sufficient information can be obtained. For instance, there may be Diaspora communities available outside of the country that can be interviewed, or other areas in the country that are accessible. If data cannot be gathered in a systematic manner across the cases, the case can nonetheless be useful and some kind of comparison can usually be made between the cases even if different types of information are used for each case. Again, explicitness in terms of the sources used and discrepancies between them, as well as an assessment of the impact, usually takes the research quite far. An analysis of why it was difficult to access certain types of sources or why there is no or little information about certain actors or events can help inform the situation and provides important clues about the context in which events are playing out and in which the research is carried out.

While textbooks – including this book – tend to stress the importance of having a clearly defined research question and focus to guide the entire project, it must also be mentioned that under certain circumstances it can be unproductive to stick dogmatically to a research question that cannot be adequately addressed due to a lack of information or difficulties in obtaining the right kind of material. Rather than abandoning the research project or inventing a new research question, it is usually possible to shift emphasis. For instance, my research on the causes and effects of electoral violence at the village level in Sri Lanka had to shift focus due to concerns about safety and access. While originally intended to be a comparative study across several locations in Sri Lanka, the escalating conflict and the sensitivity of the research topic made it more uncomfortable both for me and my local research partner to spend time in the area, to ask questions about the causes of violence, and to get access to perpetrators of violence. Fairly quickly after the inception of the field work we narrowed the scope of the study to include only one village where we had established good contacts and to focus more clearly on the effects of violence, rather than on perpetrators and causes. For a useful guide on when to redesign the project during field research, see Lynch (2004).

Concepts, measurements and language

Another challenge in a comparative research design is related to concepts, measurements and language (also see Chapters 4, 6 and 8 in this book). The comparative scholar needs to reflect on the type of terminology used in each context under study. This is warranted both for methodological reasons (so to formulate the most appropriate type of questions) and for ethical considerations (so as not to ask questions that are provocative or offensive from the respondents' point of view).

The theoretical concepts used, and how they are defined, have implications for the validity of the study. A problem arises when the same theoretical concept has different meanings in the societies of comparison. One example relates to the term democracy: 'a procedure that is "democratic" in one cultural context might be profoundly undemocratic in another country' (George and Bennet, 2005: 19). A set of concepts in peace research display similar variations in meaning, for instance forgiveness and victims.

The relationship between concepts and measurements is critical. The concern with theoretical concepts is not solely an exercise in theory (Goertz, 2006). Concepts are important because they are what Sartori refers to as 'data containers'. Without solid conceptual understanding and measurements, comparative research will fail in its efforts to advance knowledge and the theories used cannot be adequately explored or tested (Sartori, 1970: 1039). The key to dealing with these problems is to move along the 'ladder of abstraction', moving from highly abstract concepts at the theoretical level to a high level of concretization at the measurement level.[8] In this sense, the usefulness of the concepts (the 'fact-finding containers') can only be assessed at the lowest level of abstraction. Part of field research, thus, is to uncover the usefulness of the concepts and measurements: to test, adjust and retest, so that they reflect reality.

Box 7.1: Sartori on Theoretical Concepts as Data Containers

Low level of abstraction may appear uninteresting to comparative scholars. He would be wrong, however, on two accounts. First, when the comparative scholar is engaged in field research, the more his fact-finding categories are brought down to this level, the better his research. Second, it is the evidence obtained by nation-by-nation, or region-by-region (or whatever the unit of analysis may be) that helps us decide which classification works, or which new criterion of classification should be developed.

(Sartori, 1970: 1043)

For comparative research this means that concepts with a high level of abstraction at the theoretical level are needed in order to be able to make a relevant comparison between cases. But at the level of operationalization of the same concepts – what to actually observe in the real world or ask questions about – context-specific measurements are often required. For instance, when analyzing political violence, such violence can have markedly different manifestations in different societies. Whereas political assassinations of a clandestine nature were common during the peace process in Guatemala, massacres with political overtones were widespread in South Africa. Another illustration relates to violence against collaborators. In South Africa, necklacing became a manifestation of a specific type of violence commonly used against people collaborating with the apartheid regime. Necklacing was a lynching practice in which a gas-filled rubber tire was placed around the body and set on fire. In Northern Ireland such practices were not used, but instead collaborators with the other side were often subject to so-called punishment shootings, in which the target was shot in the knee. It is only with careful and context-sensitive analysis that it is possible to determine whether these two practices provide measurements of the same kind of phenomenon.

Related to concepts and measurements is the language used when in the field: the terminology used to describe and explain the research project and to ask questions in interviews, focus groups or surveys. The language used is important, since it is often politically sensitive and there may be a need to 'adapt to different political settings in the absence of neutral language' (Knox, 2001: 215). In many conflict-ridden societies, certain terms become almost provocative, such as 'forgiveness' in Northern Ireland and 'reconciliation' in Cambodia and Sri Lanka. Reconciliation, for instance, is a term that carries Christian religious connotations and has therefore been problematic to use in non-Christian countries. In other instances, terms that may appear problematic, unscientific or even derogatory by scholars of peace research – such as the use of 'tribal wars' to describe communal violence in Africa – may be commonly used and widely acceptable among those actually affected by the violence.

Conducting pilot studies can be a very useful way to test concepts and language. If it is not possible to travel multiple times to the region, terminology can be tested and discussed with other researchers with knowledge about the country either before departing for the field or as a start of the field research.

Field research: the data-gathering process

This section examines the issues that may arise in the information-gathering phase of the research process. These relate to 1) access to information, informants and respondents, and 2) risk assessment. Such issues should be considered and evaluated before field research is undertaken. Once in the country, judgement may be blurred by the mental and physical stress – due to emotional drainage, loneliness and harsh physical conditions – the researcher may be subject to. At the same time, it is impossible to fully get a sense of the local knowledge needed to make an informed judgment without being in the field.

Access to and evaluation of information

As discussed in relation to case selection, some information is difficult to get access to. Access to informants and their propensity to provide relevant information is influenced by, for instance, how trustworthy the researcher is considered to be and the sensitivity of the research topic. In general, the problems with access have to do with fear of reprisals for speaking openly about sensitive issues, a culture of silence that may be a result of repression of expression of opinions, and the stigma (shame and trauma) of having been a victim or perpetrator of violence (Feenan, 2002: 149). In certain contexts, 'many people ... believe that merely talking about conflict with outsiders can provoke it' (Tabyshalieva, 2001: 134).

In addition, for the reasons mentioned above, it can also be difficult to assess the information provided in conflict-ridden societies. Parties in a conflict have incentives to misrepresent or not to reveal information, because doing otherwise can give the opponent advantages (Fearon, 1995).[9] Due to the asymmetrical nature of many conflicts, some groups may be more accessible or available. Weaker parties, such as minority groups, may be more willing to speak with researchers because they see it as a way to channel their opinions and express their demands. There are also psychological processes at play in how information is related. Silences, evasions and inventions on part of the individuals may not be due to deliberate lying, but are coping strategies for dealing with trauma (Fujii, 2010). Again, a number of ethical questions arise when considering access: what kind of information do I really need? How will my probing into these questions influence the individual participating in the study? What right do I have to ask these questions?

The research setting in which the data-gathering is carried out will be influenced by a set of factors that are likely to vary in the different cases under study, regardless of whether the comparison is within a specific country or across countries or regions. The following questions will now be discussed in turn: the timing of the research, entry points, research fatigue, and the identity of the researcher.

Timing

The sensitivity of the research topic may depend on when in a conflict cycle the research is carried out. Box 7.2 illustrates how the research context in Sri Lanka has changed over time.[10]

With the passing of time, the sensitivity of a research topic can change with the result that people are more willing to speak about what has unfolded in the past. For instance, in the midst of or following a successful peace process, the reduction in tensions and the creation of momentum often make the research pursued less of a 'hot' topic and facilitate access to relevant informants. However, incomplete or failed peace processes are often followed by polarization and an escalation of violence, which make it difficult to gain access to informants and useful information. In such a context, the researcher dealing with armed groups can be suspected of being a terrorist sympathiser. However, it should be noted that in some conflict societies, the presence of researchers is seen as beneficial because they provide security for the community or individual who is participating in the study (Lee, 1995: 15). A new post-conflict order can also create new roles for the actors who took part in the war – power may shift from one side to another – which in turn can create incentives for them to portray the situation in a certain way.

For comparative research this means that the timing of the research will influence the willingness of individuals to participate in the research and volunteer more information. The information provided after a lapse in time – sometimes years or decades after the actual events studied were experienced – also has to be considered and assessed based on temporal proximity (see more in Chapter 3 in this book).

Entry points

In terms of gaining access to relevant networks, the importance of introduction by key people cannot be overstated. In societies where access is problematic, reliance on key gatekeepers and consent from important stakeholders might in fact be necessary (Feenan, 2002; Lee, 1995). In such cases, access to individuals can be facilitated by local organizations and it may be wise to seek partnership with a local NGO or a research institution.[11] However, affiliation with local partners should be considered carefully. In conflict situations there are few social actors who are seen as neutral. NGOs, universities and research institutes become part of the overall polarization of society. For this reason, it is important to evaluate how the organization is perceived in the local context

Box 7.2: Case Study of Changing Research Context – Sri Lanka

With the signing of a ceasefire agreement between the Sri Lankan government and the separatist Liberation Tigers of Tamil Eelam (LTTE) in early 2002, the security context improved significantly. The result was that society opened up for research on peace and conflict. However, a marked escalation of violence began in 2005 with a development into full-fledged war in 2006. The ceasefire was formally abrogated by the government in January 2008. After intense fighting during the spring of 2009, the LTTE was declared defeated in May the same year. However, the Sri Lankan state has, after the end of the war, continued to display highly authoritarian tendencies. Repression against human rights activists and journalists remains widespread. Below, the changing research context is exemplified with a comparison between the situation in 2002 and 2007–2009 on a number of aspects.

	2002	*2007–2009*
Access to war-torn areas	The opening of the A9 road in 2002 and commercial flights to Jaffna peninsula increases mobility and exchange between the war-torn north and the southern parts of the country	Land way to Jaffna peninsula closes in 2007, only few flights to Jaffna. Bus service between Jaffna in the north and the southern parts of the country opens in August 2009
Access to the country and legal issues	Obtaining a visa for peace researchers is generally unproblematic	Obtaining a visa for research on peace and conflict-related issues is increasingly difficult. Several international staff in UN agencies, embassies, etc have their visas revoked or non-renewed, allegedly due to criticism raised against government policies
Collaboration with local actors	Access to and collaboration with local universities and NGOs was facilitated by the favorable climate created for these institutions during the peace process	Local research collaboration was made more difficult due to government interference with universities and the threatening of human rights and peace promoting NGOs
Censorship and freedom of speech	Space for increased freedom of speech opens up. Sri Lanka ranked as no 51 on Reporters without Borders' Press Freedom Index	Sri Lanka ranked as no 156 in 2007, as no 165 in 2008, and no 162 in 2009 on Reporters without Borders' Press Freedom Index. Prevention of Terrorism Act and emergency regulations result in self-censorship among journalists, analysts and intellectuals

and the implications it can have for access to informants. The affiliation with a local organization can influence perceptions about neutrality and independence and make access more difficult (Howard, 2004: 9). For instance, in Sri Lanka some of the Colombo-based NGOs have a high standing with the international community and have links to high-level politics. But they may not be the most adequate channels into some of the local communities. The dilemma for comparative scholars is that in certain research settings they will be highly dependent on local partners. Such dependence may, in turn, influence the type of information available. In addition, a specific entry point may be exclusionary, since social networks in divided societies may not be overlapping. Associating with one side might prevent access to the other side. To avoid bias, an important piece of advice is to use different points of entry to individuals and networks (Cammet, 2006; Gokah, 2006).

Another matter for comparative research is that different strategies vis-à-vis local organizations may need to be adopted, due to the varying political, social and security setting in which the research is carried out. As described by Paluck (2009) identification with the NGO she was working with in Rwanda and the Democratic Republic of Congo (DRC) was made in different ways in the two research settings. Due to the high levels of violence in DRC, close identification with the NGO provided security for the research team. In Rwanda, on the other hand, she did not want the research to be too closely identified with the NGO since in local settings the NGO had close associations with the government.

Research fatigue

The 'successful' cases, or cases which for other reasons have received a large share of interest from the research community, can have an advantage in the sense that there is ample information about various aspects of the conflict. However, there is a risk that such cases suffer from what has been termed 'research fatigue' (Clark, 2008, see also Feenan, 2002). In Northern Ireland and Bosnia, the proliferation of attention from the academic community has clearly dampened interest from local communities to participate in research. In South Africa, a country that has attracted an enormous amount of interest from foreign scholars, I have encountered suspicion from local community leaders, universities and NGOs about my research. They have had bad experiences with researchers who, in their view, come to South Africa, take the information they need and leave without returning anything to the South African society or the communities they study.[12] Research fatigue can also be related to international involvement in the country and conflict in question. In situations of research fatigue, the researcher needs to attend carefully to issues of how the research is presented and be prepared to explain how the research can be of interest to those participating in the study.

The comparative scholar must thus be prepared to encounter research fatigue in some contexts and not in others, so having very different experiences of the field situation in different contexts. For any researcher, being met with scepticism and negative attitudes can be very uncomfortable. On the other hand, in countries that have experienced very little international attention, researchers – especially those from the outside – can attract interest from many different sectors within society. Such a situation can facilitate access to informants, but too much attention can sometimes also be an overwhelming experience for a researcher who wants to blend in and not draw much attention to the research as such for reasons of security.

Identity

The identity of the researcher is of particular importance in field research. How is the identity of the researcher perceived in different research settings and by research subjects? How does it influence the information shared by the participants in interviews, focus groups or surveys? Identity traits that may influence the perception of the researcher relate to nationality, age, gender and skin colour or other makers that make up part of the appearance of the researcher. Issues related to researcher identity have often been captured in the insider-outsider debate, which highlights the advantages and challenges involved in doing research as a native researcher versus being an outsider in terms of cultural context and identity (Hermann, 2001). While the native researcher may have advantages in terms of language and access due to a better understanding of how the society functions, the outsider may benefit from locals' perception of a 'stranger-value' (Gokah, 2006). The outsider researcher is in many cases seen as a sympathetic and interested person and is for this reason well-received. However, the type of information shared with an outsider may be different to that of an insider due to higher levels of trust between respondents and the native scholar. Yet, in some instances, sharing information with outsiders can be easier because they will not remain in the area or the country.

While the debate on outsiders versus insiders has raised many important questions the distinction is often difficult to apply in a clear-cut manner. For instance, a Swedish scholar doing work on Swedish peacekeepers in Kosovo is an outsider or insider depending on who is being interviewed. The researcher is an insider in terms of nationality and language when interviewing Swedish soldiers, but may also identify closely with academics in Kosovo due to a shared professional identity. This implies that other characteristics of the researcher, such as gender, profession or age, may be equally important in the interaction with the research context.[13] Thus, strategies for presenting the study and the conduct of the researcher need to be adapted to the specific research setting.

Different sides to the conflict are likely to view different nationalities or organizations as sympathetic or unsupportive of their cause. Nationality may influence the perceived neutrality and independence of the research and the researcher.[14] In many countries, the UN, NATO or other organizations play a key role and the researcher's perceived association with such organizations can influence how he or she is received (Cammett, 2006: 16). In Kosovo, for instance, NATO was generally liked by the Kosovo Albanians, while many Serbs expressed distrust towards the foreign troops. In some areas in Sri Lanka, people were sceptical of Norwegian scholars, since the Norwegian mediators were considered biased in favour of the LTTE by part of the Singhalese population. Many Tamils, on the other hand, have been supportive of the Norwegian mediation effort. In South Africa, Sweden's longstanding support for the struggle against apartheid has generally been a door opener for Swedish scholars in the post-apartheid era.

A problem which may be of greater concern for outsider researchers than native researchers is that they may unintentionally raise expectations about rewards for those involved in the research or their community. Western scholars, in particular, may be associated with humanitarian or development organizations working in the area. In any situation, research with human participants involves a give and take, which raises ethical issues. As is discussed in some of the other chapters in this volume (8, 9 and 10), financial compensation can be offered to participants for their time in taking part in a study. Yet, even without financial compensation, power relations may be changed within local communities. Being associated with a research project may in a specific context involve risks, but may in another context be associated with status and privilege, which can cause or aggravate tensions in a society or a social group. The researcher must reflect upon how his or her presence and research project may be received in different research contexts, both for ethical reasons and for reasons related to access and the information related by informants.

Risk assessment in multiple conflict zones

Considerations about access and confidentiality for individuals participating in the study are also related to the security of the researcher. In many ways, the security risks in conflict societies are highly exaggerated in media accounts. Violence tends to be localized and confined to certain geographical areas. Field researchers are not only in need of general insights, but also require information that is 'timely and accurate' (Lee, 1995: 65).

Different types of security risks are present in different countries, and in different regions within a country. In large parts of South Africa and Guatemala, violent crime is omnipresent and the risk of armed robbery is substantial. In Sri Lanka, on the other hand, crime is not the main issue; instead the security risks have been related to the political violence and the armed conflict. For instance, concerning some of the violence I have studied there are still court cases going on, and people expressed fear of disclosing information concerning these cases. Researchers working on such issues can easily be considered as a spy, a terrorist sympathizer or a human rights activist, and looked upon with suspicion by the authorities. In most research settings the most serious threats to the security of researchers relate to accidents (especially during transport) and illness (for instance malaria and dengue fever) (Lee, 1995: 10–15).

Risk assessment should be carried out in an explicit manner and the specific challenges in each case should be evaluated (Mertus, 2009). Assessments about security should include an analysis of the risks involved for individuals participating in the study and collaborating partners. Such risk assessment should, in particular, take into account local knowledge.[15] The information you get and the assessments about the security situation may vary substantially depending on who you talk to. For instance, embassies and international organizations such as the UN may be very conservative when making assessments because of a tendency for risk aversion, while local organizations may be more used to coping with the risks in a specific context. But even within a UN mission the advice on security may be very different depending on whom you consult. For instance, an assessment made by the UN staff at the headquarters engaged mainly with other international organizations is likely to be different from one made by the UN police who are patrolling the streets on a daily basis. For this reason it is important to consult and seek advice from several different kinds of sources when assessing security risks and how to cope with them.

Analyzing and publishing the material

The experience emerging from the field research has implications for the analysis of the material. The type of information obtained and its sensitivity influence how the material of the different cases is analyzed, what inferences that can be made, and how it can be published.

Analyzing the material: emotions and biases

Once the field research is over and it is time to analyze the material a new set of challenges emerge. Re-reading the material may evoke strong feelings and memories about the field experiences. The respondents may be 'living inside your heads' (Kleinman and Copp, 1993, quoted in Goodrum and Keys, 2007: 256). Some of us have had colleagues or informants who have been killed or imprisoned. Such events may create an emotional attachment to the material that may influence the motivation and ability to analyze certain cases. The researcher may feel overwhelmed by fears, guilt, sadness or even anger (Dickson-Swift *et al,* 2008). A related problem has to do with the researcher's identification with one of the sides (Armakolas, 2001).

   The result can be that a certain bias enters into the analysis, or that the researcher becomes cynical, distant or patronizing. In many instances, comparative methods can help to maintain perspective in a constructive manner. The comparison itself facilitates an analysis that relates to a broader picture and not only to one specific conflict zone or experience (Schnabel, 2001: 203).

Publishing

When the analysis has been carried out and the research is in the write-up phase, there may be uncertainties about what kind of information can and should be revealed and how it should be published. Such qualms are the result of several different considerations. First, the perspective of the academic scholar is generally different from policy-makers, NGO staff and even of the local researcher. The researcher can feel uncomfortable with the fact that the results produced were not what the research subjects had expected (Armakolas, 2001: 169–70). Second, there can be fears that publishing the findings will put informants or local communities at risk. A main concern here is that the researcher has no control over the product and how it is interpreted and used, once it has been published (Smyth and Darby, 2001: 51). Third, along similar lines, there can be fears that access to the research environment will be denied in the future if the results of the study are made public. While such instances may not be very common, there are examples of researchers who have been denied visas to enter countries because of their alleged links to the rebels based on the material in their publications.

   Concerns about how a published text will be interpreted and used can result in self-censoring on the part of the researcher. But if information is omitted in some cases, a fair comparison cannot be made and the findings may be driven in the wrong direction. The most common way of dealing with sensitive material is to omit any references and details that can reveal the identity of the informants or the community. Other ways of dealing with it are to delay publication or publish in purely academic forums. Yet in some cases the information is just deemed as too sensitive to be disclosed. Such self-censoring can be necessary to prevent the research from putting informants at risk

(Wood, 2006). Concerns about the implications of the publication of the findings are in line with the Uppsala Code of Ethics, which 'rests upon the idea that the scientist is – at least to some extent – responsible for how his/her findings are put to use in society' (Gustavsson *et al,* 1984: 313).[16]

A problem related to publication is how the difficulties in the data-gathering process should be presented in publications. Successful publication may require that the data collection is presented as an orderly process without any major difficulties (Nilan, 2002), otherwise manuscripts might be rejected by reviewers, due to the common perception that there is or should be control over the data-collection process. However, raising and discussing the information-gathering process is a sign of methodological awareness, which serious students and scholars should strive for.

Concluding remarks

To some extent the challenges involved in comparative field research are predetermined by the very nature of the questions of interest in peace research. This chapter has outlined some of the key challenges for comparative research in conflict-ridden societies. It has highlighted how the research context and the questions focused on have implications for research design, data collection and analysis of the empirical material gathered in conflict-torn and divided societies. These challenges are interlinked. The selection of cases will, for instance, influence issues concerning access and publishing. It is important to note that comparative research offers tools for dealing with some of the problems related to research in conflict-ridden countries. In particular, the comparison can help the researchers to maintain a broader perspective and prevent them from becoming too entrenched in one of the cases which may – in a worst-case scenario – introduce a bias into the data-gathering process and in the analysis of the material.

The researcher intent on pursuing comparative field research in conflict zones has to find the appropriate balance between stringency and flexibility. Most studies have financial constraints and time limitations. Due to changes in the conflict dynamics, the information-gathering process and the analysis of the material emerging from conflict zones can run into problems that were difficult to foresee when important decisions concerning research design were taken. For this reason, it is important to be open about the problems encountered during the research process. It is always useful to have a plan B since field research is sensitive to practical issues beyond the control of the individual and to make the necessary adjustments in the design of the project if required. While difficulties in obtaining information can be frustrating, the obstacles involved in the process can relate useful information about the topic under study. For instance, it can provide information about where the real power lies, or about how it has affected people in terms of expressing opinions or sharing information.

Research in conflict zones also raises ethical questions about the value, necessity and implications of research. Such issues need to be addressed throughout the research process, not only – as is often the case – during the field research.

A last point, which may seem to counter the main thrust of this chapter, is not to overestimate the difficulties of doing research in war-torn societies. Many of the problems reviewed here characterize comparative research in general. With training, experience and reflection on methodological and ethical issues, comparative field research can make important contributions to an improved understanding of the pertinent issues of peace and war.

Summary

- Find the right balance between stringency and flexibility – for research purposes a systematic approach needs to be maintained, but the research design in a comparative study needs to be adapted to the field circumstances of each case.
- Avoid unnecessary bias in case selection by being theoretically clear about the type of cases that need to be analyzed to answer the research question, before making the selection of cases based on ethical and practical considerations.
- The insecurity of the research setting is determined by the type of conflict being studied and when in a conflict's trajectory the research is carried out.
- The information accessible to a researcher is also determined by nationality and other identity characteristics of the researcher, and how such identity characteristics are perceived in the country or community under study.
- Partnering with local or international organizations may be necessary for gaining access to informants or a research setting, but in a comparative study, the strategies for identification and collaboration with an organization will depend on the local conditions.

Further reading

George, A.L. and Bennet, A. (2005) *Case Studies and Theory Development in the Social Sciences*, Cambridge, MA: MIT Press.

Gerring, J. (2007) *Case Study Research: Principles and practices*, Cambridge: Cambridge University Press.

Lee, R.M. (1995) *Dangerous Fieldwork*, Qualitative Research Methods Series Vol. 34, London: Sage Publications.

Nordstrom, C. and Robben, A.C.G.M. (eds) (1995) *Fieldwork under Fire: Contemporary studies of violence and survival*, Berkeley, CA: University of California Press.

Smyth, M. and Robinson, G. (eds) (2001) *Researching Violently Divided Societies: Ethical and methodological issues*, London: Pluto Press.

Sriram, C.L. *et al* (2009) *Surviving Field Research: Working in violent and difficult situations*, London: Routledge.

Wood, E.J. (2006) 'The Ethical Challenges of Field Research in Conflict Zones', *Qualitative Sociology*, 29 (3): 373–86.

Yin, R.K. (1994) *Case Study Research: Design and methods*, 2nd edn, London: Sage.

Notes

1. A first draft of this chapter was presented at the Department of Peace and Conflict Research, Uppsala University, November 6 2008 and at the workshop on 'Field Research and Ethics in Post-Conflict Environments', City University of New York, December 4–5 2008.
2. Some of these deal with field research generally (for instance Lieberman, 2004; Seligmann, 2005), while others specifically address research in conflict societies (for instance Lee, 1995; Nordstrom and Robben, 1995; Smyth and Robinson, 2001; Wood, 2006).
3. Those who include reflections on comparative research are, for instance, Lieberman (2004), Knox and Monaghan (2002), and Schnabel (2001). There are many useful accounts based on research carried out in one country; see for instance Armakols (2001), Gokah (2006) and Wood (2006).
4. For those new to qualitative, case-based or comparative research, the following works can be recommended: Gerring (2007), George and Bennet (2005); Mahoney (2010), and Yin (1994).
5. This is important in order to avoid selection bias. The type of selection bias that Collier and Mahoney (1996: 60) are concerned with is 'selection bias that derives from the deliberate

selection of cases that have extreme values on the dependent variable'. The issue of selection bias has generated widespread debate. See for instance King *et al* (1994) and Geddes (1990).

6. This is similar to the kind of selection bias which George and Bennet (2005: 51) refer to when discussing how 'historically important cases' have received much research attention at the expense of less 'important' cases.

7. This tendency is also linked to normative concerns driving the discipline. Peace research has its origin in the devastating world wars and was founded with the normative purpose of preventing war and building sustainable peace (see Chapter 2 in this book).

8. The meaning of concepts can be a research topic in itself, but most studies do have to make choices about the concepts used when developing the research design.

9. On the general problems associated with reporting and sources on violent conflict, see Öberg and Sollenberg (2003) and Chapters 3 and 4 in this book.

10. See also Brun (forthcoming) and Helbardt *et al* (2010) on how the field situation has changed for researchers in Sri Lanka over time.

11. Some kind of affiliation can also be important for the researcher who is on field research for an extended time period, since the affiliation also serves as a social context for the researchers who are far away from colleagues, friends and family. Scholars have reported difficulties in the relationship with local agencies in that the organization attempted to 'hijack' the project. There can also be instances where your local agency ignores those contacts that you find most important because it is not in their interest to have contacts with them (Gokah, 2006).

12. Other scholars have reported similar difficulties in South Africa; see, for instance, Kaarsholm (2006).

13. Personal conduct is also important; see Brown (2009).

14. An important debate concerning access relates to the distinction between the 'insider' versus 'outsider' researcher and the identity of the researcher; see, for instance, Hermann (2001).

15. Belousov *et al* (2007) provide an excellent overview of the security risks in their field research on the shipping industry in Russia. This article highlights the importance of local knowledge and outlines practices that can be introduced to improve the safety of the researcher.

16. A useful overview of potential problems in the post-research phase, including the protection of interviewees' identities in drafts published on websites and shared among colleagues for comments, is provided in Sriram (2009).

8 In-depth Interviewing

The process, skill and ethics of interviews in peace research

Karen Brounéus

Introduction

In-depth interviewing is used in peace research to deepen and sharpen our understanding of the complexities of conflict-ridden societies. In-depth interviews can be conducted with rebels in a remote jungle to understand their reasons to fight; with political leaders in a post-conflict country to explore how they perceive international peacebuilding initiatives; or with women who witnessed in a truth-telling process after genocide to better understand the consequences of reconciliation processes for those who participate. In an in-depth interview, the researcher 'gently guides a conversational partner in an extended discussion' (Rubin and Rubin, 2005: 4), simultaneously leading the way with well-prepared, thought-through questions, and following the interviewee through active, reflective listening.

The research method of in-depth interviewing is used to learn of individual perspectives of one or a few narrowly defined themes. The questions used to guide the interview are often semi-structured, that is the researcher has formulated a set of questions that all interviewees will be asked. Then, depending on the interviewee's answers, each in-depth interview will take different twists and turns and follow its own winding path – an important component being to have the freedom to follow up on related themes raised by the interviewees themselves. After following such new paths, the researcher then returns to the prepared set of core questions – before the interview again may begin winding out in a new direction. Most questions in an in-depth interview are open-ended, allowing the interviewees to decide if they want to give a short or long answer. The researcher is an active listener, encouraging the interviewees to give their account by using reflective listening, follow-up questions and probes, but also reflecting on when it is appropriate – and not – to continue asking, and when it is time to close.

In peace research, in-depth interviews are used to gain a deeper understanding of processes of war and peacebuilding both among elites and among different groups of the population. At the elite level, in-depth interviews are often used to follow a process, for example of elite decision-making in peace negotiations (for further reading see, for example, Berry, 2002 and Richards, 1996). At the grassroots level, in-depth interviews are used to learn from different subgroups of the population in order to better understand the challenges, possibilities and risks of peace. This chapter will focus on the latter, as many aspects of in-depth interviewing – for example issues relating to power, vulnerability and ethics – are accentuated when they are conducted with those who experience war and peacebuilding in everyday life, but who at the same time are far from the decision-making table. However, as the underlying principles of in-depth interviewing are similar regardless of who is being interviewed, this chapter is also useful for other kinds of in-depth interviewing in peace research.

In-depth interviews in peace research are usually used in combination with other methods for collecting data; they are rarely used as the sole source of data (Johnson, 2002: 104). A single in-depth interview study conducted at one point in time cannot in and by itself explain or make generalizations for other cases. However, when firmly based on and compared with previous research, that is when it is put into the realm of the 'collective enterprise' of science (King *et al*, 2004: 186), an in-depth interview study can suggest valid descriptive or causal inferences. In-depth interviewing can be used inductively, to generate new hypotheses or theory by studying a particular issue in a particular conflict or post-conflict setting. These hypotheses may later be studied and tested in other case studies, comparative case studies, surveys, or large-N studies. Alternatively, in-depth interviewing can be used deductively, to investigate whether a theory based on findings from studies at the societal or national level are applicable at the grassroots, individual level. By combining research methods, quantitative and qualitative, the analyses in peace research can at the same time be made broad and rich. So, just as the human senses give different perspectives of, say, an apple – by touching it the shape is felt; by tasting, its crispness and sweetness can be experienced; by looking at it the color is seen – so do different research methods give different perspectives on the same research question.

When is in-depth interviewing an appropriate data-gathering method? The research question helps to guide the researcher. For learning about the micro-processes of armed conflict and of peace, those at the core need to be consulted: the people. Without listening to them, the research can risk becoming shallow and not reflect the realities and challenges at stake. For this purpose, in-depth interviewing offers a unique method and source of information since it provides research with depth, detail and perspective on a certain research question, and at a certain moment in time. In contrast to secondary sources or survey research, the in-depth interview gives the researcher a first-hand account of the research question at hand. Upon such information, a deeper understanding and inferences can be made on what a theoretical concept – such as disarmament, peacebuilding, or the resource curse – actually means for those experiencing it. In-depth interviews are important to identify what theories within peace research have missed. In addition, the interviews can give color and warmth to cold facts and closeness to distant happenings. However, while in-depth interviewing provides a unique and essential type of knowledge for peace research, it is also a challenging methodology entailing reflection and responsibility on behalf of the researcher – towards interviewees, the research community and oneself.

The aim of this chapter is to explore and generate questions about in-depth interviewing to consider before, during and after they are conducted. It will do so by following the research process from preparations to publication. The chapter raises issues that are of general importance when using this research method, but also highlights specific issues to be considered for in-depth interviewing in peace research. The chapter ends by discussing two aspects of particular relevance when conducting in-depth interviews in peace research: ethics and security.

Preparation

In essence, the quality of the in-depth interviews will rely on two things; one, that the researcher is well prepared, and two, that the skill of listening is mastered (which will be discussed in more detail below). Becoming well prepared for in-depth interviewing involves the following steps: reading up on secondary sources; planning access, that is how to select and reach interviewees; formulating a draft set of interview questions; making contact and planning meetings with local counterparts and expertise; and preparing the practicalities of the trip itself. Let us go through these steps one at a time.

Studying *secondary sources* provides the theoretical and empirical foundation to build the research upon, and will form the basis for how to formulate core questions for the in-depth interview. Reading a variety of different sources, from the most recent articles to some classical writings, provides the essential research base and the historical background through which a sense of the cultural, anecdotal heritage emerges. This is important for understanding the different sentiments concerning issues such as the roots of the conflict, what tensions are wrestled with in society, and what is talked about – and not. Secondary sources give background, context, and history – empirically and theoretically. The in-depth interview picks up where these sources end by providing present, individual perspective and depth, thereby helping to develop a fuller, richer understanding of the research question at hand. It is through these sources the researcher begins to understand who needs to be consulted and what information is needed in order to probe the research question.

Critically reflecting on *who* needs to be interviewed to obtain the necessary information leads to the issue of *access*, that is considering and preparing the selection process: who will be interviewed, where and how (discussed more below). While plans might change during a research project, especially when in the field, it is useful to have a draft of the selection process or a few alternative procedures – not only for considering what perspectives will be possible to include and what will be missing, but also for planning more specifically what to ask.

Formulating *a draft set of interview questions* is both easier and more difficult than one may first expect. Easier in the way that the guiding principle is to make the core questions as simple as possible: they should be made with simple language, with a simple natural flow just as if it were a normal conversation, one question leading to the next, which leads to the next – smoothly and naturally. But to make it this simple is often quite difficult. The main research question needs to be in clear focus; to capture it the interview questions need to reflect all different aspects and angles the researcher can think of. It is a process of zooming out to be able to zoom in again. Formulating useful questions relies heavily on what comes out of the study of secondary sources, with the research question as a lucid guiding light. In many cases, the interview questions must be approved by the home university's ethical committee (or equivalent) before departing for fieldwork. The exact formulations may need to be changed upon arrival in the country or area of study, preferably after discussion with local colleagues. Minor changes and fine-tuning of questions are often permitted by the ethical committee, but each researcher needs to verify the details about these processes before starting the interviews.

Making contact and planning meetings with local counterparts and expertise is another important step in preparing for in-depth interviewing. Colleagues can often provide first points of academic and personal contact; for political contacts some researchers have useful assistance from their country's foreign ministry or representation in the country of study (for example their Embassy or High Commission). In these first contacts it will be important to introduce and inquire about the interest in the research project as anchoring the research locally is fundamental for the legitimacy of the project. It is important to establish relevant contacts at different levels and spheres in society (local/national, governmental/civil society): the proposed research project may be seen in very different ways by different people. These first contacts with *gatekeepers* will have an important role in opening (or closing) doors in sensitive environments, and it is often upon them that the feasibility of the research will depend. The question of gatekeepers will be discussed in more detail below.

Finally, there will be the often exciting step of preparing the practicalities of the travel itself. Visa and passport requirements should be checked so that no problems arise in potentially sensitive border controls. A medical check-up and vaccinations are often necessary for entering conflict or post-conflict regions in developing countries; preparing a medical kit, malaria prophylaxis, mosquito net, etc is also on the to-do list. Enquiring about the local dress code is also recommended before packing; being well-dressed is often very important and seen as a sign of dignity and respect towards the local communities. More often than not there is a restricted budget to take into account. However, safety should never be jeopardized. To cut corners for financial reasons cannot be advised as flying with the cheapest airline, staying or eating in the cheapest quarters (or sleeping in a corner of the airport), often increases the risk of accidents and diseases (such as being robbed or mugged or contracting food poisoning). Exhaustion and weariness are likely to come in any case; it is unnecessary to provoke them. Indeed, they might jeopardize the quality of the work the researcher can perform. If the budget is limited, it is worth considering making the visit shorter but genuinely productive. Local contacts can often give the best advice on accommodation and other local travel arrangements.

Box 8.1: Rule of Thumb: Be prepared!

In-depth interviewing – as for all qualitative research when used for systematic data collection – must be rigorously prepared. Here are a few things to remember when planning in-depth interviews:

- Have a clear, explicit research question based on previous research, and the aim to fill a particular research gap and thereby contribute to the academic debate. These characteristics and aims distinguish the in-depth interview from a journalistic interview, descriptive writing, or talking with a close friend or colleague.
- Make a plan for the sampling process: think through *who* would be best to speak to, *how* they may be reached, and *how many* you would like to interview. In peace research, an in-depth interview study will often include somewhere between 10 and 40 interviewees.
- Make a draft of the semi-structured interview, that is the set of core questions to ask all interviewees. Test the questions on colleagues at home to see how they work and to be able to make a first estimate of how long the interviews may take (remember, though, that the same set of 20 core questions may take 20 minutes for one interviewee and 1.5 hours for another). In general, a time-length of around 1 hour for an in-depth interview in peace research is probably not uncommon, but this varies greatly depending on the focus and scope of the study.
- Remember that even though many of the preparations may have to be altered or completely changed upon arriving in 'the field', having carefully considered different options and having a rough plan will make things much easier (just build in space for uncertainty and flexibility!)

Sampling: access and bias

The selection of interviewees for in-depth interviewing can be guided by the principle of *credibility*: what sources will maximize the reliability and validity of the results (Rubin and Rubin, 2005: 64)? If the research seeks to examine the promises or threats used in rebel recruitment, the interviews can be with the rebels who have been recruited, or the people who recruit rebels, or the families of those who have been recruited. A researcher will in such a project make limited use of interviewing a tourist in that country, or the odd person in the street. It is important that the interviewees are *'experienced* and *knowledgeable* in the area you are interviewing about': criteria that may seem obvious but nevertheless are critical (Rubin and Rubin, 2005: 64). After identifying the population of interest, the details of sampling (how to select individuals for interview from within that population of interest) can be designed (Rossman and Rallis, 2003: 136). A good design with regard to selection of interviewees is one key ingredient for making the research credible. Selection in qualitative research is all the more important as the researcher has more control over the selection process of observations than over most other factors in the research design (King *et al,* 2004: 188).

So, in contrast to, for example, random sampling, sampling for in-depth interviewing in peace research, as in other qualitative research, is done with a *purpose*. Some examples of purposeful sampling in qualitative research are typical case sampling, critical case sampling, criterion sampling and extreme or deviant case sampling (for more examples, see Rossman and Rallis, 2003: 138).

Since peace researchers are operating in politically sensitive environments, they are often dependent on gatekeepers to an even greater extent than other fields of qualitative research within the social sciences. Gatekeepers are people in a state, bureaucracy or organization, in a society or community, who decide who can or cannot have access to a specific community. As has been noted observantly,'[g]atekeepers can make or break your study. Handle them gently' (Rossman and Rallis, 2003: 163). Carefully identifying and contacting gatekeepers is important for building confidence and trust with local counterparts before departing for field research. For this step, colleagues at the home university and other contacts at home play an important role in guiding the researcher in the right direction. Contacting gatekeepers is also important because it is a first step in grounding the research locally, for building rapport and trust, and for ensuring that the research questions make sense in that particular setting. Bringing letters of recommendation to contacts is another step that can be important for opening doors and gaining access.

However, thorough preparations notwithstanding, there will often be challenges in gaining access to conflict and post-conflict environments. Due to issues such as political instability, personal power struggles in the political elite, elections, corruption, or historically-based sensitivity to outsiders, doors may be shut in one's face – for reasons far beyond the researcher. Peace research can be threatening, for example, to the political elite. In peace research, sensitive processes, assumptions and events during or in the aftermath of armed conflict are at the centre of study, and the results of the research may or may not be in line with a certain political rhetoric. In many conflict and post-conflict societies there is or has been a tradition of authoritarian rule in which the very idea of questioning is socially unacceptable or illegal. So, to tread carefully is key and even then it may be problematic. For more on challenges to access, see Thomson (2009).

Considering issues of access is also essential from the point of view of designing ethically sound field research. Potential dangers and security concerns must be taken into account when reflecting upon when the time is right, and for what. What information do I need? What do I have the right to ask? Who is it possible to approach? So, more than merely whether information can be 'accessed' there is the question of ethics and sensitivity in determining what information peace research should strive to gather. In spite of the guidelines, rules and regulations, it all boils down to the critical judgment of individual researchers. It is the responsibility of the researcher to consider issues related to ethics, not only at the outset of a research project but continuously through the research process.

Considering access also requires that the researcher reflect on some important weaknesses of in-depth interviewing, for example regarding bias and reliability. In short, researchers need to reflect upon who is willing to be interviewed – and why? Do those who are willing to share information differ from others in some particular way? In most in-depth interview studies in peace research, the number of interviewees is low. For this reason, each voice weighs heavily in the sum of the researcher's understanding and consequently the research becomes sensitive to outliers. To reflect upon and assess the reliability of the information in an interview is a further matter of concern. Are there underlying interests that may steer the interviewee's information in a particular way? Post-conflict areas can become over-researched, bringing 'research fatigue' in its wake (discussed more below), which may in turn lead an interviewee to provide the answer he/she has learnt researchers want – just to get the interview over with. Or, there may be incentives other than wanting their story to be known driving the interviewee to share information, for example, the hope of financial compensation. There is no easy answer to whether or not one should compensate interviewees; it is an area of much debate (see Dunn and Gordon, 2005; McNeill, 1997; Wilkinson and Moore, 1997). Some argue that if interviewees are taking time off from work and thereby lose income to participate in a study, they should be compensated for this loss. However, does this mean that taking time from caring for one's household, children or land plot is not worth anything financially? In conflict and post-conflict settings there is often high unemployment so many of the interviewees may not have a job. At the same time, the researcher needs to consider that if an interviewee participates only for compensation, there may be an increased risk that the information is skewed; for example, the interviewee may be more interested in hurrying through the questions and saying anything that comes to mind rather than taking the time to genuinely and carefully respond to the questions. Such a situation would diminish the validity of the inferences made from the study.

All of these considerations concerning access will lead to a certain, inescapable selection bias in the choices made in a particular study – regarding the country or countries in which the research is carried out, the specific cases in that country, and the interviewees. However, if the decisions and reasons for choices made are explicitly described – why x and y, but not z – the risks that selection bias bring are to a great extent reduced. Transparency will help delineate the boundaries and limitations of the research, and with these boundaries clearly chiseled out, the contribution of the research can be made clear.

Box 8.2: Working with an Interpreter

Peace research often brings scholars to places where they do not speak the language and they will therefore be dependent on an interpreter for conducting research. Working with an interpreter involves both challenges and benefits, and takes a bit of training:

- Speak with local colleagues: choosing whom to hire as an interpreter is both difficult and key; there are seldom professional interpreters to be found. Issues such as ethnicity, social status and gender play a critical role in how comfortable the interviewees will feel, as does the professionalism of the interpreter: can the anonymity of the interviewee and the confidentiality of the information the interviewee shares be guaranteed? It is essential the interpreter understands the importance of protecting the interviewee's anonymity, the aim of the research and the interview questions, that she or he is a good and empathetic listener, and that there is good rapport between you and the interpreter. Otherwise, no matter how well you are prepared, the interviewee will not feel comfortable talking with you.
- Practice an interview situation with the interpreter and a local colleague as an imagined interviewee. When you speak, take small sequences at a time; make sure the interpreter has time to interpret and uses the same wording and pronouns as you do. This means, for example, that if you say: 'I would like to ask you ...', the interpreter repeats in his or her language: 'I would like to ask you ...', not 'He/she wants to ask you ...'. Similarly, ask the interpreter to use the same words and pronouns as the interviewee when translating during the interview. That is, the interpreter does not say: 'He (the interviewee) is saying that he has always lived in his village ...', but translates exactly what the interviewee said, namely: 'I have always lived in my village ...'. Using the same pronouns and words, and taking care to keep eye contact with the interviewee when the interpreter is speaking, are important details for making the conversation feel as if it is in fact taking place just between you and the interviewee. Indeed, after a while, the interpreter becomes 'just' a helping voice; this is a sign the interpreter is doing a great job.
- Ask the interpreter not to wait too long to translate back to you; interpreting after every five sentences or so is good, otherwise you will lose information. When the interview becomes emotionally or intellectually charged, you also risk losing control of the interview if you do not follow the interviewee closely. But here is also where the benefit of working with an interpreter lies: the translations slow down the conversation so there is more time to really see the interviewees while listening to them or the interpretation. And sometimes, other signs we communicate with when we speak (like how we sit, or look, or don't look) can provide some more information, between the lines.

Conducting the interviews

How the in-depth interview is conducted is pivotal not only for the quality of the research, but also for the interviewee's experience during and after the interview. Creating a comfortable and encouraging atmosphere in which the interviewee feels respected and safe is important both for obtaining useful information and for conducting ethical research. Developing skills for reflective listening is central in this regard. By listening reflectively, the researcher will better understand what the interviewee is sharing, as well as understand the significance of this information for making inferences about the particular research problem at hand. For this, the researcher's most important tools include empathy, an ability to listen, and an ethical judgment of when it is time to stop.

The word 'empathy' – from the Greek *empatheia*, 'in-feeling' – means the 'ability to imagine and share another person's feelings, experience, etc' (*Oxford Advanced Learners Dictionary,* 1989); that is, to be sensitive to the feelings of someone, or to put oneself in someone else's shoes. Empathy does not mean to identify with the other or to become absorbed in the same feeling. It is to understand the other's perspective – even if we do not agree with what is being said, even if we are repelled by what is being said. It is also to understand some of what is being said between the lines. Empathy is part of how we always engage, listen and speak with each other in everyday life, without reflecting on it. But researchers can improve their ability to convey empathy by becoming more aware of the listening and communication process. The essence of reflective listening in an interview situation is to communicate to the interviewee that *'I am with you and I am listening.'*

In reflective listening, the listener seeks – through skilful listening – to understand the speaker's feelings and perspective.[1] By listening actively and with empathy to what is being said both explicitly and 'between the lines', the listener forms an understanding that then can be reflected back to the speaker for confirmation of whether this was a correct understanding, or not (Gordon, 1970). In this way, the discussion flows, the speaker speaking and the listener reflecting back and thereby sharing his/her understanding of what the speaker has said but in his/her own words, which the speaker then can confirm or clarify. Reflective listening involves using active non-verbal (nodding, 'hmm'-ing) and verbal ('tell me more …') listening techniques, but the core skills of reflective listening are the following: reflecting fact, reflecting emotion, questioning on fact, and questioning on emotion (Rautalinko *et al,* 2007).

Reflecting fact or emotion means that the listener reflects back, in short and in her own words, the facts or emotions that the speaker has shared. Questioning fact or emotion means to ask in order to clarify and understand better – not to question, with skepticism or doubt. These core skills of reflective listening involve exploring and understanding the speaker's perspective (Rautalinko *et al,* 2007). Research demonstrates that by training these four core skills, the listener becomes a better listener and the speaker discloses more emotion, in sum that the quality of the dialogue increases. In fact, even short training in reflective listening (20 hours) has proven to result in better listeners and dialogue quality (Rautalinko, personal communication, 2010). Being a good listener when conducting in-depth interviews in peace research is imperative for conducting ethically sound research: for ensuring the well-being of the interviewees and that the research does not have any adverse effects on the research participants. It is, however, also imperative for ensuring the quality of the research. If researchers are skilful listeners they will receive more and better quality information from the interviewee, understand that information better and, as a result, have an improved basis for analyzing the research question at hand.

At the same time, when being a skilful listener in peace research it is important to keep one issue in mind. In-depth interviewing in peace research may at times seem quite similar to counseling or therapy: similar listening techniques are used, profound ethical consideration is taken to care for the interviewee, and difficult and even traumatic events related to armed conflict are themes for discussion. However, the two are succinctly distinct. Peace researchers are addressing these questions because they want to contribute to a greater understanding of a particular issue, for research and for policy. It can ultimately be considered as a way to help alleviate the suffering of those affected by war, but in a very different form from therapy or counseling. It is essential to acknowledge this research/therapy gap to ensure that no harm is done to the participants: in-depth interviewing in peace research is sensitive research, but not therapy. In essence, this means that peace researchers have the ethical responsibility to conduct the in-depth interview at an appropriate level – not too shallow, but not too deep – and to hold interviewees on the interview track, not leaving them to go too deep into their own, often traumatic experiences.

Keeping the interview on track is facilitated if two things are kept in mind: the semi-structured interview questionnaire (which can help to gently guide the conversation back if it is going too deep), and the aim of the research. Determining when the conversation is beginning to probe into too sensitive issues is often not as difficult as it may sound; the signs are quite observable. For example, the interviewee may begin to speak of traumatic events that are far beyond the topic at hand and therefore not directly related to the interview. Or, the interviewee may begin to give a lot of detail about difficult events and is overcome by unexpected emotion. Or, the researcher may begin to feel very uncomfortable because he/she is no longer guiding the dialogue. In situations like these it is important to carefully guide back to the main questions of the interview to prevent the risk of negative side-effects. This can be done, for example, by making a short summary of what the interviewee has said, thanking the interviewee for sharing so much important information but then saying that unfortunately there is a need to return to a few more questions on which the interviewee's perspective is needed. So, while it is important that the researcher follows the interviewee out on some winding paths in the interview, the researcher must also mark when those paths need to end and bring the interviewee back to the main track. In other words, the researcher must remember to be the one conducting the interview – this is an ethical and professional responsibility of a peace researcher.

Keeping the aim of the research in clear focus will also help the researcher hold the interview on track. The aim delineates the boundaries of the conversation and serves as a reminder of when it is time to close one topic and move on to the next. This is a critical assessment to make when conducting in-depth interviewing in peace research because, for many interviewees, it may be the first time someone is listening to very important experiences – it is then easy to want to tell more than intended (Dickson-Swift *et al*, 2008: 8). However, it is one thing to share in this way with someone who will stay and be there to help – say a family member, friend, or a counselor. In such instances sharing can be very important in the process of soothing and healing traumatic wounds. A peace researcher has a very different part to play, namely that of learning from the interviewee, analyzing the information in the light of existing knowledge, and communicating this to the research community.

The role of being the translator between the field and the scientific community involves a further responsibility of the researcher, namely keeping a certain distance from 'the field' (Eckl, 2008). This argument may at first hand sound rather cold and unsympathetic. However, similar thinking is found in the literature on psychological therapy and counseling – without some distance the therapist or counselor cannot analyze, guide or help (Pope and Vasquez, 2007; Rogers, 2008). Theoretical and methodological knowledge in combination with empathy and an ability to listen help peace researchers find this balance when conducting in-depth interviews – creating a personal yet professional discussion, close yet with some distance.

Minding the research/therapy divide is also crucial from an ethical point of view, since in-depth interviewing unfailingly involves issues of dependency and power. When elites are interviewed, they have the upper hand and the researcher is dependent on their goodwill (Rubin and Rubin, 2005: 102). But when ordinary people are interviewed – many who have lived through violence and injustice – a researcher is often seen as someone 'important, official, or having power over them' (Rubin and Rubin, 2005: 102). It is therefore all the more important to be polite and respectful and to take meticulous care not to exploit.

Finally, it is important to be aware that researchers will experience different emotional reactions to what they are exposed to when conducting in-depth interviews. Feelings like sorrow, anger, hopelessness and anxiety are common. One of the most challenging may be the feeling of being deceived – in many instances the researcher understands or suspects that the interviewee is lying (Gallaher, 2009). It may then be helpful to keep in mind that the value of the interview is not dependent on the truthfulness of the contents (Fujii, 2009: 2010). Lying and deception can fill a very important role in politically sensitive settings; they can even be a survival strategy. However, lies can communicate important information; they provide what has been called 'meta-data'; they tell us something of what can and cannot be said, and provide information about the social and political landscape (Fujii, 2010). The most productive way of dealing with lies is probably not to challenge them. Instead the researcher can invite elaboration and use different questions, so-called 'triangular questioning', to reveal what the interviewee really thinks – and perhaps even understand something beyond the given answers (Fujii, 2009).

How to build an in-depth interview

Just as the design of the study as a whole requires ethical reflection, so too does the design of the interview itself. When planning an in-depth interview, remember to build it as a normal conversation, to find a natural flow with one question leading to the next, which leads to the next, and so on. Design the questions on the basis of theory and curiosity. You have detected a gap to fill: what are your spontaneous questions, what do you want to learn, and why is this important? Come up with a wide range of questions; then narrow them down, select the exact questions and structure them. In a way, the in-depth interview is structured as a process of building trust. It begins with easier background questions, through which the interviewee is introduced; at mid-interview, the more emotional or intellectually difficult and demanding questions are asked; towards the end, the interview tones down again – emotionally and intellectually. The interview finally ends with a summary and closure on a good note, so that the interviewee is not left with a feeling of sadness, or of being exposed and deserted.

Step 1: Introduction

Begin the interview by thanking the interviewee for taking the time to meet you. Introduce yourself, say where you are from, and describe the aim of the research, including its practical implications (for example, 'to better understand ...', 'in order to help improve ...'). Next, it is time to provide the protocol for informed consent; orally, by reading it to the interviewee and asking for his/her approval to participate, or in written form, by giving the protocol to the interviewee to read and sign. If the plan is to digitally record the interview, it is now appropriate to ask for permission to do so. Explain how the recording will be used, for example clarify that no identifying information, such as name or address, will be recorded (if this is the case), that the recording will be transcribed and the text used only for the purpose of analysis, and that it is very helpful for making sure that you have not missed any information. If the interviewee feels comfortable with this, it is useful to take notes in parallel, of details and observations that will help you remember specific passages when you later listen to the interview for transcribing. If the interviewee does not feel comfortable with recording, taking good notes will be all the more important.

Step 2: Initial questions

Questions on background (age, marital status, children, religion, ethnicity, occupation, etc) are useful for warming up; they are easy, factual questions to answer for the interviewee and give an important introduction and context for the interviewer of the life conditions of the interviewee. It is also important to begin with easy questions so the interviewee feels confident in being able to answer. The beginning of the interview is very important; it is here the tone is set, a comfortable setting is created and confidence starts to be built by, for example, reassuring the interviewee of your interest – by listening reflectively, openly and without judgment.

Step 3: Mid-interview

The interview then moves on to the more emotionally and intellectually demanding questions. This part is the heart of the in-depth interview. The questions you ask here are firmly anchored in theory – but driven by curiosity. The strength of the interview will come from how relevant the interview questions in this section are, and from the researcher's skill in asking follow-up questions. Asking follow-up questions is often a struggle for beginners because instead of actively listening to the interviewee, they are already thinking about their next question (Rossman and Rallis, 2003: 185). By using reflective listening, you can more easily pick up where follow-up questions are needed, which will give you much more thorough and in-depth information. However, it is in this section of the interview where the core questions are most important for helping to keep the interview on track, so that it does not go too deep or sway too far away. Finding the appropriate balance of using follow-up questions and making the professional judgment of when it is time to close is a learning process (with a steep learning curve in the beginning, thanks to mistakes! Johnson, 2002). It is perhaps one of the greater challenges of in-depth interviewing, but a challenge surmountable by using your empathy, your skill of listening and your ethical awareness.

Step 4: Closing the interview

Towards the end of the interview it is advisable to have some questions to round off the interview, questions that again are easy to answer, that follow on some of the themes that you have been discussing mid-interview but that are not emotionally or intellectually charged. It is good to make a short summary of the themes you have been discussing and to summarize some of the main points that the interviewee has raised. Ask the interviewee if there is anything else he/she would like to clarify or share with you before the interview finishes. End by thanking the interviewee for speaking with you, and emphasize the importance of the knowledge he/she has shared with you for better understanding the research topic at hand.

Two aspects of particular relevance for in-depth interviewing in peace research, aspects with a bearing on all of the steps covered far, will be the focus of the remainder of this chapter: ethics and security.

Ethical aspects

Considering the sensitive nature of peace research – the questions of peace and war in people's lives – the methodology of in-depth interviewing does involve particular responsibilities and challenges for the researcher. Not only do researchers need to think of what is being researched, there is also a need to consider how it is done, and possible consequences the research may bring. Anticipating ethics from the beginning, reflecting on the entire research process from an ethical perspective, and continuously making ethically-grounded decisions is therefore integral to conducting in-depth interviews in peace research. The ethical golden rule is to do no harm. Chapters 7, 9, 10 and 11 of this book provide excellent discussions on ethics in peace research and cover fundamental requirements and procedures such as seeking approval from ethical committees and permission from national and local authorities. Here, I will focus on some particular ethical aspects of in-depth interviewing.

Ethically-informed decision-making needs to take place at all stages when planning to conduct in-depth interviews in peace research: from the research design and data gathering to the analysis of data and presentation of results. Designing ethically sound field research involves reflecting from the beginning on the ethical dimensions of issues such as the selection of cases and subgroups; sampling of interviewees; timing and place for conducting the interviews; and the seemingly tiny details of how to formulate the interview questions. It is important to consider different scenarios and options, and make decisions on these issues after having carefully considered potential dangers and security concerns for all involved: for the interviewees, interpreters and the researcher.

Another ethical aspect to consider when planning the design is that of 'research fatigue'. The limelight tends to turn to certain conflicts at certain points in time and so does the interest of researchers. This may lead to the situation that many researchers are in the same place at the same time, tiring people with endless questions. Such research conduct not only leads to a type of exploitation that is deeply unethical but will also lead to meaningless research as the findings will be skewed, biased, or just plain humbug as people begin answering according to what they have learnt researchers want to hear just to get the interview over with (Clark, 2008). Such situations can be avoided by having close contact with local counterparts (and selecting another location if there is a risk of research fatigue) and thorough preparation. Considering and avoiding research fatigue is pertinent for peace research and is discussed in more detail in Chapter 7 of this book.

When planning the step of data gathering through in-depth interviewing in conflict-ridden societies, it is important to make an ethically-informed risk assessment concerning how to access interviewees in the safest possible way, and how to ensure the participants' security and confidentiality during and after the interview. In this lies, in addition to merely accessing information, the question of determining what information should be gathered. In-depth interviews in peace research involve questions related to events that have taken place during or in the aftermath of violent conflict, and it is important to decide carefully what needs to be asked to minimize the risk of doing harm. Speaking of traumatic events is difficult and may in the worst cases lead to retraumatization; by treading carefully, including only the most essential questions for understanding the research question at hand, formulating these in an open-ended manner so the interviewee can decide how much to tell, and by gently leading the interviewee back to the focus and core questions of the interview (as discussed earlier), such risks can be minimized. We will return to this question when other issues of security are considered below.

Box 8.3: Ethical Decision-making

Preparing core questions for an in-depth interview study with Rwandan women who had survived the 1994 genocide required much ethical reflection. One decision I needed to make was whether, and if so how, I should ask about their experiences of the genocide. The aim of the study was to learn how the women had experienced witnessing in the *gacaca*, the nation-wide, village-based truth-telling process. While the focus of the study was on their present experience of witnessing in the truth-telling process, having an understanding of what they had been through in 1994 could shed important light on their current experience of witnessing. I decided to do the following. At mid-interview, I asked each woman if she felt there was anything of her experiences in the 1994 genocide that she would want to tell me in light of speaking of the *gacaca* – but then left it at that. I did not use prompts or follow-up questions, only very simple reflective listening to what was being said. Some women spoke for a long time; one woman said no, there was nothing to say. Regardless, I did not encourage speaking or telling more. In this way, some very valuable background information for the study was acquired; at the same time, those who did not want to share their experiences could easily make the choice not to.

Protecting the interview data, analyzing it with care, and deciding what to publish and when, are also key to conducting ethically sound peace research. There are many options for protecting politically sensitive data: it can be done by taking simple measures like having a password for the laptop, making encrypted notes or sending the interview material directly home by email. The importance of keeping confidential, sensitive material from the eyes of authorities or, in conflict settings, at military and insurgent checkpoints is vital so that interviewees do not encounter risk after the researcher has left. The importance of ethical standards to protect interviewees during analysis, write up and publication of the research is eloquently discussed by Sriram (2009). To conduct ethically sound research also means managing the collected material with dignity and respect during analysis, and making careful, informed decisions on what and when to publish.

One aspect, which is perhaps less discussed regarding the phase of data analysis and publication of in-depth interviews in peace research, is that of the emotional turmoil the researcher may experience when working with the material upon returning home. When transcribing, it can be quite difficult to listen to the interviews again; many times they have been on emotionally challenging topics, listening to them takes the researcher back to the interview situation, and feelings that were suppressed at the time may now be felt. Or, when writing up, deciding what to leave out may feel unbearable; the sense of having the responsibility to report everything can be almost overwhelming. It is good to share these feelings with those close to you, with family and friends but also with colleagues.

Often, colleagues will have experienced something similar, which can be very reassuring. Without being aware that these reactions are normal, not dangerous and that others have been in the same situation, there is the risk that researchers turn cynical or distant. And, as the attachment to the material may influence the data analysis and the way in which findings are reported, it is important ethically to use this information of what is being felt. So, use empathy in research and do so professionally – by awareness, keeping perspective, and focusing on the aim of the research.

This leads to one last aspect that should be mentioned as an integral part of ethical in-depth interviewing, namely self-reflection. In addition to carefully considering all the steps of the research process from an ethical perspective, self-reflection must be part of the process. The researcher is often described as the 'tool' for the in-depth interview – through knowledge, experiences and empathy, the researcher learns and understands the perspective of the other, and this is conveyed to the other through an ability to listen. So, in this particular research method, the researcher plays an important role in terms of what he/she brings to the in-depth interview. In peace research, as discussed above, it also means that researchers will most probably find themselves in situations that evoke or provoke a wide range of emotions: feeling sadness when listening to stories about grave suffering, or feeling anger when learning about deep injustice or when realizing that the interviewee is deliberately lying. While the ability for feeling empathy is one of the most important assets for conducting ethically sound in-depth interviews, if researchers are not trained, it can also be a major impediment. By having reflected on individual strengths and weaknesses, by being aware of how it may affect one's work, the researcher will be better prepared – which will help both the researcher and the interviewee to keep on track, and for conducting 'responsible scholarship' (Eckl, 2008).

Security

When conducting research on sensitive topics in highly politicized or unstable settings, a main responsibility is to assess and ensure the security of the population under study. Again, the ethical fundamental is to do no harm. Wood suggests one rule of thumb: to ensure that interviewees do not run any greater risk by participating in the research (Wood, 2006: 379). By thoroughly preparing, discussing and grounding the research with colleagues and expertise, both at home and in the country of study, such risks may be assessed and avoided. For in-depth interviewing in peace research, risk assessment needs to anticipate two kinds of security, physical and emotional, for interviewees and also for oneself. The following two questions may help guide this assessment; namely to continuously consider: 1) 'What do I have the right to ask?' and 2) 'What are the potential consequences or risks for the individuals I wish to interview?'

The importance of considering whether others may be put at risk by the planned research project cannot be overstated. There are situations when ethical research cannot be conducted, when research is not called for and cannot be ethically defended (Wood, 2006: 374). There is a need to remember that research is not indispensable, despite the fact that the very impetus that motivated the research in the first place can feel all the more important when a situation is at its worst (Sriram, 2009: 67). Researchers do not provide basic needs such as food, water or healthcare to people in need. Indeed, there are situations where the presence of researchers may endanger others, for example those who help to protect the researcher. A research visit may put the interviewee at risk by leading to uncomfortable or even threatening questions from neighbors or authorities after the researcher has left. It is a moral obligation of peace researchers to make sure that the interviewees – as well as interpreters and other collaborators – are not subjected to greater risk due to engaging with the research project.

One important security measure for in-depth interviewing is the protocol for informed consent. As discussed above, informed consent may be oral or written, but the essence is always roughly the same: to explain the purpose of the research and to ensure interviewees that their participation is completely voluntary and that they can withdraw from the project at any time should they no longer wish to participate. This articulated agreement between the interviewer and interviewee may be more important than it may appear at first glance. Wood writes that although her interviewees spoke of violence and grief, she did not observe retraumatization in them, and suggests that the consent protocol she used may have helped prevent psychological retraumatization by passing a degree of control and responsibility to the interviewee (Wood, 2006: 381). Having a perceived sense of control has been found to prevent subsequent post-traumatic disorder (Herman 1997; McFarlane and van der Kolk, 1996). A consent protocol may fill an empowering function by spelling out the fact that the interview is in the hands of the interviewee. Therefore, it may indeed play a role in establishing a sense of control in the interviewee and so buffer against retraumatization.

Security also involves caring for the security of the researcher. 'Care of the self is integrally related to care for others. At the heart of both types of care is a belief in human dignity and the equal moral worth of human kind' (Mertus, 2009: 166). Guides on safety for humanitarian field workers, for example, from the International Committee of the Red Cross (ICRC), can provide valuable suggestions for researchers in conflict and post-conflict settings. The field of humanitarian assistance has long acknowledged the importance of assuring safety – both for the humanitarian field worker and for the people – as critical for delivering effective assistance (Mertus, 2009). Similar reasoning goes for the in-depth interviewer in peace research – with basic security and care, the focus can be on conducting valuable research; without security, even the attempt to do so cannot be defended as it puts the researcher and others at risk.

Finally, again, in-depth interviewing in peace research is often not only physically demanding due to the particular circumstances of conflict and post-conflict environments, but can be emotionally draining as well. A few researchers have written of the 'blues' of field research, on the loneliness of being far from home, often alone, and often in difficult situations (Eckl, 2008; Wood, 2006). These aspects are sometimes accentuated when conducting in-depth interviews, as the topics of discussion might reveal very difficult experiences on the part of the interviewee. Learning of gross human rights violations can indeed lead to 'secondary trauma', a term used to describe when a listener is traumatized by being told about the experiences of someone who himself was traumatized by the events. Having a strong social network to share experiences with is one of the most important factors for preventing psychological ill-health after difficult or traumatic experiences. This closeness is often difficult to arrange during fieldwork but, for example, writing a journal and being in as much contact as possible with family, friends and colleagues via email, telephone or Skype can be very important, so not all has to wait until returning home. Awareness of the emotional dynamics in conflict and post-conflict field research is important for safeguarding good health, and also for safeguarding the quality of the research. If unprepared for these dynamics, the researcher may become apathetic or cynical towards the interviewee as a means of self-protection. The opposite may also happen: the researcher over-identifies with the interviewees by becoming overcome by their suffering. With awareness and anticipation of such challenges, the researcher is better prepared to understand when security is at risk, when the quality of the research is affected – and to take measures continuously to minimize such risks.

Summary

- In-depth interviewing is a unique method for studying the micro-processes of armed conflict and peace; it provides depth, detail and individual perspectives to complex events. In-depth interviewing is most often used in combination with other methods for data gathering.
- In the in-depth interview, the researcher guides the discussion by asking well-prepared questions. By having core questions that are asked of all interviewees, the data gathering is systematic; at the same time each interview will be different as the questions are open-ended, allowing the interviewees to decide how much they want to share.
- Creating a comfortable and encouraging atmosphere in which the interviewee feels respected and safe is key for the quality of the in-depth interview. The researcher's listening skills will play an essential role. Reflective listening, to listen actively and with empathy, will help improve the quality of the interview and ensure that it is ethically sound.
- In-depth interviewing in peace research is a challenging methodology entailing reflection and responsibility on behalf of the researcher. To anticipate ethical concerns from the beginning, and to continuously make ethically grounded decisions is integral to conducting in-depth interviews in peace research. So is remembering the ethical golden rule to do no harm.

Further reading

Dickson-Swift, V., James, E.L. and Liamputtong, P. (2008) *Undertaking Sensitive Research in the Health and Social Sciences: Managing boundaries, emotions and risks*, Cambridge: Cambridge University Press.

Herman, J.L. (1997) *Trauma and Recovery*, revised edn, New York: Basic Books.

Rubin, H.J. and Rubin, I.S. (2005) *Qualitative Interviewing: The art of hearing data*, 2nd edn, London: Sage Publications.

Smyth, M. and Robinson, G. (eds) (2001) *Researching Violently Divided Societies: Ethical and methodological issues*, London: Pluto Press.

Sriram, C.L. *et al* (eds) (2009) *Surviving Field Research: Working in violent and difficult situations*, London: Routledge.

Wood, E.J. (2006) 'The Ethical Challenges of Field Research in Conflict Zones', *Qualitative Sociology*, 29 (3): 373–86.

Note

1. Reflective listening grew out of nondirective, client-centered counseling that emerged in the 1940s as a reaction to psychoanalytic approaches. Carl Rogers is one of the founding fathers of nondirective counseling; the term 'Rogerian counseling' is also used (Rogers, 1975). However, reflective listening has increasingly come to be used in other counseling approaches as well, such as cognitive behavioral therapy, and by professional helpers in other areas.

9 Focus Groups

Safety in numbers?

Johanna Söderström

Introduction

In this chapter, the use of focus groups in post-conflict settings is discussed as are the particular possibilities and challenges that arise from working in such a context. Focus groups are commonly defined as 'a research technique that collects data through group interaction on a topic determined by the researcher' (Morgan, 1997: 6). This research technique will be discussed on the basis of my own research with ex-combatants in post-conflict Liberia.[1] Focus group interviews are a data collection method that has recently made inroads in the social sciences broadly defined, but which is still underused and under-discussed in peace research. In part this relates to a failure to grasp the type of data one can obtain from using focus groups and the potential advantages of focus groups in post-conflict contexts. But it also relates to a conflation between the practices of practitioners and researchers, as focus groups can often be used in peace-building efforts and for policy guidance. Hence, this chapter will deal with focus groups as a research tool and nothing else.

As a group interview, this data collection relies not only on the questions posed to the group in generating the data, but also the group interaction itself. The role and importance of the group in this form of data collection cannot be overstated. This data collection method allows the political and social context in which the research is carried out to be present in a different way than individual interviews or survey data do. As will be discussed in this chapter, it is from this aspect that most challenges and advantages of focus groups arise. As participants respond to the moderator (the interviewer) other participants will respond and react to other participants' statements as well. The degree of involvement by the moderator will differ considerably between different research projects, which will temper the type of interaction brought forth in the groups. Thus, this chapter will take the reader through the different aspects of conducting focus groups, such as designing group composition and size, recruiting participants, the role of the moderator, order and type of questions, as well as analysis, while paying specific attention to issues of importance in a conflict context. In particular, the conflict or post-conflict context heightens security concerns for the individuals involved in the data-gathering processes, but it also means that the research questions are usually concerned with aspects of conflict. These issues play out differently in relation to focus groups and regular interviews. As the title of this chapter suggests, focus groups can, on the one hand, create a sense of safety, especially in relation to the researcher, where individuals can hide behind the group. On the other hand, conducting interviews in a group of people also exposes the individual participant to the discretion and interests of the other participants, and the possible security risks associated with that. These issues among others will be addressed in this chapter.

The chapter starts with a delineation of some of the reasons why one might use focus groups. The bulk of the chapter is, however, concerned with the more practical aspects of conducting and using focus groups in research. First, group composition issues are discussed, followed by recruitment issues and choice of location, then the role of the moderator and question guide are explained, and finally a few things that can go wrong when using focus groups are described (and ways that they can be handled).

Why use focus groups?

While there are several reasons why one might choose to use focus groups, it is important to make sure that the data collection method chosen corresponds with the research question posed in a student thesis or research project. For this reason it is important to understand what kind of data focus group discussions can, and cannot, generate.

Focus groups are often used to study attitudes and opinions, perspectives and experiences, behavioral choices and motivations (Morgan, 1997). Focus groups are also valuable when researchers want to evaluate why a certain program or policy worked or failed (for an example of such a use, see Jennings, 2007). The contrasting and comparing among the participants help to better elucidate motivations and reasoning, especially if the topic at hand has been a group experience. Sharing and comparing will help to clarify the important turning points in the development of a particular experience. Focus groups can also be used to track a line of argument or capture what kinds of words are used to describe a certain phenomenon in a particular setting. Focus groups thereby offer a means to understanding the production of meaning. This latter part explains why focus groups are often used in exploratory studies, particularly prior to designing a survey: researchers want to make sure that the types of questions and phrases used in a survey reflect the context of interest. However, while focus groups have often been used as an exploratory method (often as a preamble to survey data; see Bratton and Liatto-Katundu, 1994, for an example of this), they are also a valid data collection method on their own. Focus groups are for instance often deemed to be superior to other forms of data collection in certain areas of study, for instance in the study of norms (Bloor, 2001: 4–8).

The group context conditions this data collection method and research technique in several ways. The group interaction usually entails the participants developing and redefining their opinions during the discussion. This is especially useful if the topic is such that not everyone will have a ready-formed opinion, or if the topic is such that it requires new reflection because it is not a question participants pose to themselves every day. Also, the group interaction allows the participants to more clearly define their own position, since hearing the comments of others in the group will either lead to exclamations of ,'Yes, I totally agree, I had the very same experience', 'True, but for me it was slightly different, and here's how ...', or 'For me it was very different, almost the opposite in fact, especially when it comes to ...'. This contrasting back and forth is at the heart of focus groups.

However, there is also another element that may be overlooked but is equally important. In a focus group, the participant does not have to voice an opinion on everything. Compared to the individual setting, whether a questionnaire or an interview, the participants in a focus group are exposed to less social pressure to say something, no matter what, when they may not have a response, knowing that others will fill the void. This aspect of focus groups makes them more appropriate when a less intrusive data collection method is required. This might be the case because the researcher wants the data to be more 'natural', reliable (in the sense of being an actual reflection of what people feel or think rather than just the filling of a void) or because data is collected about a group in society that, for some reason, has a power disadvantage.

While there may be less pressure to say something in a focus group, the social desirability bias (see Box 9.1), common to all interviews, does not disappear. This tendency, however, does not only pertain to the moderator, but also to the others in the group. Depending on the research question and focus of the study, this tendency might be in the researcher's favor. Discussing in a group of peers entails conditioning the data collection to take place in the social context in which the participants normally exist. Thus the comments voiced will be filtered, and the filter through which this process occurs is the social reality and norms of the group that is being interviewed (Söderström, 2010). Depending on the research goals and ontological and epistemological claims of the study, this will either be an advantage or a disadvantage of focus groups.

Box 9.1: Social Desirability Bias

Human subjects interpret and interact with the researcher and the context in which the research takes place. Social desirability bias relates to the situation in which interviewees filter what they answer in face-to-face interviews or surveys. Sometimes it is a question of wanting to appear *better, more normal* or *more acceptable* in the eyes of the interviewer. To please the interviewer or others in the group, participants in a study may underreport certain behaviors or expressions of deviance, or in some way conform to the norm they believe is in existence. This is not done out of malice, and can be driven by an anticipation of and will to ensure that the researcher finds what he/she is looking for. The issue comes into play in all human interaction, and should be considered in relation to the wording of questions in surveys, as well as in individual or group interviews. As a researcher it is a question of being aware of the existence of the phenomenon, the potential risks involved and the kind of bias that may be introduced in the material. Much of the discussion concerning social desirability bias rests on the assumption that there is a core truth that is filtered through a lens and thereby altered. Whether such a view is subscribed to or not ultimately depends on one's view of human nature and its autonomy (for more details concerning this discussion, see Gubrium and Holstein 2002: 12).

The group context also influences the balance between researcher and those participating in the study, simply because the interviewees outnumber the moderator. In contexts of power hierarchies and conflict, collecting data in this format can tilt the power balance in favor of those who are interviewed, simply because of their sheer number. Depending on who is interviewed, this can be very valuable. With a marginalized group, this tendency will allow trust between the moderator and group to develop much faster than in a regular interview. As long as the group is composed of peers,[2] the trust they share in each other will envelop the entire group, including the moderator. In a sense, if the moderator treads carefully then he/she can catch a ride from tapping in to the trust already in existence among the peers.

The group context also raises the issue of consensus. Concerns have been raised about the problem of group think, or enforced consensus, or excessive group conformity. However, this risk has been refuted by focus group methodologists and is only a real threat when the groups are forced to come to a decision beyond sharing their different opinions (Morgan and Krueger, 1993: 4–8) – in such cases we often refer to this as 'group think'. Note, however, that depending on how consensus-oriented the political culture is in the country where the research is carried out, this issue needs to be given attention. The legacy of political censure and the experience of the conflict itself may heighten this concern. The purpose of the research, and the particular context in which it is carried out, may lead researchers either to avoid focus groups in favor of individual interviews, or to actively use focus groups to study the degree of consensus tendencies. In my own research with ex-combatants I found that focus groups could help me explore this aspect in detail, as has been noted elsewhere as well (Morgan, 1997: 15). For a further discussion, see Box 9.2.

Box 9.2: Consensus or Dissent?

Focus group settings can be used to study the degree of consensus-forming tendencies in each group. In my own work with ex-combatants in Liberia, the degree to which they accept dissent or try to create consensus was of theoretical interest. Democracy is highly dependent on the existence of differences of opinion and the toleration of dissent. In this case, I could use the focus group interaction itself to study this phenomenon. In addition to opinions voiced in the groups, I also paid particular attention to how opinions were voiced and responded to and whether people held on to their opinions when they met with disagreement. Did the group tend to polarize concerning different themes, or was there a tendency toward coalescing the views in the group? Were these patterns particularly noticeable concerning some areas compared to others? And were there issues that were more sensitive than others and more effectively silenced? This kind of study would not have been possible with any means other than focus groups. Of course, extended participant observation may have contributed similar observations, but not nearly as focused or systematic (for more details concerning this study see Söderström, forthcoming). For a discussion on the display of disagreement in focus groups, see Myers (1998). See also della Porta's study on social movements for a similar discussion on the use of focus groups to access and study group processes (2005: 78).

The conflict or post-conflict context often entails a research interest in rather sensitive topics, such as war-time experiences or participation in truth and reconciliation commissions. The lived experiences of conflict, or even of peace-building can be quite arduous. Interviewing in such a context can therefore be quite a challenge, and sometimes the use of focus groups can be one way of dealing with it. The issue of discussing sensitive topics is often deemed impossible within focus groups by those not using them. However, my own experience, as well as those of other users of focus groups, tends to raise concerns about the opposite. Being among peers sometimes makes it easier to divulge sensitive information than a one-to-one interview would allow. The context of the focus group often implies that one is not alone with a certain experience and this makes it easier to discuss the particulars of this experience. In fact, there is often a danger that the participants may relate too much information, because the discussion can be experienced as liberating. Again, in accordance with good focus group practice, no one should be put on the spot and forced to answer a question. Thus a person who is uncomfortable talking about a certain experience can take a step back and only participate nominally. While topics such as rape or the experience of violence should be handled with care and by a well-prepared moderator and researcher, there is no topic that should *a priori* be deemed unfit to be raised in a focus group. Sometimes topics that an outsider perceives as sensitive are already part of the public collective experience in a post-conflict context; at other times they are not – it all boils down to knowing the context and preparing for the interviews carefully based on such knowledge. What is politicized or sensitized varies from community to community and over time.

Related to the issue of sensitive topics and whether they are appropriate within a group context or not, is the issue of anonymity. The group context changes the ability to keep information anonymous, and while the need for keeping a discussion anonymous and private will vary between topics and the individuals participating in the interview, this needs to be considered seriously. Researchers cannot promise complete anonymity for the individuals participating in a focus group as the group context ultimately means that others are included in the discussion and are privy to what is said. These last two issues, limited anonymity and an interest in sensitive topics, highlight the importance of informed consent (see Box 9.3), but also the difficulties for the participants of making an informed decision about participation. The psychological repercussions are usually harder to anticipate than the physical ones, but even here risk assessments may change over time as the conflict landscape changes.

Box 9.3: Informed Consent

Informed consent refers to the participants being able to make an informed decision about their participation in a particular research project, especially in terms of the risks involved for them personally but also as to the purpose of the research. Depending on the regulation that applies in each case, written consent from the participants may be required. The crucial aspect of this principle is the empowerment of the research participants, which may not necessarily be fulfilled through the signing of a written form in, for instance, a mostly illiterate context. Researchers have an ethical responsibility to ensure that participation is voluntary and knowingly entered into. Ensuring that this is the case can be problematic and has inspired a broad debate; see for instance Thorne (1980) and Fluehr-Lobban (1994).

While there are ways of handling issues of anonymity and informed consent in focus groups, as will be discussed later on in this chapter, these are serious matters that raise ethical concerns about our research. A research project involving individuals in a conflict or post-conflict context will in most cases need to be scrutinized by a research ethics committee or similar. Praxis and regulation differ between countries, and it is the responsibility of each researcher that he/she is following the guidelines set out by their department and the country where the research is conducted. However, the overarching principle of doing no harm always applies – and the responsibility of the researcher to consider these issues is continuous throughout the research process; it is not a one-off evaluation that is subsequently relegated to the side. In this book, research ethics are discussed in several of the chapters (see, for instance, Chapters 7, 8 and 10). In this chapter I have tried to highlight how and when such issues become actualized when working with focus groups.

In the following sections I discuss and cover questions that arise during the different stages of working with focus groups, from design issue, to recruitment and other logistical questions, moderation and question guides, and finally how the material should be analyzed and presented.

Group composition

Who should be included in a focus group? Again, this depends on the research question. Usually the relevant group is identified in the research question, or in the initial stages of the research process. The relevant group may for instance be ex-combatants, rebel leaders, UN personnel, refugees, civil servants or NGO personnel. Depending on the nature of the question, the participants may either be strangers or already know each other. From a recruitment perspective, it may be tempting to rely on the participants to bring others along; however, such procedures for recruitment are not always appropriate. Consider how previous relations may influence what the participants say in the group, or avoid saying, but also what risks are involved if people they know hear them comment on the questions raised in the focus group. While researchers involved in the focus group may be able to ensure anonymity on their part, the other participants also share in this responsibility. What incentives do they have for sharing the information they received in the group discussion, and could this endanger the anonymity and safety of any of the participants? In a conflict context, the research interest usually pertains to conflict-related aspects. Hence, the information revealed in a focus group session can – in a very real sense – put the participants at risk if it spreads beyond the focus group.

Sometimes the focus of the research dictates whether or not the participants know each other. For instance, the interest may be in the experiences of a certain faction, village, community, work team, members of a certain organization etc, in which case it is very likely that at least some of the participants know each other in advance. If that is the case, the researcher should be diligent as to the types of questions posed. Consider for instance how detailed the information from the participants needs to be – does it matter for the research whether specific events and individuals are identified (events and individuals that may be known to others in the group)? Issues of confidentiality and anonymity with the group can also be raised before starting the discussion. Normally, all participants share an interest in keeping the anonymity of the group intact, if they are made aware of the problem.

How many groups?

Another issue related to group composition is how many groups should be organized. The number of groups convened clearly depends not only on the goal of the research, but also on the time and resources available to complete the focus group sessions. If the research is more exploratory in nature, three to five groups is usually an adequate number, but may vary substantially depending on the research topic. In exploratory studies, one usually aims for theoretical saturation; that is, the point where an additional group no longer produces different findings compared to the ones emerging from earlier sessions. However, if the interest is in comparing across groups – such as different rebel groups or between men and women – more groups are usually required. A study with an exploratory aim can also contain comparative design elements, but often such a study is yet to discover which forms of group membership are relevant. This brings us to the discussion of composition within and across groups.

Segmentation

The composition of the groups concerns both differences in composition within a group as well as across groups. Within a group the aim is usually to make them as homogenous as possible with respect to the criteria believed to matter in that particular case. Thus, at times it makes sense to keep women and men separate, and other times not. Common criteria here include gender, age, ethnicity and social membership, but with these criteria homogeneity of opinions does not necessarily follow. The key issue is to make sure that the participants feel at ease and are in a group of peers. How peers are defined in each case depends on the topic of research, but generally it would, for instance, be inadvisable to mix members belonging to different parties of a conflict.

Homogeneity is, however, not always a goal for composition across groups. A difference may be introduced between groups because it is of theoretical interest. For instance, do the Revolutionary United Front (RUF) members differ in their experience of the war in Sierra Leone compared to members of the Civil Defense Forces (CDF)? At other times a difference between groups is introduced because of an interest in covering a range of experiences and backgrounds. The criteria believed to be relevant within the groups are often referred to as 'control characteristics', whereas the differences between groups are often referred to as 'break characteristics' (Knodel, 1993: 39) or segmentation (Morgan and Scannell, 1998: 63–7). When designing the study, it should be clear that the more characteristics that are to be compared, the more groups are needed. For an example of a study using segmentation, see della Porta (2005).

Group size

The question of size of the group is also a reoccurring issue in focus group research. What is the minimum number of people required, and what is the maximum possible number of people to have in a group? Clearly, giving set limits is futile, but numbers between three and 20 are not unusual. The most common size for a focus group is perhaps between six and 10. The size of the group also depends on the kind of topic under discussion. The more data needed from each individual participant, the fewer people should be included in the group. By extension, if the interest is in life narratives, then focus groups are usually inappropriate and individual interviews should be considered instead. A general recommendation is that the more the participants have to say on the topic at hand, the fewer participants are needed. If, on the other hand, the topic of discussion is somewhat unusual, odd or peripheral (at least to the participants), more participants need to be included. While a small group is more adept at handling sensitive questions, they also have certain problems, such as being more sensitive to group dynamics and dominant voices. In contrast, in a large focus group there is a risk of having several parallel conversations at the same time.

Getting the right people … in the right place … at the right time

The logistical aspects of conducting focus groups can be a more daunting task than expected, and should not be underestimated. This is especially true in a conflict environment. For one, how do you get in touch with people? And before that, how do you know they exist? Lists, records and means of contact are usually fairly limited. This means that calling potential participants or sending them a letter inviting them to the group is often not possible. Issues of recruitment and choice of location are discussed next.

Recruitment

Recruiting the right people for a focus group is sometimes challenging, especially if the group profile of interest is difficult to define or locate. The identities of interest are often not the identities people advertise openly, especially if there is a stigma attached to the group targeted for interview. For instance, approaching an ex-combatant or a member of a group that has been portrayed as the perpetrator in a conflict, out of the blue, is often difficult and not advisable.

Another issue to consider is how to make sure that potential recruits genuinely belong to the group of concern. In some instances, self-identification is sufficient. At other times, the researcher has a very set definition of the group, in which case ways to screen people before inviting them to the group are needed. Consider the complexities of the concept 'ex-combatant': are ex-combatants those who actually fought during the war, or those who were classified as combatants in the disarmament process, which would include women associated with the fighting forces? How is such an issue dealt with in the recruitment process? If satisfied with the latter definition, then those who participated in the disarmament process can be approached.

It is important to ensure that individuals identified as being of interest for the study will not be placed in harm's way by the format of the recruitment process. For this reason, be aware not to direct potentially sensitive questions to locate recruits in a situation where others may listen in. A way to alleviate some of these concerns in the recruitment process may be to use a snowball sample: identify one person who knows or belongs to the group in question, and then ask that person to suggest others for the group. However, when using a snowball sample it is important to try to use multiple access points for the potential participants, thereby avoiding the sample being too dependent on certain individuals.

Depending on the form of recruitment, the participants may need additional screening before the group session can be started. Do they really fit with the planned composition of this particular group? Depending on the precise characteristics needed, those selected for participation can either briefly be asked to respond to a few questions when they arrive. If they can read and write they can be asked to fill out a short questionnaire. If nothing else, the researcher or moderator can make clear in the introduction who should be there, and hope that individuals who do not meet the criteria will make themselves known. However, at times certain individuals will want to participate even when they do not meet the criteria of the group. For various reasons, such deception can be difficult to detect. One way of addressing such concerns is to pose knowledge questions that only the group in question will be able to answer, either during the recruitment process or screening.

The recruitment process is usually strategically guided rather than being a random sampling process. Sometimes a broad range of experiences and backgrounds in the groups is desired, but achieving a representative sample is problematic. The need for certain types of groups and the overall composition of groups often requires careful planning and strategizing about who to approach and how to approach potential recruits. Having a clear idea of whom to include to obtain the information needed to answer the research question, is pivotal. While it may be tempting to ask people to join a focus group at random, this implies losing control of who actually ends up in the groups. Knowing who is in the group will not only make it easier to ask the right questions, but will also avoid wasting the participants' time. See Agar and Macdonald (1995) for the importance of having control over the recruitment process.

If the researcher has the possibility of inviting participants ahead of time, it is advisable to invite around 20 per cent more people than actually needed. Showing up on the actual date and time of the focus group may not always be feasible for all those invited. However, sometimes it is not viable to invite people for a group taking place at a later date, either because the time in the area is limited or because the ability to make such promises is limited for the group of interest, or simply because too few actually show up for the planned groups. In such cases direct recruitment into a focus group may be required. Such recruitment is easier if the initial recruitment and the holding of the focus group are done in the area where the participants live, or if the researcher is utilizing an event the participants normally attend. The issue of location will be revisited in the next section. In either case, the researcher needs to make sure that informed consent is obtained from the participants in the focus groups (see Box 9.3, above). In particular, the potential participants need to be informed about the voluntary nature of participation in the study and the possibility of opting out. This is particularly important where recruitment is carried out immediately prior to the holding of a focus group.

Should researchers compensate the participants for their time and effort? This is a difficult question. Focus group research often offers some compensation to participants, especially because the researcher is more dependent on the participants showing up at the right time and place compared to when conducting regular interviews. If nothing else, reimbursement for travel to the group discussion is usually offered. There are other ways to show participants appreciation for the time they take to participate in the focus group, such as offering snacks during the discussion (which is advisable for other reasons anyway; see the section on building rapport). Simply showing enthusiasm and genuine interest can also be an important way of expressing gratitude.

In situations where it is difficult to recruit participants to the focus groups, the researcher needs to consider what incentives are offered for participation. In some instances monetary compensation is appropriate, but in other instances the problem may lie more in the way the research topic is described, or the way the focus group is set up. Does participating in the study sound like it could be any fun or interesting at all? Is it obvious to them why the topic is important? If the research resonates with potential participants on these grounds they are more likely to be persuaded to participate. Is the timing and location of the focus group appropriate for the group being recruited? Is the time devoted to the focus group discussion too long given the situation and/or occupation of the participants? If monetary compensation is used to entice participation, be sure to consider how it might affect who actually shows up. Will it rule out certain people, and are certain people more likely to show up? Are such differences between people important to the research topic and if so, will it introduce a bias in the material collected?

Determining the level of compensation can be difficult. Wages may vary considerably, both over time and between people. One way to ensure the compensation is at an appropriate level is to ask local people during the early stages of field work. What do the people participating in the study normally earn in a month? What does it cost to get from one place to another? Alternatively, can the researcher arrange for transport? For a further reasoned discussion of compensating respondents, see McKeganey (2001).

Location

Finding the right place for holding a focus group discussion is a challenge, as is getting the right people to that place. Ideally, the location should be neutral, safe, comfortable and private, as well as easily accessible. Again, attention to the type of questions asked during the group discussion and the composition of the group is critical in determining the appropriateness of a site. For some, meeting at the local church is neutral and for others it is the complete opposite. Sometimes using a room at a university building is an option, at other times such a location is either intimidating or implies a certain political stance. The main thing is that the location is convenient for those participating and preferably private enough during the discussion. However, sometimes the most convenient place is in the center of a village under a tree, or in a café during the quiet hours, in which case privacy is more problematic. Ensuring that others in the village respect the privacy of the event often entails telling key stakeholders what the research is about and the reasons why it needs to be private. Operating in secrecy is not always appropriate and usually it is advisable to be up front and explain why the discussion is private, and why not everyone can participate. This does not mean, however, that it is necessary to give those interested in the event all the details as to who and why these particular individuals were invited to participate; rather a general description that does not stigmatize or endanger the safety of those participating can be provided.

In terms of the seating arrangement, a circle is preferable. Avoid placing the moderator at the head of a table. A table to sit around can help put people at ease, as participants then have a barrier of sorts to take cover behind. Without a table people will usually be more self-conscious, which may result in diminished attention to the discussion.

The moderator and questions

The moderator is the person who leads the discussion with the participants. For anyone undertaking moderation, it is wise to conduct a pilot group first since it might be a somewhat awkward – perhaps even scary – experience the first time it is done. This pilot group, which could be conducted at home before going into the field, is a way to become familiar with the role as a moderator, and to feel more at ease with moderation techniques. A pilot group may also be needed in the context of the research, to test if the questions play out as planned. An advanced student who uses focus groups in his/her thesis is unlikely to have the resources to hire someone to act as the moderator for the group discussion, but advanced researchers may also have reasons to do the moderation themselves.

The style of moderating depends yet again on the research focus, and in particular on the kind of question guide, which has been prepared in advance. If the study is more exploratory in nature, then merely introducing a theme for the conversation may be enough. Explorative studies typically involve a rather low-key role for the moderator, in which case the moderator will mainly prompt the participants if the conversation halts, or suggest where he/she might want additional information and depth to the discussion, or make sure they stay on topic (broadly defined). The more specific the research question is, however, the more control the moderator usually must exert on the group. This also tends to correspond to having a fairly detailed and structured question guide for the groups.

When deciding the order of the questions there are a few rules of thumb. Start with more open questions and then let the questions become increasingly detailed. It is often a good idea to have a round of introductions when starting, but this does not have to be confined to simply stating names. The participants can also be asked to briefly describe their experience with the phenomenon at the focus of the research, or something concerning their background that is relevant to the study. If it is important in the analysis to distinguish different participants from each other, a more extended round of introductions serves as a strategy for voice identification if the interview is recorded, since to continually re-state the participants' names throughout the interview becomes unwieldy and awkward.

In terms of the order of the questions, placing the more sensitive ones toward the end is also recommended, as the earlier discussion can help to create a comfortable and trusting atmosphere. However, when designing the question guide, think outside the box – perhaps using visual material or objects instead of direct verbal questions might aid the discussion (see Box 9.4). The question guide should note what questions need to be posed in all groups, but also indicate potential follow-ups or ways to probe the group if more detail is needed.

It should now be clear that the time spent on a focus group can vary substantially, from anywhere between 30 minutes to three hours. Consider how much time it is reasonable for the participants to devote to the process. A group running as long as three hours is usually the result of a very engaged group that found the discussion stimulating, in which case the length of the discussion was not a problem. A more reasonable length is perhaps around an hour or two. Be sure to limit the number of questions posed to each group so that there is enough time to discuss the questions in detail. Getting a sense of how much time the questions might take is another reason for conducting a trial group before starting the real data collection.

Building rapport

In order for a focus group to function properly, both participants and moderator need to feel at ease. Many students often feel uncomfortable taking too much control of a focus group and, no doubt, finding the right balance is not easy. Again, trying to conduct a focus group prior to field work will be beneficial. All of this will be assisted if at the onset of the interview the participants are informed of the moderator's role, what the moderator will and will not do, and what is expected from the group. For instance, it might be emphasized that the interest is in their specific experiences and that any differences between them are especially important, so for this reason displaying differences of opinion is ok. But it might also include informing the participants that on occasion the moderator will interrupt the group because of a need to move on to the next question, or because more details are needed. In this preparatory phase of the focus group, offering some snacks is also useful, as this will relax the situation for everyone involved. It will decrease the formality of the situation and express the researcher's

Box 9.4: Photos and Election Experiences

In order to study the election experiences among ex-combatants in Liberia, I used photos of the election in 2005 as a way to stimulate the discussion. The photos depicted people standing in line to vote, political campaigns (both presidential candidates Ellen Johnson Sirleaf and George Weah), and people voting. These photos served two purposes. First, they acted as a memory bridge, taking the participants back to the situation at hand. As the interviews were carried out almost three years after the event, it was important to focus their attention on this particular period. Secondly, they allowed the participants to voice the aspects of their election experience that were most important and salient to them. When presented with the photos, they were simply asked what they thought about when they saw the photos and how it made them feel. As the pictures presented a spectrum of experiences from the election, they allowed the participants to voice spontaneous thoughts and ideas in relation to the pictures. All of the groups responded well to the photos, and it was often fun and relaxed. The groups became at times quite excited as a new photo was handed out. Had I instead posed them a direct question about their experience of the election in 2005, I would have at least been forced to frame it as a question about *elections*. Instead the photos allowed several different associations, while clearly resonating with events surrounding the elections in 2005. (For more details concerning this study, see Söderström, 2010.)

Photo by Catarina Fabiansson.

appreciation to the participants. Biscuits, sandwiches, fruit – just make sure the snacks are appropriate for the group being interviewed, and are easy to organize. It often makes sense for the moderator to discuss the purpose of the research, introduce him/ herself and discuss questions of anonymity and possible recording while the others snack, if there are any ground rules or simply encourage voicing different perspectives. Having prepared them in this manner will undoubtedly make the moderator more comfortable directing the discussion in the way laid out without feeling intrusive. The group is convened for research purposes, and unless it is directed in the way the research requires, the researcher's and participants' time will be wasted.

Undoubtedly the person acting as a moderator for focus groups will develop skills throughout the data collection, but a moderator can also use inspiration from similar group discussions that he/she has participated in, like a seminar or a workshop. How did they work? How were participants encouraged to talk if they were quiet? How can those who tend to dominate the discussion be handled, and how can people be encouraged to develop their ideas? Lessons from such situations are often transferable, and can be used as a source of inspiration.

Being an outsider

Quite often, in peace research, research is carried out in an environment where the researcher is an outsider. In focus group research, this can mean that the moderator has noticeably different traits from the group being interviewed. Being an insider or an outsider, or at least being perceived as such, has an impact on the group interview. There are advantages and disadvantages to both, but the issue of trust is crucial for both types of moderators. If the moderator appears to be like those interviewed it will help create an acceptance and trust in the moderator, but an outsider may have greater license to ask odd questions for clarification and details, indeed to question things that are normally taken for granted. As an outsider, it is sometimes easier to gain access to certain groups. Although an insider may be more adept at locating potential participants, often the outsider has an easier time in convincing them to join the group – simply because it is more exciting to talk to someone from somewhere else. Having an outsider involved may give the situation an air of importance. In addition, in a conflict context, being an outsider may help to disassociate the research from either party in the conflict. In this sense, an outsider can gain the trust of a group, since he/she has no prior involvement in the conflict. In a similar sense, being non-threatening may also be particularly useful in a conflict context – although determining who appears as non-threatening is not always obvious. Sometimes being young and female constitutes such a person, at other times it is just the opposite. Again, it all comes down to knowing the context in which the focus groups are set.

In some projects, different moderators can be used for different groups. For instance, in certain circumstances it can be an advantage to have a male moderator for male groups and a female one for female groups. But often the disadvantages of having more than one moderator will outweigh the benefits. Many other aspects will undoubtedly vary between different moderators so it will be hard to claim that these differences are only based on gender. To make the data from different groups comparable, the group activities need to be carried out in a similar manner, which is a challenge when using several moderators.

In many cases it is not feasible to conduct focus groups in a language that the researcher is fluent in. Having a translator present to translate for the moderator usually disrupts the flow of the conversation and removes most of the advantages of using focus groups. If the researcher is fairly confident in the language of the participants or if the participants use a language that is not their first language, it can be wise to have a translator standing by. The researcher can also engage a moderator who speaks the language, although this adds a layer of complexity. It entails not only transcribing the discussions afterwards, but also translating the transcripts. Transcribing is arduous work, and to add translation is even more cumbersome. If the research has a particular interest in the phrasing and choice of words among the participants, the focus group discussion needs to be conducted in a language the researcher understands. However, if the details of the talk produced are of less importance, someone can be hired to take notes during the discussion and then have these translated. This option still entails a huge amount of logistics and the data will have gone through several filters (the moderator, the note-taking and the translation) before the researcher can analyze it.

Sensitive topics

It was earlier pointed out that being among peers with similar experiences can make it easier for participants to discuss sensitive topics, and there is a risk that participants in a focus group divulge more information than they would actually like to. For this to happen everyone in the group needs to know that they are all similar or have similar experiences at some level. Such commonalities among participants can, for instance, be established through the way the research aims are presented. Setting the stage so that such important topics can be discussed freely is one important aspect, but the moderator also has a responsibility for protecting the participants. The moderator needs to make sure that during the discussion the group does not go too far into a sensitive or vulnerable discussion that is not needed for the research at hand that puts the participants in harm's way. If such a discussion is part of the research focus, the researcher needs to make sure that each of the participants feels alright when they leave. It is also useful if the researcher has contact details for someone the participants can be referred to should they need further assistance. The researcher and/or the moderator cannot be expected to be a psychiatrist but should ensure that the participants are not left out in the cold.

In relation to the issue of sensitive questions, it is also reasonable to discuss the advantages and disadvantages of recording the focus group session. Again, the field of peace research often implies that the topics of discussion are sensitive in several ways. Some of the participants may therefore be hesitant about recording the conversation. For research purposes, however, recording the discussion is often crucial. If recording is not possible, the researcher needs to rely on notes. Taking notes while simultaneously leading the discussion is clearly a difficult task. If the discussion cannot be recorded, it is wise to have assistance, either for the moderation or for note-taking. The experience of many researchers is that if the issue of recording is discussed openly and in detail, most groups have no problem with it. The group needs to be informed why recording is necessary and useful for the research process, how the recording will be stored, and who will have access to it. Such information allows for an informed decision. Again it is important to highlight that keeping the discussion confidential is a joint responsibility. In my research in Liberia, several ex-combatants expressed a concern at being recorded in relation to their possibilities for future travelling. They had already been through a cumbersome registration in the disarmament process, and were worried that they would end up in a file somewhere, which would make it impossible for them to travel to the USA. Such concerns need to be taken seriously and the participants must be given time to talk about their concerns. If there are only one or two individuals who object to being recorded and the recording is essential for the research, those who are uncomfortable with recording can leave the group.

Analyzing and presenting the material

Having completed the focus groups, the next step is analyzing the material and then presenting the findings. In practice there are as many ways of analyzing focus groups as there are ways to analyze individual interviews, if not more. Again, the type and level of analysis depends on the research question. The analysis, however, is highly dependent on the types of transcripts of interviews the focus groups have generated.

Working with transcripts

Transcribing interviews is often necessary. However, the amount of detail in the transcripts can vary quite substantially. It is not unusual that transcribing a focus group takes at least four times as long as the original interview and a two-hour interview can easily produce 50 pages of transcripts. By their very nature, focus groups are more difficult to transcribe than a regular interview, as the discussion needs to be differentiated between various speakers. If there is an interest in the turn-taking, pauses, positioning among participants and the details of the participants' arguments, the researcher needs to factor in this part of the process when designing the study. If there is an interest in the group interaction as such, then transcripts are needed that will allow an analysis of such interaction. Here the content of what was said may not be of primary importance, but rather how things were said and in what context (see Agar and Macdonald, 1995, and Myers, 1998, for more details and examples). A complete overview of the various choices and alternatives at this stage of the research process cannot be provided within the confines of this chapter, but any standard textbook that deals with text analysis or regular interviews can be informative for analyzing and presenting focus group material.

A grounded approach, as found in Reilly *et al*'s study (2004), entails reading and re-reading the transcripts in search of common themes and perspectives. Such an analysis will allow categories to develop solely based on the transcripts themselves. However, if the research aims are more detailed and precise, the categories and hypotheses needed to confront the data are usually already defined. There is computer software that can be used for indexing transcripts, but indexing can also be done manually – on paper copies of the transcripts or by cutting and pasting in a word-processing program – if the number of groups is fairly limited (see Frankland and Bloor, 1999, for further discussion of these issues). If the analysis is also concerned with differences across groups, the researcher needs to pay attention to whether descriptions or arguments differ systematically across any or all of the segments included in the focus groups. With a segmentation design, the group comparisons are crucial, but be aware that it involves a lot of work and continually checking the reliability of the conclusions.

Generalizing?

Generalizing findings in qualitative research is always a challenge, but focus groups are amenable to the same strategies appropriate for individual interviews or ethnographic research (such as least and most likely cases). However, one additional aspect comes into play, namely whether the findings are true for the entire focus group or only for the individual in question. Do the opinions expressed indicate the opinion of everyone in the group? Such inferences can often be difficult to make, as not everyone in the group will make their position known on everything. Thus, based on the group interview, can claims be made about the entire group, a majority, or only in relation to those that were vocal about their stance? Drawing clear boundaries here is often filled with difficulties, unless we have encouraged participants to clearly voice disagreement during the focus groups (Söderström, 2010). Researchers can often benefit from focusing on the advantages of mapping out certain types of experiences or opinions (in which case it does not matter as much if these were voiced by different people or not), rather than trying to argue for the representativeness of the findings.

Unit of analysis

A reoccurring problem for the focus group researcher is the question of unit of analysis. Is it the individual or the group? Different researchers and different research projects will inevitably have different answers to this question. However, I and others (see e.g. Morgan, 1997: 60) maintain that there is a vacillation between the two, and that there is interplay between these levels of analysis. Again, depending on the research project, the focus may lie more with one than the other.

If we suspect that the group is particularly relevant for the attitude or perspective we are interested in, then focusing on the group interaction and the group-produced expressions make sense. If the group displays differences in opinion, or the experiences of the participants turn out to be less than homogenous, then the researcher needs to consider how relevant that particular group label is. If the focus is solely on the individual, then the question is whether the use of focus groups is appropriate to begin with. However, sometimes focus groups are used to grasp the views of individuals because the researcher believes more reasoned and detailed responses will emerge from the participants if they are set in a group context. In other instances, these deliberated answers are of interest because the researcher is particularly interested in the logic of someone's argument and the chain of meaning that they construct. If the research is located closer to the individual as the unit of analysis it is also common to use focus groups in combination with other forms of data collection (such as surveys or in-depth interviews).

Presentation

Presenting the research results can also be done in many different ways, but it is always advisable to be as explicit and transparent as possible. Sometimes it is necessary to quote passages at length to give the reader a good sense of how the discussion was structured, thereby allowing the reader to evaluate any claims made. But obviously there is a limit to this use of quotes. If claims are made about group differences, then findings need to be structured by group rather than by theoretical themes. If such group comparisons are less important, then structuring the results according to set categories is more appropriate. This was done by McEvoy (2000) in her study of notions of peace and community in Northern Ireland. An alternative is to let the data structure the presentation more directly, as was done in a study by Reilly *et al* (2004).

What can go wrong?

When conducting focus groups there are many things that can go awry. Below are a few examples and suggestions for how to avoid or deal with them.

Intruders

If the focus group discussion takes place in a communal area or outdoors, people who have not been invited to the discussion often want to join. For those not invited, a focus group discussion may appear like fun, and the presence of a researcher may signal something new and interesting. Often the researcher does not have the option of a location that prevents others from noticing and approaching the group. If someone comes too close, so that they can overhear the conversation, or if someone actually tries to join the group, the advice to the moderator is to be firm yet courteous to the intruders. The moderator needs to inform them that the conversation is private, and that there unfortunately is no time to talk to everyone in the community. The moderator should take care to be smooth and polite when asking the intruders to leave, as offensive behavior can create antagonism between focus group members and outsiders.

The wrong people

Despite efforts of screening, the wrong people may still end up in the focus groups. Depending on the study and how this particular person is a wrong fit for the group he/she attended, this can be a serious problem or something that has little influence on the quality of the research. However, if the researcher discovers during the discussion that someone should not be there, it is usually more disturbing to remove them than to keep them in. If they are different from the rest of the group, the researcher can pay particular attention to their interaction with the rest of the group and whether their comments differ radically or sway the group's opinions. If it does not seem as if they have made a huge impact on the group's discussion then the problem was not that severe.

Silence

Sometimes during a focus group the conversation grinds to a halt. If this happens despite a well-designed question guide, there are a few things one can still try to do. If someone in the group indicated a topic of interest, the moderator can ask the person to go into more detail, or ask if other participants have similar or different experiences, or suggest that in other groups people have felt differently or thought differently in order to create a reaction. The more experience the moderator has, the easier it will be to give prompts that fit with both the research aim and the specific conversation that has already taken place. If the participants have a difficult time relating the experience to their own circumstances, the moderator can ask them what they think people like themselves would feel, do or say in a similar situation. A different strategy is to wait in silence and thereby motivate someone to fill the silence with additional comments. While this works in many situations and will most likely trigger a similar response in a focus group, there are reasons to advise against such usage. To deliberately allow long pauses in a focus group will change the atmosphere and disrupt the feeling of a conversation. If the conversation seems to come to a natural halt and the moderator has no more follow-up questions then one has to accept that the discussion on a specific topic has come to an end. If the moderator indicates to the group that the discussion will move on to the next question/theme, this might also elicit some final comments from the group. In any case, it is good to indicate that the participants are welcome to return to any of the questions at the very end of the session if they have anything more to add. It is always wise to have a round of last comments, where the participants are given the opportunity to add to what has already been said before the session is completed.

Dominant voices

In some focus groups there are one or two very dominant participants who tend to always speak first and vehemently so. Such dominant people risk pushing the discussion in one particular direction. There are several ways to deal with dominant participants, and I have found two methods to be fairly effective. One is to indicate the name of someone else in the group and ask them to comment first. This will give the moderator more control over the turn-taking in the group and the more dominant members will heed the call to give the floor to someone else. However, if the domination of one or two participants continues despite the moderator's efforts, the problem may need to be brought to the group's attention. They can be reminded of the importance of everyone getting to voice their opinion. Lightly, and perhaps jokingly, it can be indicated that someone has been given too much attention. If this is done with charm most participants will not be offended or react negatively.

Summary

- Good research always boils down to finding the data collection method that works best with the research questions and subject matter at hand. Be sure to be familiar with the options available and what kind of data they can produce before deciding.
- Focus groups are particularly apt for studying norms, attitudes, opinions, perspectives and experiences, behavioral choices and motivations.
- The group interaction is at the heart of focus groups. This interaction matters for what is said in each group and holds the potential for both advantages and disadvantages of this form of data collection. This chapter has highlighted some of the areas where this interaction comes into play, such as the social desirability bias, decreased pressure to voice any opinion, the power balance between the moderator and the group, as well as in the creation of trust in the group. The group context also has implications for the sense of security and ease with which difficult topics are discussed as well as the type of anonymity the participants can expect.
- When designing a study, consider group composition not only within a certain group but also across groups (segmentation). The more comparisons aimed for, the more focus groups need to be conducted.
- The type of questions posed to the group will determine the optimal number of participants in each group; the more *odd* or *thin* the topic is, the larger the group needs to be.
- Be conscious about how the research and data collection strategies will influence and possibly endanger the participants. This is especially important in terms of recruitment, choice of locality and the topics covered in the focus group.

- Focus groups can often lead participants to divulge too much information about themselves or an experience. The moderator and the researcher need to make sure that this does not happen and will need a plan for dealing with such issues if it happens.
- Do try this at home! Conducting focus groups is an art and practice makes perfect.

Further reading

Agar, M. and Macdonald, J. (1995) 'Focus Groups and Ethnography', *Human Organization*, 54 (1): 78–86.
Kitzinger, J. and Barbour, R.S. (eds) (1999) *Developing Focus Group Research: Politics, theory, and practice*, Thousand Oaks, CA: Sage Publications.
Morgan, D.L. and Krueger, R.A. (1993) 'When to Use Focus Groups and Why', in D.L. Morgan (ed.) *Successful Focus Groups: Advancing the state of the art*, Newbury Park: Sage Publications.
Myers, G. (1998) 'Displaying Opinions: Topics and Disagreement in Focus Groups', *Language in Society*, 27 (1): 85–111.
Smithson, J. (2000) 'Using and Analysing Focus Groups: Limitations and Possibilities', *International Journal of Social Research Methodology*, 3 (2): 103–19.
Ward, V., Bertrand, J.T. and Brown, L.F. (1991) 'The Comparability of Focus Group and Survey Results', *Evaluation Review*, 15 (2): 266–83.

Notes

1. I want to thank all those involved in the qualitative method seminar at the Department of Government at Uppsala University for their useful comments, throughout my work with focus groups as well as on this text in particular. I would also like to extend my appreciation to Robert Kimball for his critique of this chapter.
2. Peers who are aware of being peers; for instance, if it is believed that membership in specific rebel groups matters for the trust between individuals: it is important for the participants in the group to know that they all belong to the same rebel group.

10 Survey Research in Conflict and Post-conflict Societies

Kristine Eck

Introduction

In recent years, researchers have increasingly come to employ surveys as a way of studying topics within the field of peace and conflict research. By interviewing individuals in conflict-stricken regions, researchers are able to study new questions and approach existing topics from different angles. Surveys in conflict and post-conflict areas can help to address questions like why some people participate in armed rebellion while others do not (Humphreys and Weinstein, 2006), or what effects exposure to conflict has on political engagement in post-conflict society (Blattman, 2009). The nature of conflict often makes it very difficult for researchers to collect data on many issues, and researchers have discovered that conflict surveys can provide enormous leverage in obtaining data on issues relating to the use of violence that are otherwise difficult to collect. Surveys facilitate the study of the microfoundations of war because they allow researchers to obtain fine-grained data on variations in individuals' attitudes and behaviors. Indeed, researchers have only begun to scratch the surface of the research opportunities that surveys offer.

Surveys provide a systematic means for gathering information from a sample of entities (usually individuals) for the purposes of describing attributes of the larger population (Groves *et al,* 2004). Surveys are often thought of as quantitative in nature because they result in quantifiable data that can be used in statistical analysis. But the data that surveys generate are based on interviews, so surveys exist at the intersection of qualitative and quantitative methodologies.[1] As such, they require skills related to both methodologies, such as case study and fieldwork experience as well as knowledge of database management and regression analysis.

There is an extensive body of literature on survey methodology. In designing surveys, researchers seek to maximize their ability to generalize from the sample to the population with a minimum of error, while at the same time best addressing the research question of interest; in other words, maximizing validity and reliability. The existing survey design literature does a very good job of covering topics like drawing different types of samples, reducing error, questionnaire design, data collection, bias and so on. But little has been written on how to undertake survey work in areas that have recently experienced armed conflict. This chapter is meant to complement existing sources on survey design by focusing on the issues that arise in the context of surveying in conflict areas. A basic knowledge of survey methodology itself is assumed and the focus is instead on the practical aspects of designing and implementing surveys in conflict-ridden areas.[2]

Before embarking on a survey, researchers should carefully consider if it is the optimal means for gathering data on the research topic of interest. Surveys are costly, both financially and in terms of the time investment necessary to ensure that they are done correctly. This is particularly true for surveys undertaken in post-conflict areas, which combine not only all of the difficulties of survey work, but also the difficulties of working in developing regions and in insecure environments. Surveys in conflict regions can take a long time to complete and will often be fraught with setbacks. Researchers should be prepared to invest a good deal of their time in managing the survey. Hopefully this chapter will give prospective survey researchers an idea of some of the issues they will face when undertaking survey work in conflict and post-conflict regions.

Finally, throughout this chapter conflict surveys are generally discussed in the context of individual or household surveys undertaken in conflict-ridden countries. In these types of surveys, households are visited by enumerators, who are the individuals who collect the survey data by conducting the interviews with the respondents. Enumerators verbally ask respondents the questions on the questionnaire and record their answers. In most developing countries, and certainly those that have experienced conflict, it is rarely possible to send out questionnaires that respondents fill out themselves and send back; households must be visited. In addition to household/individual surveys, there are innumerable other possible research designs that could be used to study facets of violent behavior. One is to change the unit of analysis; for example, one can conduct community-level surveys as a way to determine refugee flows, intra-community conflicts, overall levels of conflict damage to the community and so on (cf. Bozzoli and Brück, 2009; Bundervoet *et al,* 2009). One may also be interested in conflict issues but choose not to survey in conflict areas. For example, for some research topics it might be more relevant to survey refugee populations who have resettled elsewhere; in these cases, other approaches to data collection, such as sending out questionnaires, may be feasible. This chapter focuses on household surveys in conflict areas mainly because these are the most logistically challenging types of conflict surveys, but many of the topics covered in this chapter are relevant for these other variations of conflict surveys as well.

Getting started

As with any research project, the researcher must consider the research question and the planned contribution when designing the study. In addition to asking how the planned research fits into the existing literature, one should also consider the question of whether there are any other similar survey projects ongoing. To do so, the researcher should familiarize him/herself with the researchers who regularly conduct post-conflict surveys, as well as the researchers who work in the region of interest. Useful places to look are the Household in Violent Conflict Network (HiCN, www.hicn.org), Post-Conflict and Ex-Combatant Surveys (2010), and Afrobarometer (www.afrobarometer.org). If other survey projects are underway, the researcher should seriously consider the possibility of collaboration; given the costs associated with survey work, it is more efficient to add a set of questions to an existing survey than to conduct a separate one.

Because of the high costs of survey data collection, the researcher should also begin by scouring the internet and literature for data that already exist. A clearly defined research question anchored in a solid understanding of existing literature makes it easier to identify what data are relevant and what are not. It may be that the data needed by the researcher are already available in an existing household survey. Often it is not necessary to conduct a new survey since there is a great deal of existing data that are rarely used in academic analysis. Governmental agencies, NGOs and international organizations like the UN often conduct surveys or gather other types of systematic data that they do not make publicly available but can be accessed with permission. Knowing that these data exist and obtaining them often requires an intimate knowledge of the country and organizations of interest; the importance of in-depth case knowledge is a point to which I will return and is one that cannot be overemphasized.

Most surveys are one-shot investigations of a single country/region. But comparative designs are also a possibility, such as cross-sectional/cross-national or longitudinal (that is, when individuals are studied at multiple points in time). Such designs may provide analytical leverage, but their usefulness is dependent on the research question. Klandermans and Smith (2002) provide a discussion on the advantages of such designs for the study of social movements. If the researcher does decide to take a longitudinal approach, he/she should be careful to design the first wave of the study so that it will still be useful in and of itself. It is good if the entire research project does not depend on obtaining longitudinal data since it is not always possible to conduct a follow-up survey. Political situations in post-conflict countries are apt to change quickly and obstacles may arise. With a shift in leadership, permission to survey may be retracted, or a decline in the rule of law may pose insurmountable security problems that prohibit a second wave. Researchers should plan the first round of surveying with this eventuality in mind. In some situations, it may be possible to create a longitudinal study by running a second wave of an existing survey to study variation over time. In such situations, it is advisable to consult closely with the research team that conducted the initial study.

Composing the research team

Surveys are usually conducted by a research team rather than a single researcher, and for good reason. To do a survey well requires an in-depth knowledge of the theoretical literature driving the research question, the country or region that is to be sampled, and survey methodology itself. It is rare that one person is expert in all of these areas, so it is wise to collaborate with other researchers whose skills complement one's own.

Theoretical expertise is necessary not only in the general design process of preparing a research question and determining the project's contribution, but also for formulating questions that adequately measure the concepts of interest. Problems can also arise in the implementation phase that require the researchers to shift the research focus. For example, the research team for the Nepal Peacebuilding Survey (NPS) planned to interview both civilians and ex-combatants, but political developments led rebel leaders to sour on the idea of allowing their troops to participate in the survey, leaving only the civilian population to survey. To address this, the research team removed questions intended to study participation in rebellion and instead added a section aimed at measuring the effect of conflict exposure on a number of social, economic and political attitudes and behaviors. The researchers were able to make these changes relatively late in the planning stage because of their familiarity with the theoretical literature; they were able to quickly identify another research gap that would be feasible to study within the constraints they faced.

Country expertise is essential to designing a good survey. All of the researchers on the team should familiarize themselves with the country of interest by reading news reports and anthropological, political and other literature on the country. But the team should also have someone who has done fieldwork in the country before and is familiar with the lay of the land, in both literal and figurative senses. Personal connections are often crucial for obtaining permission to survey in many countries, necessitating someone on the team with an existing network to draw upon. A country expert will also ensure that the questions and answers in the questionnaire are appropriate to that country. Determining whether the planned project is realistic in terms of practicalities like permission, timing, budget and security concerns also requires case knowledge.

Finally, it is also necessary to recruit someone familiar with survey methodology, preferably someone who has led survey work in a similar setting before. Survey methodology is a large literature and the solutions to many common problems are becoming increasingly sophisticated. While a team can get some assistance from an implementing partner (for example, a professional survey agency), there are many reasons not to delegate methodology to such a partner. One is that it is not always the case that such organizations are aware of current advances in survey methods and accepted best practices in the particular research field of interest, a point to which I will return later. But most important, methodological decisions are driven by theoretical interests; a hired survey agency does not know what is best for studying the research question. For this reason it is essential that someone on the research team has a solid grasp of survey methods.

Of course, one researcher may have several of these skills. Indeed, it is desirable for all of the researchers on the team to have at least a good basic understanding of the relevant theory, case and survey methods. Collaborating to pool expertise allows the research team to vastly improve the quality of the survey and to better achieve the aims of the research project.

Designing the instrument

One of the most important aspects of survey work is designing the questions that are included in the questionnaire (this is often referred to as 'the instrument'). The questions should naturally be driven by the aims of the research question, but they will also be affected by practical constraints and ethical considerations. Will the respondents be able to answer the questions? What is the risk of dishonest answers? Can the asking of some questions have adverse effects on the respondents?

There is a substantial body of literature that addresses the basics of how to formulate survey questions, covering topics like open-ended versus closed-ended questions, double-barreled questions, and so on. In addition to all of these considerations, there are other factors one should take into account when designing a conflict-related questionnaire. Luckily, researchers do not have to start from scratch since a number of conflict surveys have already been conducted. The instruments from conflict surveys in Sierra Leone, Burundi, and elsewhere are publicly available,[3] as are standard demographic health survey instruments.[4] Many questions from existing DHS and conflict surveys can be adopted into the instrument, saving the researchers a great deal of work. These questions should naturally be adjusted for the context in which the researchers will operate, for example, questions about the actions of paramilitary groups may be relevant in a country like Colombia where paramilitaries are active, but not in a country like Nepal which has not seen paramilitary groups. In addition to easing the workload of the researchers, using the same questions can contribute to standardization of conflict surveys, and over time allow researchers to undertake comparative analysis using different surveys.

While the researchers are advised to familiarize themselves with existing instruments and lend from them as they wish, this does not mean that existing instruments are always relevant for the research question at hand, or that they cannot be improved upon. The researchers should be alert to issues like whether to have a separate conflict module or to integrate conflict questions into other modules (cf. Bundervoet *et al*, 2009), and how to sequence the questions to avoid order effects. Researchers should also consider how various words will be interpreted in the area they are planning to survey. In some countries, certain words or topics are considered unacceptable by authorities and so one must speak of these topics with the use of euphemisms. Speaking of 'demobilization' in Nepal or 'democracy' in Singapore may result in authorities rejecting a researcher's request to survey; knowing that 'security sector reform' and 'rule of law' are acceptable synonyms can greatly improve the researcher's chances of being allowed to implement the survey.[5] Similarly, terms like 'democracy' can carry vastly different meanings in different contexts; the case expert on the research team should be familiar with which terms tend to be understood differently in the country compared to the researchers' understanding.

Probably the issue of greatest concern when designing instruments to be used in conflict settings is that of sensitive topics. Will respondents be willing to answer questions about certain topics? How can the researchers improve response rates and minimize the risk of dishonesty when asking sensitive questions? Again, expertise in the country of interest will help to inform the research team as to exactly which topics are potentially problematic. This issue can be addressed both in the planning and in the implementation phases. In terms of planning, sometimes the problem can be solved by broaching the topic indirectly. For example, in their survey of former fighters in Sierra Leone, Humphreys and Weinstein (2003) read a list of things that 'soldiers sometimes did during the conflict' and told the respondent that 'for each one I would like you to tell me whether a combatant at your level in the unit would get in trouble for doing these things without the permission of his commander'. Actions like raping someone, killing someone from the same group, etc were then included. Another option is to use list experiments (Keeter, 2005; Kuklinski *et al*, 1997), in which the sample is divided randomly into two groups. Both groups are read a list of (non-sensitive) behaviors and asked how many – *but not which* – they have engaged in. The lists are identical except that the second group has one additional behavior listed – the item of interest for the researcher. Any difference in the mean number of behaviors between the two groups is attributable to the additional item presented only to the second sub-sample.[6] While this approach allows researchers to gauge the incidence of the sensitive behavior for the sample, it cannot identify the individuals who engage in that behavior. This limits the researcher's ability to draw inferences about the characteristics of individuals who engage in the behavior. Scacco (2008) provides another alternative. In her study of ethnic riots in Nigeria, she ensured that enumerators did not know whether they were interviewing rioters or not because participants filled out the sensitive part of the questionnaire themselves behind a screen. The questions were read aloud to the subjects and they were required only to make tick marks to indicate their responses.

The problem of sensitive topics can also be addressed at the implementation level; exploring sensitive topics is greatly helped by using local enumerators who have been appropriately trained to gain respondents' trust. It is important to also consider the attributes of the enumerators and whether they will invite the confidence of respondents. Researchers may prefer, for example, to have female enumerators interview female respondents, especially for victimization studies (Paluck, 2009, notes, however, that respondents in her surveys discussed rape just as easily with male and female enumerators). Similarly, respondents may not be as forthcoming to members of other identity groups (Hatchett and Schuman, 1975; Norman, 2009; Paluck, 2009).

Sampling strategies

A sample is a sub-set of the population. The term 'sampling' refers to the way in which researchers select the individual units that compose the sample (people, households, etc) in order to reproduce the characteristics of the population as closely as possible. The first step in devising a sampling strategy is to establish the survey frame. A survey frame is a list of all units (individuals, households, etc) that comprise the population from which the sample is to be drawn. Many countries conduct censuses and that is one place to start looking, but the researchers should consider the accuracy of the information. Record-keeping varies considerably in accuracy from country to country. In areas ravaged by intense fighting, there may have been dramatic population shifts and migration out of the country since the last census was conducted; for countries that have seen many years of fighting, no recent census data may exist at all.[7] In some countries, voter registers constitute another source for population lists, but in many areas a considerable portion of the population consists of non-citizens and is therefore not listed on voter registers. These individuals may be of interest but will be missed if voter registers are used as the sample frame. The researchers must consider carefully the source used for constructing the sample frame. Since the researcher should already be familiar with all of the data sources available for this country, they should know what the options are for composing the frame.

In many cases, no viable list exists. In such situations, researchers often employ spatial sampling. This practice is common in developing countries. In spatial sampling, the sampling is based on geographic locations. Kumar (2007) describes the use of GPS in spatial sampling for demographic and health surveys, but the most prominent use of spatial sampling in conflict studies comes from the well-publicized excess mortality studies conducted by Les Roberts and his colleagues in the Democratic Republic of Congo (DRC) and Iraq. Even when opting for spatial sampling, researchers may run into the problem that good maps do not exist for the areas to be sampled. In these situations, researchers usually employ random walk sampling, in which they map the area of interest themselves and then choose random points at which to begin. Mapping, although time-consuming, is important because if random points are chosen without a map, it is likely that they will not be truly random: they will be points that are easier to access. After a point is chosen, enumerators are instructed to work in circles, for example by turning left after every third turn-off. The use of sampling frames versus spatial sampling can have important consequences and the optimal method has resulted in debate, for example, over excess mortality estimates in Iraq (see Box 10.1).

Conflict surveys are much like household surveys in developing countries, but there are two additional difficulties that arise in the former. The first is that the researcher should keep in mind the changing household composition over time because of migration; the researcher needs to know where household members live and what happened to them during the conflict, since many people migrate out of conflict-ridden

---

Box 10.1: The Iraqi Mortality Estimate Controversy

No conflict survey has generated as much controversy as the Burnham *et al* (2006) estimate of excess mortality in Iraq. Released just prior to the 2006 US midterm elections, Burnham *et al*'s study suggested that approximately 650,000 violent deaths occurred as a result of the war. By means of comparison, the WHO-led Iraq Family Health Survey (IFHS, 2008a, 2008b), which covered basically the same period, found only 151,000 violent deaths. The IFHS figure was based on a much larger sample (9,345 households compared to Burnham *et al*'s 1,849) in far more clusters (1,086 clusters compared to Burnham *et al*'s 47). The sampling strategies of the two surveys also differed in other ways. While the IFHS used a sampling frame based on census and other governmental data, the Burnham *et al* study used a spatial sampling approach in which the researchers selected 40 households on a cross-street to a main street. Critics have charged that this approach leads to a 'main street bias' (Johnson *et al,* 2008) because main streets are more likely to see patrols, convoys, police stations and other natural targets for violence; residents of households on cross-streets to main streets will thus be more exposed to violence than those living further away. Other methodologies for ascertaining fatality numbers, such as surveillance-based methods (Öberg and Sollenberg, Chapter 4, this volume), find approximately 51,600 violent fatalities in Iraq (Iraq Body Count, 2010), a number that is more in line with the IFHS estimate. The Burnham study was also heavily criticized for violating ethical prerogatives (Hicks, 2006; Spagat, 2010); for this, Burnham had his privileges to serve as a principal researcher suspended by his employer, the Johns Hopkins University (JHSPH, 2009). The literature on this case provides insightful reading into the issues of survey versus surveillance methods for generating conflict fatality estimates, spatial versus frame sampling, household selection, and ethical behavior.

---

areas. The second difficulty arises in accessing ex-combatants. If the research topic concerns only the civilian population (e.g. civilian attitudes towards peace-building, reconciliation, etc) then this is not problematic. But those interested in explaining participation in conflict or the behavior of (ex-) combatants in any way will need to access ex-combatants. Ex-combatants or other sub-groups of interest (ethnic minorities, etc.) represent a small portion of the population, and so researchers are unlikely to sample many of them if they sample purely randomly. The margin of error for this group will then be very large. To deal with this, researchers deliberately over-sample key groups of interest so that they can more precisely draw conclusions about this group.[8] This over-sampling is then corrected for in the analysis through the use of weighting, a process that is discussed in all survey textbooks.

In some places it is easy to find ex-combatants, for example through the official demobilization registers or in camps, but in other areas they will constitute a 'hidden population'. There are a number of techniques available for finding hidden populations, which are increasingly sophisticated (cf. Salganik and Heckathorn, 2004), although using these techniques is not always feasible and researchers may have to compromise on this point, for example by instead using a convenience sample. What is important is to be aware of the consequences of such decisions on the ability to draw inferences for the population (cf. Mvukiyehe and Samii, 2009).

Most conflict surveys go beyond simple random surveys to employ stratification and cluster sampling. Researchers often want to sort people into strata, or groups, of interest. If the variable they are interested in takes on different mean values in different sub-populations, they can obtain more precise estimates by using a stratified random sample. These strata do not overlap, and they constitute the whole population, so that each sampling unit (such as a household) belongs to exactly one stratum (cf. Lohr, 1999). This type of stratified random sampling allows the researcher to ensure that the sample he/she draws matches the population on this particular characteristic. The drawback is that stratification adds complexity to the study and requires additional information on how many and which units of the population belong to each stratum. The characteristic that is used to stratify the sample is specific to the research question and theoretical aims of the study; for example, the NPS sample was stratified on the basis of exposure to conflict (Samii *et al,* 2009). Researchers should think carefully about these issues and consult existing studies for guidance.

The most common method of selecting households from the frame uses a two-stage design. At the first stage, selection is from a list of 'clusters' of households, and then the households are selected at the second stage. Clusters are often administrative units like villages or districts. Once the clusters are chosen, households are selected directly from the survey frame. If the frame does not provide sufficiently detailed information, then all households in the selected clusters can be listed prior to the second stage (Deaton, 1997). Thus, like a stratum, a cluster is a grouping of the population. But unlike stratification, clustering can lead to decreased precision in the sample because individuals within a cluster are likely to be more similar to each other than randomly sampled individuals: 20 households on the same block are likely to be less diverse that 20 households selected at random. Because clustering increases internal homogeneity, it underestimates the true population variance. Researchers use clustering nonetheless out of practical necessity, especially when surveying in developing countries where travel can be difficult and time-consuming. Cluster sampling cuts costs and increases convenience considerably. Researchers use clustering despite its decreasing precision because it can be corrected for afterwards in the statistical model. As with stratification, this topic is well-covered in statistical textbooks.

The planning necessary to create a multistage sample using stratification and clustering techniques requires not only methodological knowledge but also a solid knowledge of the theoretical literature the research question is based upon as well as an in-depth knowledge of the country. The researcher should not treat these questions as technical fixes that can be handled by, for example, a survey agency but should instead be actively engaged in designing these facets of the study.

Bias

There are many types of bias that researchers must be aware of; most are discussed thoroughly in the survey methods literature. Some examples include *non-response bias* (when the characteristics of those who do not respond to the survey may be systematically correlated with a variable of interest; Lohr, 1999, devotes a chapter to methods for dealing with this); *acquiescence bias* (when certain people, such as those with little education, are more likely to acquiesce to an enumerator's suggestions rather than disagree); and *social desirability bias* (when individuals understate behaviors they may be ashamed of and overstate those they are proud of). These are just a few examples of biases with which researchers should familiarize themselves; they are well-covered in the survey methods literature.

Two other sources of bias deserve special attention because they are particularly problematic in conflict settings. The first is *survivorship bias*. This type of bias refers to the fact that many individuals are killed in armed conflicts.[9] For retrospective mortality surveys, the mortality rates are underestimated when whole families are killed and there are no survivors to report to the enumerators what happened. Moreover, the researcher is unable to know the characteristics of those who died, and whether a variable of interest is systematically correlated with mortality.[10] While there is no perfect fix for this problem, one survey project in Uganda provides an example of current best practice (Annan *et al*, 2006; Blattman, 2009). To obtain a random sample, researchers first created a retrospective household roster. They then sought to actively track down youths who had moved elsewhere in the country (the team was successful in tracking 84 per cent of these youths). For those unfound, as well as for those youths who died, surveys were completed with the families to gather demographic data and data on current activities and well-being. The research team then used these data to create weights in line with Fitzgerald *et al* (1998); they noted that even with this correction there was still a risk for bias due to any unobserved traits that influence migration or survival as well as potential outcomes (Blattman, 2009). This type of solution to survivorship bias is becoming increasingly common but is still only occasionally implemented for the simple reason that it greatly increases the time, cost and complexity of the survey.

The second type of bias of particular concern is *recall bias*. Recall bias refers to the fact that respondents make mistakes in recalling past events and that the probability of making mistakes systematically increases with time. Recall bias is a problem in all self-reporting surveys. Spagat *et al* (2009) note that in the case of wars, fatalities that occur during war are not necessarily the same thing as fatalities caused by war, but the two types of fatalities may be confused by respondents, especially if many years have passed. The Standardized Monitoring and Assessment of Relief and Transitions (SMART, 2006) guidelines on survey methodology state that recall periods longer than one year are inadvisable, and that the beginning of the recall period should always be a date that everyone in the population remembers (for example, a major holiday or festival, an episode of catastrophic weather, an election, etc).[11] Related to this point is the fact that the chaos of war can produce added strain on individuals to rationalize past behaviors, and may lead them to respond incorrectly to a question. This type of response bias can be affected by the security concerns prevalent in post-conflict environments as well as by subsequent political events. The post-conflict environment is arguably special and has not been subject to validation studies of recall, making it unclear whether and to what extent bias or error is present. Researchers are currently studying this issue using longitudinal designs to examine how answers differ between first and second waves. The results of this work may help to provide researchers with some idea of the extent and form of recall bias in conflict settings.

Ethical aspects

The fundamental ethical guideline is to do no harm. Conflict surveys often raise topics that are emotionally-charged for respondents, such as experience with victimization and the death of loved ones. Researchers must consider what questions are appropriate to ask and whether there is any risk of retraumatizing respondents by probing certain topics. In many cases, people express a feeling of relief at being able to share their experiences or have their stories heard by a wider audience. But this topic requires sensitivity and consideration on the part of the research team. In addition to emotional risks, the researcher also must consider whether participation in the survey can itself pose a risk to the physical security of respondents. Researchers should always keep respondents' answers confidential by storing identifying information separately from respondents' answers. Indeed, there is no need to gather identifying information at all if the researcher is not planning on a longitudinal study. But considering physical security goes beyond this, and the researcher must ask whether the very act of being selected by the enumerator can put the individual at risk. Will a respondent risk retribution simply for being interviewed? This is one critique that was leveled against a mortality survey of Iraq; by having children spread the news of the enumerators' presence to the entire neighborhood, the enumerators became exceedingly visible in the community. As a consequence, the security of the respondents may have been compromised since local militia members would know who had spoken to the researchers (Spagat, 2010).

Enumerators should always precede questioning by reading a protocol and obtaining informed consent from individuals. A protocol spells out the purpose of the survey and the risks involved in participation. It also makes clear what will be expected of the individual if he/she chooses to participate, as well as whether the respondent's replies are confidential. The protocol also emphasizes the voluntary nature of participation and that the individual can refuse to answer questions or cease participation at any time he/she wishes. Researchers can also take this opportunity to explain to potential respondents why he/she should give her/his time to the researchers. Answering survey questions can take a considerable amount of a respondent's time; household surveys often take one to two hours to administer. In many places people are quite pleased to share their stories, and most conflict surveys report low levels of refusal; in some areas that have received a lot of attention, however, people may suffer from research fatigue (see Chapter 7, this volume). Finally, the researchers should make their contact information and institutional affiliations available, indicate whether they will compensate respondents for their time,[12] and provide potential respondents an opportunity to ask questions. Informed consent can be either oral or written.

Most universities require that research projects are approved by an Institutional Review Board (IRB) or other type of ethical approval committee. While the exact process for obtaining IRB approval varies, they share a number of commonalities. As part of the application procedure, IRBs will want to see the research proposal, which should contain a discussion on the potential for harm during the study, and how the researchers will seek to prevent this. As much as possible, researchers should try to anticipate and address ethical challenges in advance in order to preempt concerns from the IRB. Part of the submission will include a draft of the instrument and the protocol. Most IRBs understand that the exact wording of questions can change somewhat after pre-studies have been undertaken in the field, and are ok with such changes as long as the general procedures and questions remain the same; researchers should of course learn their IRB's policies prior to departure. IRB approval can be a time-consuming process since review boards often send back the application for further clarification before granting approval. Researchers should familiarize themselves with the ethical guidelines of their respective university, country and professional associations. For instance, the Code of Professional Ethics and Practice of the American Association for Public Opinion Research (AAPOR) (www.aapor. org) provides a wealth of resources concerning ethical standards, IRB applications, informed consent forms and so on.[13]

Institutional Review Boards usually focus on the risk to respondents, but researchers must keep in mind that they also have an obligation to ensure the physical and mental security of themselves and their staff. In many areas where work is scarce, enumerators will be willing to take excessive risks to complete the survey; they also often become committed to the goals of the project. Researchers should not equate willingness on the part of the enumerators to enter dangerous areas with the idea that this is then acceptable ethical practice. Researchers have an obligation not to send enumerators into areas that would put them at risk, and to rein them in should they seek to enter such areas. There are some well-publicized examples of researchers bragging about smuggling themselves over borders, being shot at, and putting themselves and their teams in grave danger. Such behavior is not to be emulated. The risks to researchers in hot zones are very real; for example, one of the authors of the Iraqi Family Health Survey was shot and killed on his way to work. I will return to the topic of security shortly, but it is important to keep in mind that security for the team is not only a matter of practical concern but is also central to the ethical obligation for a researcher to do no harm.

Obtaining permission

In addition to getting permission from the IRB before proceeding to the field, researchers normally face additional hurdles with local authorities. Any of the following might need to sign off on the project: central government officials, local government officials, local militia leaders or warlords, former rebel leaders, and so on. If possible, researchers should get official, written copies of permission, as well as phone numbers to authorities that can be contacted in case problems arise in the field. In some areas, even if permission is granted by officials in the central government, the research team may also have to secure permission from local authorities, be they governmental or non-governmental. In many cases, the survey permission is granted easily. In other cases, researchers must work hard to convince local stakeholders that the survey will not cause disruption. How does one win the trust of these decision-makers? A lot depends on what they have at stake. When approaching authorities, researchers should envisage the project from their perspective and try to imagine whether the authority potentially has anything to lose from the survey work or its results. Researchers should also consider what the stakeholders may have to gain from the survey. Sometimes, for example, the survey can be presented as a way for the record to be set straight on a number of important issues. Researchers can give back to these stakeholders in other ways, as well, to gain trust. In Nepal, a researcher from the NPS held a session for former rebel leaders on how security sector reform worked in another setting the researcher had been involved in. This topic was high on the former rebels' agenda and the seminar helped engender goodwill towards the team.

Authorities will often want to see the instrument and find out about the sampling strategy (that is, who the team wants to talk to) in advance. As discussed previously, the wording of certain questions may cause problems with authorities if the questions tread on topics authorities find threatening. The best solution is usually creative re-phrasing, but at times this is not feasible. The problem of authorities censoring the survey is a difficult one. While there may be some leeway for negotiations, researchers are usually not inclined to compromise the integrity of the study completely. At the same time, it is essential to procure permission from authorities in advance. Researchers have an obligation to ensure that the study is not perceived as threatening by local security forces who could generate problems for enumerators and put the civilian population at risk of recrimination for participation. Some individual officials may attempt to extort bribes in exchange for permission, particularly at the local level. There is no single way to deal with this; familiarity with local practices and the help of local partners may help to determine how best to deal with such situations. It is best that researchers consider this eventuality in advance so as not to be taken off-guard should such a request come.

Implementation

There are two types of collaboration the research team will need to consider in conjunction with the implementation phase. The first is whether to collaborate with a local partner who can provide various forms of assistance and advice. The second is whether to collaborate or hire another organization to undertake the enumeration. Sometimes the same organization can fill both of these functions, but I will address them separately.

The first question the research team should consider is whether to seek out a local partner who can provide assistance and advice. These are often local organizations like NGOs, but international organizations like the United Nations (UN) or Médicins Sans Frontières (MSF) may also be appropriate. The advantage of having a local partner usually has to do with its networks and resources. Local partners can often provide information on the security situation in areas that are planned for surveying and can provide assistance with logistics. Many local partners have regional offices or contacts in the field, which provides an additional resource for the enumeration teams should problems arise. They can also advise the team on how best to obtain permission from various authorities, and sometimes partnership with a local organization is in fact necessary to obtain permission. If the team opts to recruit and train its own enumerators, a local partner can also be a source for finding qualified enumerators. Researchers need to consider the question of local partnership carefully. International organizations like the World Bank or the UN have enormous resources and can open many doors for the research team, but in areas where these organizations are controversial, the team can become unwittingly associated with unpopular policies. The same questions arise vis-à-vis locally-based organizations like NGOs. Some NGOs may be perceived as being associated with various political actors, and any affiliation the NGO has will be cast on the activities of the research team (cf. Paluck, 2009). In some situations this may be an advantage, but in many others it will not be. It is essential to know how individuals from various sectors of society react to the potential local partner in order to ensure that the research team will be perceived as independent, neutral and credible. These two factors – the resources that the organization can contribute that are needed by the team, and the public perception of the agency – should guide the research team in deciding whether to enter into a local partnership and if so, with whom. There is always the option of forgoing a formal partnership but still obtaining some assistance from an organization.

The second question is how to compose the enumeration teams, and there are essentially two options. The first is that the research team hire, train and supervise the enumeration themselves. The second is to delegate the enumeration process to another body, usually by hiring a survey agency, or using the local partner if it is proficient in survey methods (for example, the UN, Statistics Sweden, etc). This often comes down to a question of experience and time. Researchers who are unable to spend long periods in the field or who have little or no experience leading surveys will probably opt to employ an outside organization for the job. The disadvantage to delegating data collection is that organizations have often developed bad habits or become set in their ways. They may make decisions based on convenience or cost rather than on what is most methodologically sound; for example quota samples[14] are the dominant practice for many data collection agencies. If researchers choose this path, they will need to be very clear about the methodology and engage in a dialogue with the survey agency about the sampling strategy and their expectations for the enumeration process.

The research team can be very hands-on even if it has contracted the enumeration to a survey agency; the team can determine the areas to be sampled, train the enumerators (or participate in their training to ensure quality control), etc. It is also possible for the research team to follow the enumerators into the field. There are a number of advantages and disadvantages in doing so. Supervising the enumerators in the field allows the researcher to maintain a close eye on what is happening and ensure that corners are not being cut. It also allows the researcher to answer questions that arise. But having a researcher in the field, particularly if he/she is a foreigner to the country, can also lead to problems and confusion vis-à-vis the local population. The decision boils down to a trade-off between trusting the enumerators and risking the distortion of locals' perceptions. One option is for researchers to conduct random spot-checks during enumeration or to follow up by re-visiting a selection of the sampled households to ensure that the enumerators have been carrying out their job faithfully. The American Statistical Organization (ASA, 2003) provides an excellent set of guidelines for preventing and detecting interviewer falsification.

Box 10.2: Lost in Translation

During pre-testing of the Nepal Peacebuilding Survey, the research team visited areas that had been surveyed by enumerators the day before. At one village, the research team was surprised to learn that villagers had thought that the enumerators were connected to the US visa lottery. After piecing together the story, the researchers discovered that the confusion came about because the term 'random sampling' does not translate well into Nepali. That, plus the fact that the enumerators mentioned that there were Americans on the research team, led villagers to make a connection to the US visa lottery. By instructing the enumerators to use layman's terms and to take more time in explaining the purpose of the study, the team was able to avoid further confusion.

Pre-testing the questionnaire is one way to minimize the chance that enumerators will face difficulties once in the field. Pre-testing consists of administering the draft questionnaire to a small set of respondents drawn from the population in the same way as planned for the study. Pre-testing allows the research team to determine if the phrasing of questions is working and identify questions that may be causing confusion or problems for respondents. It also helps researchers get an idea of how long each interview will take; often this is longer than anticipated, forcing the researchers to edit the instrument. By pre-testing, the researchers will hopefully discover problems before sending the enumeration teams out into the field; these problems can have to do with the questionnaire itself, timing issues, methodological concerns, practical constraints and so on. Even researchers who have invested enormous amounts of time in preparation cannot anticipate everything, and pre-testing helps illuminate such problems (see Box 10.2).

Some other issues that arise when preparing for the implementation phase include when to conduct the survey. In some regions, this will be dictated by weather or other seasonal patterns (like seasonal labor migration, etc). In Nepal, for example, many areas are only passable in the spring and early summer before the monsoon rains arrive; after that, respondents are unavailable during the fall holiday season, and then the winter snow makes roads impassable. This narrow window had a number of important implications for the NPS. First, it narrowed the available range of implementing partners; since surveys can only be conducted in a narrow window, many agencies were already pre-booked to conduct other annual surveys. Second, it put pressure on the team to obtain permission, train enumerators, and conduct pre-tests by a set deadline; delays risked postponing the survey for a year. Researchers should consider what sort of timing constraints they will face and how delays, etc could impact implementation.

Translation of the instrument is another issue researchers must consider. As Box 10.2 highlights, not all terms are translated easily into foreign languages, and unless the research team has local language skills, this may be difficult to catch. It is advisable that the research team hires reputable and experienced translators and that the instrument is back-translated by a different translator to detect whether there are any problems. Researchers will also need to consider how many languages are spoken by the people who are to be sampled and whether the instrument needs to be translated into minority languages. Allowing the enumerators to translate on the spot is inadvisable since it means that exact wordings will vary from interview to interview and interviewer to interviewer.

Security issues

The research team will need to consider security prior to deployment. A familiarity with standard risk assessment procedures as practiced by the UN and International Committee of the Red Cross (ICRC) may help the team to organize this analysis (cf. Mertus, 2009). Researchers need to ensure that they have access to up-to-date information on the security status of areas into which enumerators will travel. Local NGOs often have access to information that the UN and news agencies do not; this varies, however, from country to country (and even within countries). Again, this becomes a question of knowing the country well enough to find an organization (whether the local partner or another body) that is willing to collaborate and share this information. All credible indications of security problems should be taken seriously. Sometimes events can transpire that could not have been predicted. In one post-conflict country, an enumeration team was caught in a mêlée when ex-combatants spontaneously protested about the non-payment of benefits; as a result, the town was under siege and the researchers lost contact with their team for a day. While the team returned unscathed, this incident highlights the fact that law and order cannot be taken for granted in most post-conflict countries. In addition to trying to obtain good information on the security situation, researchers can also try to protect their teams by providing them with contacts in all of the areas they enter so that they have a local connection who can help them should troubles arise; such connections can often be provided by a local partner.[15]

Surveys, particularly excess mortality surveys, have been conducted in conflict zones like Democratic Republic of Congo and Iraq. Most of these surveys are accompanied by stories of threats, emergency evacuations and even fatalities. Working in a hot zone raises enormous concerns about the researchers' ethical responsibility to not put respondents, their team or themselves in danger. Moreover, it is unlikely that researchers will be granted permission by the government to work in areas where security forces are actively engaged in military operations. There are exceptional circumstances that provide windows of opportunity for surveys in conflict areas, such as ceasefires or negotiation processes, but the usually short durations of these events are rarely sufficient for the long process of preparing and implementing a survey. Since ceasefires often break down without warning, there are no guarantees for safety; if anything, they may only instill a false sense of minimal risk.

Instead, most conflict surveys take place after the warring parties have ceased hostilities, usually due to a negotiated settlement. Researchers often want to conduct the survey as close in time as possible after an agreement has been reached since this ensures that respondents' memories will be fresh. But to do so is challenging because the more recently the country has experienced civil war, the greater the potential security risks. They also tend to impose more political and security complications since decision-makers are working in a new and insecure environment. Indeed, it is not necessarily the case that post-conflict countries are more secure than when the warring parties were fighting; the proliferation of ex-combatants and arms often results in rampant criminality and the rise of other forms of organized violence, such as militias. Such violence may be even more unpredictable than it was during the armed conflict. This is not the case in all areas, of course; many countries see peaceful transitions and a return to relative security. The point is that the researchers must assess the risk for security problems, and should not be lured into a false sense of security because a peace agreement has been signed.

The big picture

The aim of this chapter was to give prospective survey researchers an idea of some of the issues they will face when undertaking survey work in conflict and post-conflict regions. There are many aspects of the survey that must be planned well in advance. Indeed, many of the preparations described in this chapter take place concurrently: as researchers draft the questionnaire, they also prepare the sampling design and begin making contact with potential local partners. The American Statistical Organization's 'What is a Survey?' flowchart (ASA, 2010) provides an overview of the temporal dimensions of the process.

Surveys are enormously resource-intensive. Their planning and implementation require a considerable investment in time. They also require funding for their implementation and, depending on the region to be sampled, this can be considerable. Surveys are logistically complicated, and even without unforeseen delays it is not unusual for them to take years to get from the initial planning stage to the data analysis stage. The process is greatly facilitated by researchers planning well in advance and maintaining a flexible attitude towards the process. Moreover, many people are involved in making a survey come to fruition: the research team is usually composed of multiple people, and the team generally collaborates with local partners and hires a survey agency or else directly hires enumerators. The end result is that many people are involved in critical roles in the survey project, hence the importance of choosing these collaborators wisely. Researchers without the means or inclination to conduct an original survey can consider collaborating with an existing project, for example by having questions or a module inserted into an ongoing project. This approach is much more efficient for the individual researcher, but has the drawback of giving the researcher less control over how the survey is implemented. Still, it may be a viable solution to those lacking time or funding. This chapter provides such researchers with an idea of what questions they should pose to their collaborators, and what implications the existing design may have for their ability to draw inferences.

Surveys offer a wealth of opportunities to study peace and conflict issues from a new perspective and using a different type of data than has been common in the past. Researchers have been keen to leverage these opportunities and post-conflict surveys are a burgeoning field. Researchers contemplating undertaking survey work should be aware of some of the issues that will arise and take care to avoid methodological and practical pitfalls that can threaten the project; this chapter has mapped some of these topics.

Summary

*   Be familiar with and take advantage of existing resources, especially other data-collection efforts.
*   Work in a team, and compose it carefully.
*   Consult other experts before the implementation phase.
*   Do a pre-study.
*   Attend to potential biases.
*   Surveys take a long time and require a lot of resources: be prepared for the long haul.
*   Make a back-up plan for every possible eventuality, and be prepared to face unexpected obstacles.
*   Attention to detail is critical for the success of a survey.

Further reading

Blattman, C. (2009) 'From Violence to Voting: War and political participation in Uganda', *American Political Science Review*, 103: 231–47.
Deaton, A. (1997) *The Analysis of Household Surveys*, Baltimore: The Johns Hopkins University Press. Online at: <http://www.worldbank.icebox.ingenta.com/content/wb/937> (accessed 12 April 2010).
HiCN (Households in Conflict Network) (2010) Online at: <http://www.hicn.org/> (accessed 12 April 2010).
Humphreys, M. and Weinstein, J. (2006) 'Handling and Manhandling Civilians in Civil War', *American Political Science Review*, 100: 429-47.
IHSN (International Household Survey Network) (2010) Online at: <http://www.surveynetwork.org/home/> (accessed 21 April 2010).
Lohr, S. (1999) *Sampling: Design and Analysis*, Pacific Grove: Duxbury Press.
UN (United Nations) (2005) *Household Sample Surveys in Developing and Transition Countries*. Online at: <http://unstats.un.org/unsd/hhsurveys/> (accessed 21 April 2010).

Notes

1. While surveys are based on interviews, there are differences between surveys and in-depth interviews. First, survey data is analyzed using quantitative methods and is designed

specifically to be generalizable from the sample to the population; data from in-depth interviews in which the interviewees are not selected according to established sampling procedures cannot be demonstrated to be generalizable to the population in the same way. Second, surveys use primarily closed-ended questions; to the extent that open-ended questions are used, responses are usually recorded by the person administering the survey as belonging to a particular category. In-depth interviews, on the other hand, facilitate open-ended questions and extensive responses.

2. Readers new to survey methodology are recommended to read Lohr (1999) and Groves *et al* (2004) for a background on survey methodology, and Deaton (1997) and UN (2005) for household surveys (with an emphasis on developing countries). Korn and Graubard (1999) provide an overview of the analysis of survey data. ASA (2010) provides a good summary of practical matters and the IHSN (2010) provides an excellent collection of resources relating to all facets of survey work.

3. See for instance Afrobarometer (www.afrobarometer.org) and Post-Conflict and Ex-Combatant Surveys (http://www.columbia.edu/~mh2245/XCSURVEYS/).

4. See for example Demographic and Health Surveys (DHS) (www.measuredhs.com) and International Household Survey Network (IHSN) (www.surveynetwork.org).

5. Paluck (2009) describes being prohibited from using the term 'ethnicity' in Rwanda, with officials instead suggesting the word 'people'. Because Rwandans were used to speaking in code, her research assistant was confident that respondents would nonetheless understand the meaning.

6. This approach can of course also be used for studying sensitive attitudes (see Kuklinski *et al*, 1997, for an example).

7. Even when census data do exist, researchers should keep in mind possible problems with frame coverage (cf. Deaton, 1997).

8. A common question concerns how to determine the optimal size of the sample. This topic is discussed extensively in existing survey literature; interested readers should consult the literature on power analysis (Cohen, 1988).

9. This is best understood as a special type of *attrition bias*, which is a common problem in panel studies (cf. Fitzgerald *et al*, 1998).

10. For example, Blattman (2008) notes that the 'impact of abduction will be biased if personal qualities that determine survival also influence later social and political behavior. Plausible candidates include intelligence, self-confidence, or the tenacity to resist abduction'.

11. Research on recall bias in other settings suggests that it is a function of both time and saliency, cf. Auriat (1991), Pearson *et al* (1992), Smith (1984), Tourangeau (2000).

12. Research teams may wish to offer a small cash payment or gift to respondents to compensate them for their time. Such payments should be appropriate vis-à-vis local standards.

13. Many IRBs have as policy that researchers should also obtain permission from ethical boards in the country in which the research will be conducted. Often this is impossible, either because such entities do not exist or because in many areas ethical research boards only handle research within the natural sciences. In these cases, IRBs will usually either waive the requirement or stipulate that other arrangements be made.

14. In quota sampling, the population is first segmented into mutually exclusive sub-groups, just as in stratified sampling. But quota sampling usually allows the interviewer discretion in selecting the subjects from each segment based on a specified proportion. A quota sample is thus a convenience sample with an effort made to insure a certain distribution of demographic variables. Quota samples are problematic because they do not provide any basis for estimating sampling error and may be subject to selection bias. While they are often used in marketing, they are not considered appropriate for academic studies.

15. Les Roberts recounts a harrowing description of being caught in a tense Kisangani where violence was about to break out. His collaborating partner, MSF Holland, provided advice on the security situation and sheltered him in the MSF house (CNN, 2000).

Part IV

Conclusions

11 Improving Information Gathering and Evaluation

Kristine Höglund and Magnus Öberg

Introduction

Good information is the basis for relevant analysis and for making appropriate inferences. Yet a challenge in any social science is to obtain complete, accurate and unbiased information. In peace research, the difficult research context and the dynamics of violent conflict – which include propaganda, suppression of information, fear and insecurity, etc – may compound these problems. However, peace research can be significantly improved by increased awareness of the general challenges involved in gathering information in conflict-ridden societies and knowledge about how to evaluate sources. In addition, successful research requires a well-developed strategy for actually gathering the data.

In this chapter we highlight the common themes and guidelines for improving information gathering and evaluation that emerges from the previous chapters. First, we discuss some general principles for improving information quality. Second, issues related to the collection of information are outlined. Third, the ethical considerations are highlighted. Finally, we emphasize the importance of knowing the general dynamics of conflict and the specific context in which the research is conducted.

Improving the quality of information

Four issues are of special concern when seeking to improve the data quality: validity and reliability, documentation, source criticism, and triangulation. These issues are common to all methodologies and approaches discussed in this book.

Validity and reliability

The relationship between concepts and measurement is central to data collection. Information is collected about some aspect of conflict or conflict resolution that interests the researcher; it does not involve gathering information about anything and everything. Whatever the topic of interest may be, information about it should not be collected before the key terms involved have been conceptualized and operationalized. Thus, data collection efforts begin with theory and theoretical concepts.

Whether the research project sets out to map a phenomenon empirically, or to test or develop theory, the key concepts of the study should be defined. First, the meaning, or connotation, of the concept needs to be defined so that it is clear what it means on a theoretical level. Second, to make the concept measurable it needs to be operationalized.

To operationalize the concept is to define its empirical referent, specifying its concrete manifestations. Thereby it is made clear what the concept refers to in observational terms. The operational definition of the concept can be used to construct indicators that measure the concept.

The validity of a measure is the degree to which it captures the essence of the concept it purports to measure. Thus, validity will be affected in part by how well the operational definition matches the theoretical definition. The nature of the operational definition will also affect how consistently it can be applied to the source materials and thus the reliability of the measure. The reliability of a measure is the extent to which applying the same procedure in the same way will yield the same result.

Constructing valid indicators is sometimes challenging. Theoretical concepts often have aspects or components (like intentionality) that are either difficult or impossible to observe directly. Thus, a direct 1:1 correspondence between the theoretical definition and the indicators is sometimes hard to achieve. War, for example, is commonly defined theoretically as 'large-scale organized violence for political purposes'. 'Large-scale organized violence' is relatively straightforward to operationalize and measure, but constructing indicators of 'political purposes' involves trying to measure the intentions of the belligerents, and intentions cannot be directly observed. Thus, one has to find some proxy indicator, or indirect measure, for intentions, such as the stated goals of the belligerents. The validity of the measure then depends on how well this proxy actually discriminates between 'large-scale organized violence for political purposes' and 'large-scale organized violence for other purposes'.

The type of indicator that can be used also depends on the type of sources and data-collection method. The researcher usually has fewer options for getting at the hard-to-observe or unobservable – such as intentions, attitudes and motivations – when using news resources and other secondary material. Interviews and surveys usually provide opportunities to make more valid measures since it is often possible to ask about such matters. Note, however, that unobservables are still not directly observed, and that the people being asked may not reveal their true intentions or motivations.

There is also often a tension between validity and reliability in measurements (see Chapter 6). Reliability is maximized by having a simple, directly observable and unambiguous operationalization that can be applied without room for interpretation. It will yield the same results every time it is applied to the same source material. But such a measure typically runs into problems with validity. Concepts of interest for peace researchers, such as democracy and peace, are complex phenomena. Inevitably the concepts that interest peace researchers often contain nuances and unobservable dimensions that require some interpretation and judgment. Typically there are also variations in the concrete manifestations – for instance of violence – in different contexts. Thus, while high validity and high reliability should always be strived for it is not always possible to have both to an equal extent. In practice, the researcher need to strike a balance, in effect making trade-offs between validity and reliability. What that balance looks like depends on the nature of the research project, including the research question, the available source materials and the data-collection method.

In doing comparative or large-N research, it is also important to develop measures that travel well across cases that have different cultures, languages and histories. The same concept may have different meanings in different societies and it may also have different concrete manifestations (see Chapters 6, 7, 8 and 10). Similarly, the use of a concept can vary, both in terms of its meaning and empirical referent, across cases and over time (see Chapter 4). Thus, in constructing the instrument used to measure the concept, whether it is an interview question, a survey question, or a coding rule for a large-N data project, researchers need to take into account potential problems arising from how the concept is used and understood in the relevant research context and source materials.

Developing valid and reliable measurements that are useful in practice often requires plenty of thought and some experimentation. Doing a pilot study is helpful in developing good indicators because it is rarely possible to foresee and take into account all the complexities and variations in the real world (see Chapters 6, 7 and 10). It is only in the actual empirical application of a measure that all its strengths and weaknesses become clear, and revisions are often necessary. Even after serious consideration, experimentation, pilot studies and revisions, there will always be borderline cases that do not fit the operational definition but which intuition tells us should be included. This makes it tempting to stretch the operational definition, but that temptation is often best resisted. Stretching the definition is likely to invite as many problems as it solves and it undermines the reliability and integrity of the measure. It is better to go back to the drawing board and re-design the operational definition (see Chapter 6).

Documentation

The value of thoroughly documenting the data-collection procedures cannot be overstated (see Chapters 4 and 6). Documentation is important for several reasons. First, research should be publicly available and replicable. Without proper documentation it is neither. Second, to evaluate reliability and validity of the information gathered, the procedures and sources used to obtain the information must be known. This includes details such as exactly what search strings were used in electronic searches, which sources were used, how and why these sources rather than some other sources were selected, when and under what circumstances interviews were conducted, who is present during the interviews, exactly what questions were asked, and what coding rules were employed. Finally, without detailed documentation of the data-gathering process it is all too easy for the researcher to lose track or become confused about exactly what was done, how it was done, and why. Data collection usually involves a process of trial and error, often over fairly long periods of time. After a while recollections of different searches, interviews, trial rounds and versions are easily mixed up. It takes a very special kind of memory to keep track of all the details. A good practice therefore is to keep a continuous record – a research diary – which can be used as the basis for the final documentation. Having a record of the paths tried but rejected and the reasons for making particular choices or coding decisions is very helpful when someone asks about it months or years later.

Source criticism

The chapters in this book describe different methods for collecting information in peace research and the particular challenges confronting each of them. Regardless of which information-gathering method is used, a critical task facing the researcher is to evaluate the veracity of the information obtained. While it may never be possible to establish the facts with certainty, researchers can and should systematically attempt to identify and reduce uncertainty and bias in the information they gather. To this end, source criticism is an indispensible tool. Source criticism is a methodology originally developed by historians to identify and estimate error and bias in sources.

In applying source criticism researchers are asking questions about the source and about the relationship between the source and the genesis of the facts it relates. Source criticism consists of several steps, each designed to help the researcher assess the reliability and bias of the source. The importance of source criticism is discussed in detail in Chapter 3. It outlines the four criteria for source evaluation, which begins with identification of the source and then continues with three broad criteria for evaluating the source: proximity, dependence and bias. Box 11.1 outlines the criteria and key questions involved in source criticism.

Box 11.1: Checklist for Source Criticism

Identification	• Who is the source of information? • Is this person or agent authentic? • Linked to conflict parties?
Proximity	• How close in time and space is the source to the information related?
Dependence	• Is the source giving first-hand information or is it dependent on second-hand information?
Bias	• Does the source have incentives to misrepresent the information provided? • Is it likely that certain types of information are exaggerated or left out?

Identification

The first task is to identify the source and determine whether it is authentic or not. Who is providing the information? Is that person or agent who/what it claims to be; that is, is it authentic or not? How does the source relate to the conflict parties? The second task in identifying the source is to find out how the source obtained the information and as much as possible about the origin of the information provided by the source. Finally, it is important to know about the context in which the source provides the information. All of this matters for how the source and the information it provides will be assessed using the following criteria.

Proximity

A first question concerns the proximity of the source to the fact. In short, this affects how well the source can know the facts it is relating. In general, sources closer to the facts of interest – in time, space and agency – are more reliable than sources further away. For example, information about an event provided by a reporter who personally observed the event is likely to be more reliable than information provided by a reporter who did not observe the event first hand but has been told about it by informants. First-hand information is generally more reliable than second-hand information. Similarly, reports of an event that took place a long time ago are liable to be less reliable than reports that are contemporaneous. The centrality of the source to the facts of interest is also important. For example, the actual decision-maker usually has more reliable information about the decision than do outside observers.

Dependence

Is the source a primary source of the information or is it dependent on some other source, that is, is it simply relating information that comes from some other source? It is important to know if the source is the original source of the information. Primary sources are preferable to higher order sources because information is liable to be selected and corrupted as it travels from primary to secondary to tertiary and higher order sources. Thus, second- or third-hand information is prone to be incomplete and/or corrupted. To understand how information may have been selected and/or corrupted along the way, it is important to know who or what the original source was, and also how the information travelled from the primary source to the higher order source. It is, moreover, important to know whether different sources are interdependent, that is if they depend on each other and if they have a common original source. If they are interdependent, then the corroboration is of no added value. On the other hand, a piece of information corroborated by a second independent source greatly improves the credibility of that information. Hence, the classical rule in journalism is that information is only trustworthy if two independent sources corroborate the information.

Bias

How likely is it that the source gives us a biased picture of the facts? To assess bias, researchers must consider if the source has any incentive for misrepresenting the facts; does it have a tendency or bias? For example, decision makers, or the conflict parties, usually have strong incentives for misrepresenting the facts to put themselves in a more favorable position, or their actions in a favorable light. But the reasons for bias may be more subtle than simple self-interest. A source may misrepresent facts to protect or elevate someone else's standing, or it may be dependent on an audience for which it is providing the information. The audience may also have particular interests that affect the information provided. Roughly speaking there are two kinds of bias. The first, and obvious, is that the information provided is systematically distorted or false; the second and less obvious is that while the information provided is undistorted, particular types of information are systematically left out. It is therefore always a good idea to think about what information is related and what is or may have been left out, and why this may be so. The general world-view of the source may also be thought of as a subtle (or not so subtle) form of bias. This is sometimes evident in the choice of labels ('bandit', 'terrorist', 'freedom fighter' or 'insurgent'), framing, and language used by the source. But it may also be more subtle, influencing what is emphasized or downplayed, included or left out. Note that bias may affect not only facts but also explanations provided by a source.

Source criticism and different sources

Source criticism is important for all data gathering, but the specific problems vary across different types of sources and methods for gathering data. Identifying the source of the information and determining its authenticity and relation to the conflict parties is often not a major problem, but it can be difficult. As discussed in Chapter 4 on news reports, identifying and assessing the authenticity of websites is often difficult. News reports from news agencies usually state the original source of the information, making identification easier, but many other news reports fail to do so. In written narratives, like biographies and memoirs, the original source of most information is often known, thus facilitating identification (Chapter 5). Interview-based methods like those covered in Chapters 8 to 10 facilitate identification in principle, and some questions can be sorted out in the interview situation. However, in interview-based methods, participant selection also presupposes at least some degree of identification. For elite interviews this rarely poses a problem, but for interviews with less well-known individuals (such as former soldiers or victims of violence) identification can be demanding and require much more detailed knowledge of the local context. As discussed further in the section on research ethics, anonymity and confidentiality are often important to protect the participants in the study and may hamper identification of sources.

The proximity of the source depends on the research question. When gathering information through interviews, proximity criteria are important in selecting interviewees. The centrality of the source to the facts being investigated is important, so the interviewees should be knowledgeable about the questions being researched. Temporal proximity may be more difficult to achieve in interviews that often take place some time after the facts of interest. Long recall periods potentially undermine reliability because of how people's memories work; memories fade over time and details may be lost. Long recall periods may also introduce bias as memories are adjusted in view of new information. This problem is also a prominent problem in some written narratives such as memoirs. News reporting is mostly second-hand information, but the original source of the information in news reports often comes from the central actors scoring high on proximity criteria and the information is typically current (proximate in time).

Different methods for collecting conflict information are also associated with particular forms of selection bias that are rooted in the type of sources used or in the method itself. Non-response bias (a form of selection bias) is associated with survey methods, but it also should be considered in interview and focus-group studies. Acquiescence bias and social desirability bias are also associated with interview-based methods, including surveys and focus groups (see more in Chapters 9 and 10). In news reporting, selection bias induced by audience considerations works in a way similar to acquiescence bias and social desirability bias in interviews. In certain written narratives, selection bias is often compounded by the lack of temporal proximity. In memoirs and biographies, especially, facts tend to be selected for inclusion based on hindsight; matters that in retrospect seem important or successful are included, while facts that in retrospect appear less important or inconvenient are excluded.

While the possibility of getting the facts wrong can never be completely eliminated, source criticism suggests ways to reduce problems with reliability and bias, thereby improving the chances of getting it right. However valuable the guidelines offered by source criticism are as tools for assessing information, they cannot substitute for commonsense, experience and a substantive knowledge of the problem at hand.

Triangulation

Triangulation is another tool for assessing and improving information. Triangulation in terms of corroborating information with multiple independent sources is described above. However, it is also possible to triangulate different types of sources to improve construct validity and to detect bias (see Chapters 3, 4 and 8). Multiple types of sources, source materials and information-gathering methods may provide information on different aspects of the same phenomena. Combining sources and methods can therefore be one way to improve validity in the measurements. For example, news reports can be used to obtain information about what events took place and which actors were involved, while interviews may provide information on what motivated the actors, what their interests were, and how they reasoned. Even when using a single method of data collection, a richer and more nuanced picture can be obtained, for example by consulting sources with different partisan bias, news reports produced with different audiences in mind, selecting interviewees from different social strata or levels within an organization, or by comparing elite surveys with grass-roots surveys on the same issues. Thus, a multitude of aspects and perspectives on the same phenomena can be observed, providing a richer picture while simultaneously making it easier to detect bias in the source material.

Improving the practices of information gathering

Issues related to the practice of information gathering are important in all the different stages of a research project. Access is typically the main issue of concern. The amount of data available will influence the focus of a research project, how it will be planned and implemented, and the inferences that can be made. The challenges related to access will vary substantially depending on whether the research is primarily based on desk research or field research. For the desk researcher it is a matter of identifying relevant sources, determining which sources are most adequate for the study, and considering what might be the best strategy given the resources and budget available. As discussed in Chapter 1, there are a number of issues for which there is little available information and data-gathering on-site is required. For field research, there are not only practical aspects (time, budget, logistics, security, etc) related to access, but also considerations related to how participants are recruited for interviews, focus groups, or surveys. In addition, in the field, researchers should plan carefully to obtain the best possible information from the participants, as well as reflect on ethical issues.

Recent developments in technology have made many sources of relevance for peace research quite easily available. Archives, reports by international and local organizations, government documentation, and websites of conflict parties are available on-line. Skype, mobile phones and emails assist the planning of field work, as well as offer researchers an opportunity to follow up on missing information once they have returned to their home university after the field work. Yet, the long-term ramifications of these developments are difficult to assess. Citizen journalism – with the use of mobile phones, blogs and other types of local reporting – is becoming important for finding out what transpires on the ground during crises and conflict. But there are serious difficulties in evaluating the authenticity of sources on the internet (see Chapters 3 and 4).

Availability of information can vary quite substantially between countries (see more in Chapters 4, 6 and 7). Also within a country, some groups may be more accessible. It is not uncommon that weaker parties, such as minority groups, display a greater propensity to meet with researchers than government officials, since speaking with researchers gives them an opportunity to voice their demands.

Language as an impediment to access

Language barriers are obstacles to information in both desk and field research. Without appropriate language skills, there may be biases in the type of sources that are consulted. For large-scale data collections, skills in one of the world languages besides English (for example Arabic, Chinese, French or Spanish) will undoubtedly have the potential to generate more even and comparable material for the cases. Another problem is that if the sources cannot be accessed via the original language (written and oral alike), there will be an extra layer of interpretation that will make source criticism more difficult. In field research – where the interaction with human subjects is at the core of the data-gathering process – language barriers can place serious restrictions on the type of information accessible.

For field research, the challenges regarding language will vary depending on the type of information-gathering technique utilized. If the researcher is not fluent in the language in question, interview-based research will often require interpretation on-site. Working with an interpreter involves a number of issues that call for consideration and are described in more detail in Chapter 8. Since practically no one is considered 'neutral' in a conflict setting, the researcher should assess how the identity of the interpreter will influence the interview situation (gender, local affiliations, etc). Attention must also be given to ensuring that the interpreter uses the same words and phrasing as in the interview guide. Consulting with colleagues with local knowledge and to practice the interview situation with the interpreter will improve the quality of the interview. In focus group research (as discussed in Chapter 9), using a translator can be very difficult, because doing so will clearly disrupt the natural flow of a conversation, which is the aim of the focus groups. A moderator who knows the language can be used, but this will add another filter to the information, since the focus group discussion will not only need transcription but also translation. In survey research, the questions may need to be translated to local languages so as to be able to target the populations of interest for the study. Sometimes it may be difficult to translate specific terms into foreign languages, and care must be taken to ensure that the translation works as intended. Chapter 10 gives an example of how flaws in the translation in a pilot survey carried out in Nepal contributed to confusion about the purpose of the entire research project because 'random sample' became mistaken for 'lottery'. By conducting a pilot study the researchers were able to detect and correct this problem.

Field research and access

For the field researcher, there are a number of issues related to access – logistical and practical arrangements, security for researcher and informants, and choice of collaborating partners – which need careful consideration and planning before the data gathering is carried out. During field work, negotiating access can take substantial time and resources.

In a context of conflict, access is inextricably linked to issues of trust and relationships with key organizations, individuals and gatekeepers who can facilitate contact with a larger network of participants in a study. The first time a researcher visits a new country or region, or if research is initiated on a new topic, a substantial amount of time will inevitably be devoted to developing useful contacts and finding the right channel for gaining access to the groups of people targeted in the study. Academic colleagues can often provide a first contact with local academics or NGOs in the country. For outside researchers, embassies or development agencies can be another way forward. It is very difficult to assess which contacts will actually be most useful when in the field, so researchers should strive to develop a broad network of contacts. The need for local partners (usually a university, research institute, or NGO) will vary depending on the type of field work conducted, and the country or region in which the work is carried out. In some instances, local partners are critical in identifying participants and legitimizing the research; in other instances they can provide help with logistics or security. Even if no formal relationship is formed, an organization can still be of important assistance in providing contacts, local assistants, or merely serving as a discussion partner in terms of the direction of the research project. Finally, personal connections can be essential for gaining official permission for the research, especially for surveys where government permission is often required.

It is important to identify and build rapport with so-called *gatekeepers*, individuals with the power to determine who can or cannot have access to a specific community. The general advice regarding gatekeepers is to have multiple access points to ensure a sample that is not too biased due to reliance on only a few individuals. However, in extremely polarized situations and when research is conducted across the conflict divide, gaining the trust of a broad range of gatekeepers can be a difficult balancing act, since contact with one can exclude contact with another.

Gaining access to the information needed for a study is not only a matter of making contact with the relevant people, but also one of convincing them to talk about the topic of interest in the research. Since peace research almost exclusively deals with sensitive issues, this entails ethical questions, which are discussed in the next section. However, there are several ways in which a researcher can improve the data quality. For all types of research involving interviews, the order in which questions are asked, how the questions are formulated, and the setting of the research are important. For both in-depth interviews and focus group discussions, it is usually advisable to start with some warm-up questions before probing more sensitive issues. Chapter 10 provides suggestions on how to capture sensitive issues in survey research, by for instance approaching the topics in a more indirect way. In any type of research in conflict societies, the veracity of information is difficult to evaluate. Conflict actors may have incentives to intentionally mislead or portray themselves in a more favorable light. But there will also be several psychological processes at work during an interview situation. The participants may be influenced by experiences of fear and sometimes severe trauma. Interviewees may be silent on certain topics, avoid talking about others and invent narratives to make sense of what has happened to them. These evasions, lies or rationalizations may not be due to deliberate processes to mislead the researcher, but are coping strategies for dealing with difficult experiences. With the passing of time, the probability that participants will make mistakes in their recollections increases and the turmoil of conflict and crises is usually not helpful. As a way to bridge the memory to the experiences that the researcher is interested in – and as described in Chapter 9 – photographs or the like can be important to help the participants recall past events. In survey research, the advice is to never extend the recall period beyond a date that everyone participating in the study can remember (an election, a major holiday or celebration, etc) and to use this event as a way to bridge the memory (see more in Chapter 10).

A related issue is how the person conducting the interview is perceived by potential participants. Interviews are usually conducted by the researcher her/himself, but enumerators often assist in collecting data in surveys, and local moderators may be used in focus groups. Adequate training is essential, but the situation can also be influenced by the attributes of the researcher or local research assistant/s. How does gender, age, or the ethnic, racial and religious identity influence who will be willing to participate in the study and the type of information related? In many instances it might be exciting to talk to an outsider, but the participant may be careful in what type of information he/she actually shares. The researcher should also consider how the identity and characteristics of the respondents influence the sample. There may be a propensity to spend more time with people with whom the researcher feels comfortable or to award more importance to those interviews where the researcher felt rapport or sympathy with the interviewee.

Another important aspect related to access is how much attention the conflict has received. Access is one of the reasons why some topics and cases receive disproportionate attention, which in itself can result in a bias in the types of cases studied (see Chapter 7). Such attention has different ramifications for data gathering and will also vary across cases. On the one hand, international attention – with substantial involvement in terms of donor aid, mediation, or international peacekeeping – usually ensures that there is a great deal of documentation about the case. Yet it must be kept in mind that reports issued by international organizations like the United Nations or the World Bank have an intended audience as their target. A substantial international presence often allows for better access for researchers, and international organizations may be willing to assist both with contacts and logistics. On the other hand, there is a risk of 'research fatigue' (see Chapters 7 and 8). Communities that have received too much scholarly attention may find themselves over-researched. The risk is that people will not be very interested in meeting researchers, and if they do agree to meet, that they will respond to the questions either without much reflection or respond in accordance with what they think the researcher wants to hear.

Several chapters emphasize the importance of how the timing of the research can affect access (see especially Chapters 7 and 10). Issues related to security and how accessible people are to participate in a study will be influenced by the dynamics of the conflict. Risk assessments should be done on a continuous basis and the type of security threat may vary substantially between countries and across locations within a country (see more in Chapters 7 and 10). Even if a research project will include several rounds of information gathering, ideally each trip should be planned to generate useful data in case it will be difficult to return. The timing of the research can also have implications for the more practical aspects of access. In some countries or regions the seasons dictate, for instance, when roads are passable and thus when it is possible to travel.

In sum, the researcher should reflect upon how different biases in the material arising from access will influence the study. These are issues related to language, who the researcher prefers to talk to, who the participants prefer to talk to, and who prefers to talk about which subjects. The international and local affiliations a researcher has should also be considered: given the polarization and politicization of conflict societies, how are the contacts of the researcher perceived in society and how may this have influenced the information?

Peace research and research ethics

The importance of pursuing ethically sound research has been emphasized throughout the book. The idea of 'doing no harm' is the main guiding principle, but what this means in practice for an individual research project may not always be so clear-cut. There are real ethical dilemmas confronting peace researchers. Research ethics become especially acute for field research that involves direct interaction with the research subjects (as respondents in individual, group or survey interviews), but they require reflection in any type of research.

Ethical frameworks and guidelines

Peace researchers are guided by several more or less detailed ethical frameworks and guidelines issued by professional bodies or universities. In many countries research projects need approval by an ethics committee or equivalent before commencing the research. These guidelines are useful starting points for ethical reflection and in cases where research proposals need to be submitted for approval, the proposal itself is often a useful instrument for preparing the field work in terms of formulating interview questions, consent protocols, etc. However, these guidelines are never comprehensive or likely to list all the different ethical issues that should be considered. In particular, these guidelines are usually focused on the integrity, safety and wellbeing of the participants of the research project and less on the safety and wellbeing of the researcher actually conducting the research and the local research assistants, interpreters, transcribers, enumerators and other people involved in making the research possible.

Protecting participants

In the planning of a research project, the researcher has to consider if the questions and topics posed in the project and to the participants – regardless of data-gathering technique (survey, focus groups, in-depth interviews, etc) – may have an adverse impact on the respondents. The topics and questions raised in peace research may be sensitive in two different regards: first, they may be emotionally charged, and second, they may be sensitive because of security concerns. To assess the risks of retraumatization and insecurity for the research subjects, it is usually a good idea to consult experienced researchers, or people working in the field, who have local knowledge. How may the research participants and society at large react to the questions? As suggested in Chapter 9, what constitutes a sensitive topic is not always clear-cut, and issues that may seem sensitive from an outsider's point of view may already be part of the public collective experience. In addition, what is sensitized may vary from community to community, over time, and between individuals, so the researcher should make these assessments for each case studied and for each interview conducted. Often the respondents express gratitude for the interest shown by the researcher, that their story is being listened to, and the discussion can be a 'liberating experience'. Yet, it is the responsibility of the researcher to make sure that the respondents do not reveal sensitive information that is not required for the research (see more in Chapters 8 and 9). As described in Chapter 8, '[d]etermining when the conversation is beginning to probe into too sensitive issues is often not as difficult as it may sound; the signs are quite observable' and may include too much detail off the topic, or unexpected emotion on the part of the interviewee. It is important to keep in mind that the ethical obligations relating to emotional and physical wellbeing go beyond the respondent and include other people participating in the conduct of the research, such as research assistants, enumerators, translators and transcribers.

There are several measures that a researcher can take to minimize risks and prevent the research from having adverse effects on the participants' emotional and physical wellbeing. A first matter is informed consent (see more below), which has been suggested as a strategy to ensure that the research will do less harm, by giving the participants a sense of control and empowerment. As discussed in Chapter 8, a sense of control is an important way of preventing post-traumatic disorder.

A second matter relates to anonymity and confidentiality. To ensure confidentiality, it is advisable to store respondents' answers separate from identifying information. It is important that research assistants, interpreters, enumerators and other people involved in the research process are equally informed about the importance of confidentiality and their responsibility in ensuring it. In focus groups, it becomes the responsibility of the group to ensure confidentiality, although the researcher has the responsibility of raising the question for discussion and emphasizing its importance. In some cases, identifying information is not important for the research purpose and it may not be necessary to collect it at all. Anonymity and confidentiality of sources is a principle that seemingly runs counter to the academic principle of transparency and documentation of sources. But the protection of respondents is always the overriding priority and it cannot be compromised.

A third matter is to find a situation were the respondents feel safe and comfortable. While individual interviews are usually the preferred data-gathering method the more private and sensitive a research topic is, Chapter 9 argues in favor of focus groups as an underused method in peace research. For many questions, the group context makes people feel more comfortable with the researcher, since the participants outnumber the researcher and since focus group research also makes it easier for participants to opt out from responding to specific questions ('safety in numbers'). The researcher should keep in mind that participation and responding to questions are always voluntary. Finding a place where the participant/s feel safe and comfortable is also important. In individual interviews this can be in someone's house or a place of their choice. For focus groups, which involve multiple participants, it might be more difficult to find a good place that is spacious, private and easily accessible for the participants (see more in Chapter 9).

Informed consent

As part of conducting ethical research, informed consent is required from the research participants (see Chapters 8, 9 and 10). Informed consent includes fully informing the respondents about the research and its purpose, how the information will be used, and how the data will be stored. This information serves as a basis upon which potential participants can assess the risks involved and make an informed decision about participating in the study. Consent can be given orally or through a written consent form, and ethical committees (or equivalent bodies) can have specific guidelines on how such consent is best obtained. The critical aspect of informed consent is that the participants themselves are empowered. It also needs to be fully clear that participation is voluntary and can be discontinued at any time. It is thus important as part of the protocol to leave contact details so the participants can contact the researcher should they change their mind about the project.

Compensation and giving back

An issue of some controversy in the social sciences – also discussed in Chapters 8 to 10 – is whether or not participants in a research project should be compensated. In many cases it might seem appropriate for interviewees or respondents to be compensated for the time and effort they use to participate in the study. Yet, there are concerns that compensation might bias the answers and that a select type of people will seek to participate in the study. While in many instances compensation is a method for enticing participation, there are also ethical aspects related to compensation. Usually compensation is offered for travel costs, not least because one of the ethical principles is to conduct the interview in a place where the participant is comfortable in discussing the topic at hand, which may be away from the home village or workplace. Researchers using focus groups are also more likely to offer compensation to participants because in focus groups there is a need to gather a group of people together and the entire interview falls apart if people do not show up as scheduled. What might be appropriate as compensation varies between different research contexts and has to be adapted to what is reasonable in that particular community (see Chapters 7 to 10). It must also be kept in mind that even without direct financial compensation, the presence of a researcher can change power relations in local communities, since being associated with a research project may imply status and privilege, which has the potential to generate conflict and tensions. The field researcher must also be prepared to deal with expectations that a research project will bring aid or other benefits to society, and of being mistaken for a humanitarian or development worker.

Another discussion relating to compensation is that the ethical obligation of peace research should move beyond the principle of 'doing no harm' to 'doing good' – the research should not only benefit the academic community or further knowledge in general, it should also benefit those who are participating in the study (individuals and communities). Especially during field work, researchers may develop strong emotional bonds to one side in the conflict, blurring the objectivity of the data-collection effort and analysis. Yet, as pointed out in Chapter 8, the researcher role is different from that of a therapist or a humanitarian worker. At a general level, peace research has a normative drive to understand how violence can be reduced and peace achieved. For this reason, peace researchers usually seek to build a policy-relevant perspective into the research that indirectly seeks to benefit the communities under study. Researchers also often feel a great deal of gratitude toward the communities in which the research has been carried out and may want to thank those who have participated in the study. One way of doing so is to make sure that the findings of the research are disseminated to a wide audience (including the participating individuals or organizations). Publishing policy briefs, as well as engaging in discussions with policymakers and practitioners, is important for ensuring that the research at least has the potential to benefit a broader audience.

Protecting the researcher and co-workers

Security and wellbeing for oneself are also an ethical responsibility of researchers. Field work can be a physically and mentally draining experience, with long working hours, new impressions, and an unfamiliar social and cultural context. In addition, learning of traumatic events through the research can lead to so-called *secondary trauma,* 'a term used to describe when a listener is traumatized by being told about the experiences of someone who himself was traumatized by the events' (Chapter 8). If researchers do not take care of themselves there is a risk that judgments will be blurred or that the project cannot be followed through, neither of which is useful from an ethical point of view. Taking time to relax; remaining in contact with friends, family and colleagues at home; keeping field notes or a diary to process experiences; and discussing and reflecting on the field experience in a comfortable and safe environment (usually among peers), are some suggestions on how to safeguard the wellbeing of the researcher.

Ethically sound research often produces better quality research. An example highlighted in Chapter 8 is that improving listening skills makes it easier to make judgments about when to stop an interview to prevent the research from being harmful to the respondent. Improving interview techniques will also give the researcher better quality information. The aspiration to acquire information always needs to be weighed against the ethical obligation researchers have of doing no harm.

Concluding remarks – know the context

In improving the practice of information gathering, there is no better investment for a researcher than to become familiar with the broader dynamics of the society and conflicts under study. Frames of reference – in terms of knowing the historical background of conflicts, current tensions and the actors and grievances – are essential for source criticism. Without at least a basic understanding of the context and dynamics of the conflict, biases and other issues related to source criticism are difficult to evaluate.

For desk research, especially large-scale data collections, knowledge about the cases, topic at hand and the context will increase the effectiveness of the data collection. It will help the researcher to design effective search strings and to pinpoint what is important amongst vast amounts of information.

For those collecting primary material through in-depth interviews, surveys, or focus groups, secondary sources are indispensible for understanding the context in which the data collection takes place. Reading up on a variety of sources (ranging from the most recent news reports to classical works about the history of the country or conflict), as well as talking to area experts and practitioners with different types of experience will facilitate the planning of the research in more than one way, maximizing returns from the field visits. It will help the researcher in formulating adequate questions and the most appropriate design of the study, in preparing the practical aspects of field work (logistics, permissions, budget, security), as well as understanding the boundaries for ethical research in the country in question (what is culturally acceptable, whether compensation is appropriate, what the sensitive issues are, etc).

The growing interest in peace research has been accompanied by an expansion in the types and numbers of sources of information available on issues of concern for peace research. This wealth of information helps researchers gain an improved understanding of the context to which their specific research question relates. To improve the quality of the data and the practices for obtaining it, conducting a pilot study is advisable in both desk and field research. Only when the theoretical concepts are applied and tested against the empirical material can what is realistic in terms of the planned project be assessed. Finding an appropriate research design always entails a process of trial and error, of testing, redesigning and adjusting. But the errors and mistakes can be minimized with improved knowledge, practice and experience.

Bibliography

AFP (2003) 'Powell UN Briefing Fails to Budge World Opinion on Iraq', *Agence France-Presse*, February 6.

Agar, M. and Macdonald, J. (1995) 'Focus Groups and Ethnography', *Human Organization*, 54 (1): 78–86.

Annan, J., Blattman, C. and Horton, R. (2006) *The State of Youth and Youth Protection in Northern Uganda: Findings from the Survey for War Affected Youth*, UNICEF Uganda. Online at: <http://chrisblattman.com/documents/policy/sway/SWAY.Phase1.FinalReport.pdf> (accessed 10 April 2010).

Armakolas, I. (2001) 'A Field Trip to Bosnia: The dilemmas of the first-time researcher', in M. Smyth and G. Robinson (eds) *Researching Violently Divided Societies: Ethical and methodological issues*, London: Pluto Press: 165–83.

ASA (American Statistical Organization – Survey Research Method Section) (2003) *Interviewer Falsification in Survey Research: Current best methods for prevention, detection and repair of its effects*. Online at: <http://www.amstat.org/sections/SRMS/falsification.pdf> (accessed 12 April 2010).

ASA (American Statistical Organization – Survey Research Method Section) (2010) 'What is a Survey?'. Online at: <http://www.whatisasurvey.info/> (accessed 12 April 2010).

Auriat, N. (1991) 'Who Forgets? An analysis of memory effects in a retrospective survey on migration history', *European Journal of Population*, 7 (4): 311–42.

Azar, E.E. (1990) *The Management of Protracted Social Conflict: Theory and cases*, Hampshire: Dartmouth Publishing Company.

BBC (1999) 'Transcript from TV show Panorama', 19 April. Online at: <http://news.bbc.co.uk/hi/english/static/audio_video/programmes/panorama/transcripts/transcript_19_04_99.txt> (Retrieved 11 August 2010).

Belousov, K. *et al* (2007) 'Any Port in the Storm: Fieldwork difficulties in dangerous and crisis-ridden settings', *Qualitative Research*, 7 (2): 155–75

Berry, J.M. (2002) 'Validity and Reliability Issues in Elite Interviewing', *Political Science & Politics*, 35 (4): 679–82.

Blattman, C. (2008) 'From Violence to Voting: War and political participation in Uganda', Households in Conflict Network, Working Paper 42. Online at: <http://www.hicn.org/papers/wp42.pdf> (accessed 20 April 2010).

Blattman, C. (2009) 'From Violence to Voting: War and political participation in Uganda', *American Political Science Review*, 103 (2): 231–47.

Bloch, I. de (1899) *The Future of War*, New York: Doubleday and McClure.

Bloor, M. (2001) *Focus Groups in Social Research*, Thousand Oaks, CA: Sage.

Bozzoli, C. and Brück, T. (2009) 'Identifying Conflict and Its Effects Using Micro-Level Surveys', Households in Conflict Network Research Design, Note 13. Online at: <http://www.hicn.org/research_design/rdn13.pdf> (accessed 14 April 2010).

Bratton, M. and Liatto-Katundu, B. (1994) 'A Focus Group Assessment of Political Attitudes in Zambia', *African Affairs*, 93 (373): 535–63.

Brounéus, K. (2008) *Rethinking Reconciliation: Concepts, methods and an empirical study of truth telling and psychological healing in Rwanda*, Uppsala University: Department of Peace and Conflict Research.

Brown, S. (2009) 'Dilemmas of self-representation and conduct in the field', in C.L. Sriram, J.C. King, J.A. Mertus, O. Martin-Ortega and J. Herman (eds) *Surviving Field Research: Working in violent and difficult situations*, London: Routledge.

Brun, C. (forthcoming) '"I Live My Soldier": Developing responsible and ethically sound research strategies in a militarised society', in D. Mazurana, K. Jacobsen and L.A. Gale (eds) *A View from Below: Conducting research in conflict zones*.

Brzoska, M. (2008) 'Measuring the Effectiveness of Arms Embargoes,' *Peace Economics, Peace Science and Public Policy*, 14 (2), Article 2: 1–32.

Bundervoet, T., Nillesen, E., Verwimp, P. and Voors, M. (2009) 'Integrating Conflict Questions in a Household Survey: An example from Burundi', Households in Conflict Network Research Design, Note 12. Online at: <http://www.hicn.org/research_design/rdn12.pdf> (accessed 14 April 2010).

Bundeswehr (1999) 'Operation "Hufeisen" (Potkova)', Retrieved 27 April 1999 from http://www.bundeswehr.de/kosovo/hufeisen.html.

Burnham, G., Lafta, R., Doocy, S. and Roberts, L. (2006) 'Mortality After the 2003 Invasion of Iraq: A cross-sectional cluster sample survey', *The Lancet*, 368: 1421–8.

Buzan, B and Waever, O. (2003) *Regions and Powers*, Cambridge: Cambridge University Press.

Cammett, M. (2006) 'Political Ethnography in Deeply Divided Societies', *Qualitative Methods: Newsletter of the American Political Science Association Organized Section on Qualitative Methods*, 4 (2): 15–18.

Clark, T. (2008) '"We're Over-researched Here!": Exploring accounts of research fatigue within qualitative research engagements', *Sociology*, 42 (5): 953–70.

CNN (2000) 'The Man Who Did the Counting. Les Roberts' Personal account of his mission in the Congo', June 21.

Cohen, J. (1988) *Statistical Power Analysis for the Behavioral Sciences*. 2nd edn, Hillsdale, NJ: Lawrence Erlbaum Associates.

Collier, D. and Mahon, J.E. Jr (1993) 'Conceptual "Stretching" Revisited: Adapting categories in comparative analysis', *The American Political Science Review*, 87 (4): 845–55.

Collier, D. and Mahoney J. (1996) 'Insights and Pitfalls: Selection bias in qualitative research', *World Politics*, 49 (1): 56–91.

Collier, P. (2009) *Wars, Guns and Votes: Democracy in dangerous places*, London: Bodley Head.

Conca, K. (1997) *Manufacturing Insecurity: The rise and fall of Brazil's military-industrial complex*, Boulder, CO: Lynne Rienneter.

Correlates of War Project (2008) 'State System Membership List, v2008.1', Online at: <correlatesofwar.org> (accessed 31 August 2010).

Cortright, D. (2008) *Peace: A history of movements and ideas*, Cambridge: Cambridge University Press.

Cortright, D. (2009) *Gandhi and Beyond: Nonviolence for a new political age*, 2nd edn, Boulder, CO: Paradigm Publishers.

Coser, L. (1956) *The Functions of Social Conflict,* New York: Free Press.

Das Parlament (2000) 'Das Hufeisenplan existiert', Das Parlament 16. Online at: <web.archive.org/web/20041119005944/http://www.das-parlament.de/2000/16/Kulissen/2000_16_010_836.html>, April 13 (retrieved 7 May, 2000).

Deaton, A. (1997) *The Analysis of Household Surveys*, Baltimore, MD: The Johns Hopkins University Press. Online at: <http://www.worldbank.icebox.ingenta.com/content/wb/937> (accessed 12 April 2010).

della Porta, D. (2005) 'Making The Polis: Social forums and democracy in the global justice movement', *Mobilization: An International Quarterly*, 10 (1): 73–94.

Derriennic, J.-P. (1972) 'Theory and Ideologies of Violence', *Journal of Peace Research* 9 (4): 361–74.

Deutsch, K.W. *et al* (1957) *Political Community and the North Atlantic Area: International organization in the light of historical experience*, Princeton, NJ: Princeton University Press.

Dickson-Swift, V., James, E. and Liamputtong, P. (2008) *Undertaking Sensitive Research in the Health and Social Sciences: Managing boundaries, emotions and risks*, Cambridge: Cambridge University Press.

Diehl, P.F. (1983) 'Arms Races and Escalation: A closer look', *Journal of Peace Research*, 20 (3): 205–12.

Dixon, J. (2009) 'What Causes Civil Wars? Integrating quantitative research findings', *International Studies Review*, 11 (4): 707–35.

Druckman, D. (2005) *Doing Research: Methods of inquiry for conflict analysis*, Thousand Oaks, CA: Sage.

Dulić, T. (2004a) 'A Reply to Rummel', *Journal of Peace Research*, 41 (1): 105–6.

Dulić, T. (2004b) 'Tito's Slaughterhouse: A critical analysis of Rummel's work on democide', *Journal of Peace Research*, 41 (1): 85–102.

Dunn, L. and Gordon, N. (2005) 'Improving Informed Consent and Enhancing Recruitment for Research by Understanding Economic Behavior', *JAMA*, 293 (5): 609.

Eck, K., Sollenberg, M. and Wallensteen, P. (2004) 'One-Sided Violence and Non-State Conflict', in L Harbom (ed.) *States in Armed Conflict 2003*, Uppsala: Universitetstryckeriet.

Eckl, J. (2008) 'Responsible Scholarship After Leaving the Veranda: Normative Issues faced by field researchers – and armchair scientists', *International Political Sociology*, 2: 185–203.

Etzioni, A. (1967) 'The Kennedy Experiment', *The Western Political Quarterly*, 20 (2): 361–80.

Farmer, P. (2004) 'An Anthropology of Structural Violence', *Current Anthropology*, 45 (3): 305–25.

Fearon, J.D. (1995) 'Rationalist Explanations for War', *International Organization*, 49 (3): 379–414.

Feenan, D. (2002) 'Researching Paramilitary Violence in Northern Ireland', *International Journal of Social Research Methods*, 5 (2): 147–63.

Fitzgerald, J., Gottschalk, P. and Moffitt, R. (1998) 'An Analysis of Sample Attrition in Panel Data: The Michigan Panel Study of income dynamics', *The Journal of Human Resources*, 33 (2): 251–99.

Fjelde, H. (2009) *Sins of Omission and Commission: The quality of government and civil conflict*, Uppsala University: Department of Peace and Conflict Research.

Fluehr-Lobban, C. (1994) 'Informed Consent in Anthropological Research – We are not exempt', *Human Organization*, 53 (1): 1–10.

Frankland, J. and Bloor, M. (1999) 'Some Issues Arising in the Systematic Analysis of Focus Group Materials', in J. Kitzinger and R.S. Barbour (eds), *Developing Focus Group Research: Politics, theory and practice*, London: Sage.

Fruchart, D., Holtom, P., Wezeman, S.T., Strandow, D. and Wallensteen, P. (2007) *United Nations Arms Embargoes: Their impact on arms flows and target behaviour*, Solna: Stockholm International Peace Research Institute. Online at: <http://books.sipri.org/files/misc/UNAE/SIPRI07UNAE.pdf> (accessed 29 June 2010).

Fujii, L.A. (2009) 'Interpreting Truth and Lies in Stories of Conflict and Violence', in C.L. Sriram, J.C. King, J.A. Mertus, O. Martin-Ortega and J. Herman (eds) *Surviving Field Research: Working in violent and difficult situations*, London: Routledge.

Fujii, L.A. (2010) 'Shades of Truth and Lies: Interpreting testimonies of war and violence', *Journal of Peace Research*, 47 (2): 231–41.

Gallaher, C. (2009) 'Researching Repellent Groups: Some methodological considerations on how to represent militants, radicals, and other belligerents', in C.L. Sriram, J.C. King, J.A. Mertus, O. Martin-Ortega and J. Herman (eds) *Surviving Field Research: Working in violent and difficult situations*, London: Routledge.

Galtung, J. (1959) 'Pacifism from a Sociological Point of View' *Journal of Conflict Resolution*, 3 (1): 67–84.

Galtung, J. (1964) 'A Structural Theory of Aggression', *Journal of Peace Research*, 1 (2): 95–119.

Galtung, J. (1965) 'International Programs of Behavioral Science: Research in Human Survival', in M. Schwebel (ed.) *Behavioral Science and Human Survival*, Palo Alto, CA: Science and Behavior Books.

Galtung, J. (1967a) *Theory and Methods of Social Research*, Oslo: Universitetsforlaget.

Galtung, J. (1967b) 'Peace Research: Science or politics in disguise?', *International Spectator*, 21; reprinted in J. Galtung (1975) *Essays in Peace Research*, vol. 1, Peace: Research, Education, Action, Copenhagen: Ejlers.

Galtung, J. (1969) 'Violence, Peace, and Peace Research', Journal of Peace Research 6 (3): 167–91.

Galtung, J. (1971) 'A Structural Theory of Imperialism', *Journal of Peace Research*, 8 (2): 81–117.

Galtung, J. (1996) *Peace by Peaceful Means*, London: Sage.

Galtung, J. and Naess, A. (1955) *Gandhis Politiske Etikk*, Oslo: Tanum.

Galtung, J. and Ruge, M. (1965) 'The Structure of Foreign News: The presentation of the Congo, Cuba and Cyprus crises in four Norwegian newspapers', *Journal of Peace Research*, 2 (1): 64–91.

Gantzel, K.J. *et al* (1986) *Die Kriege nach dem Zweiten Weltkrieg bis 1984*, Munich: Weltforum.

Geddes, B. (1990) 'How the Cases You Choose Affects the Answers You Get: Selection bias in comparative politics', *Political Analysis,* 2 (1): 131–50.

George, A.L. and Bennet, A. (2005) *Case Studies and Theory Development in the Social Sciences*, Cambridge, MA: MIT Press.

Gerring, J. (2007) *Case Study Research: Principles and practices*, Cambridge: Cambridge University Press.

Gleditsch, K.S. and Ward, M.D. (1999) 'Interstate System Membership: A revised list of the independent states since 1816', *International Interactions*, 25 (4): 393–413.

Gleditsch, N.P., Wallensteen, P., Eriksson, M., Sollenberg, M. and Strand, H. (2001) 'Armed Conflict 1946–2000: A new dataset', paper presented at the conference on 'Identifying Wars: Systematic Conflict Research and Its Utility in Conflict Resolution and Prevention', Uppsala University, 8–9 June.

Gleditsch, N.P., Wallensteen, P., Eriksson, M., Sollenberg, M. and Strand, H. (2002) 'Armed Conflict 1946–2001: A new dataset', *Journal of Peace Research*, 39 (5): 615–37.

Goertz, G. (2006) *Social Science Concepts: A user's guide*, Princeton, NJ: Princeton University Press.

Gokah, T. (2006) 'The Naïve Researcher: Doing social research in Africa', *International Journal of Social Research Methods*, 9 (1): 61–73.

Goodrum, S. and Keys, J.L. (2007) 'Reflections on Two Studies of Emotionally Sensitive Topics: Bereavement from murder and abortion', *International Journal of Social Research Methodology*, 10 (4): 249–58.

Gordon, T. (1970) *Parent Effectiveness Training*, New York: Wyden.

Gronow, J. and Hilppo, J. (1970) 'Violence, Ethics, and Politics', *Journal of Peace Research*, 7 (4): 311–20.

Groves, R.M., Fowler, Jr, F.J., Couper, M.P., Lepkowski, J.M., Singer, E. and Tourangeau, R. (2004) *Survey Methodology*, Hoboken, NJ: John Wiley.

Gubrium, J.F. and Holstein, J.A. (2002) 'From the Individual Interview to the Interview Society', in J.F. Gubrium and J.A. Holstein (eds), *Handbook of Interview Research: Context & method*, Thousand Oaks, CA: Sage.

Gurr, T.R. (1980) *Handbook of Political Conflict*, New York: Simon & Schuster.

Gustavsson, B., Rudén, L., Tibell, G. and Wallensteen, P. (1984) 'The Uppsala Code of Ethics', *Journal of Peace Research*, 21 (4): 212–16.

Hampson, F.O. (1996) *Nurturing Peace: Why peace settlements succeed or fail*, Washington DC: USIP Press.

Harbom, L., Högbladh, S. and Wallensteen, P. (2006) 'Armed Conflict and Peace Agreements', *Journal of Peace Research*, 43 (5): 617–31.

Harvey, C. (2010) 'The Web as a Reporting and Research Tool'. Online at: <http://www.newsline. umd.edu/italy/reportingtool.htm> (accessed 30 August 2010).

Hatchett, S. and Schuman, H. (1975) 'White Respondents and Race-of-Interviewer Effects', *Public Opinion Quarterly*, 39 (4): 523–8.

Helbardt, S., Hellman-Rajanayagam, D. and Korff, R. (2010) 'War's Dark Glamour: Ethics of research in war and conflict zones', *Cambridge Review of International Affairs* 23 (2): 349–69.

Heldt, B. (1993) 'Armed Conflicts over Government and Territory 1989–1991', in B. Heldt (ed.) *States in Armed Conflict 1990–91*, Uppsala: Repro-C.

Herman, J.L. (1997) *Trauma and Recovery*, revised edn, New York: Basic Books.

Hermann, T. (2001) 'The Impermeable Identity Wall: The study of violent conflict by "insiders" and "outsiders"', in M. Smyth and G. Robinson (eds), *Researching Violently Divided Societies: Ethical and methodological issues*, London: Pluto Press, 77–91.

Hettne, B., Inotai, A. and Sunkel, O. (eds) (1999) *Globalism and the New Regionalism*, Basingstoke: Macmillan in association with UNU/WIDER.

Hicks, M. (2006) 'Mortality After the 2003 Invasion of Iraq: Were valid and ethical field methods used in this survey?' Households in Conflict Network Research Design, Note 3. Online at: <http://www.hicn.org/research_design/rdn3.pdf> (accessed 15 April 2010).

HIIK (Heidelberg Institute for International Conflict Research) (2009) *Conflict Barometer 2009*, Department of Political Science, Heidelberg University.

Hill, M.R. (1993) *Archival Strategies and Techniques*, Newbury Park: Sage.

Hobbes, T. [1651] (1996) *The Leviathan*, Oxford: Oxford University Press.

Höglund, K. (2008) *Peace Negotiations in the Shadow of Violence*, Boston, MA: Martinus Nijhoff.

Höglund, K. and Söderberg Kovacs, M. (2010) 'Beyond the Absence of War: The diversity of peace in post-settlement societies', *Review of International Studies*, 36 (2): 367–90.

Howard, M.M. (2004) 'Obtaining and Recording Data', *Qualitative Methods: Newsletter of the American Political Science Association Organized Section on Qualitative Methods*, 2 (1): 7–10.

Howell, M. and Prevenier, W. (2001) *From Reliable Sources: An introduction to historical methods*, Ithaca, NY: Cornell University Press.

Hultman, L. (2008) *Targeting the Unarmed: Strategic rebel violence in civil wars*, Uppsala University: Department of Peace and Conflict Research.

Humphreys, M. and Weinstein, J. (2003) 'Sierra Leone Ex-Combatant Survey #1', Online at: <http://www.columbia.edu/~mh2245/Survey.pdf> (accessed 4 April 2010).

Humphreys, M. and Weinstein, J. (2006) 'Handling and Manhandling Civilians in Civil War', *American Political Science Review*, 100 (3): 429–47.

Humphreys, M. and Weinstein J.M (2007) 'Demobilization and Reintegration', *Journal of Conflict Resolution* 51 (4): 531–67.

ICTY (2000) IT-95-14-T (Blaškić, T.).

ICTY (2004) IT-95-14-A (Blaškić, T.).

ICTY (2005) IT-2005-87 (Milutinović *et al*).

IFHS (Iraq Family Health Survey) Study Group (2008a) 'Violence-related Mortality in Iraq from 2002 to 2006', *The New England Journal of Medicine*, 358 (2): 484–93.

IFHS (Iraq Family Health Survey) (2008b) *Iraq Family Health Survey 2006/7*. Online at: <http://www.emro.who.int/iraq/pdf/ifhs_report_en.pdf> (accessed 26 April 2010).

IHSN (International Household Survey Network) (2010) Online at: <http://www.surveynetwork. org/home/> (accessed 21 April 2010).

Iraq Body Count (2010) Online at: <http://www.iraqbodycount.org/database/> (accessed 15 April 2010).

Jarrik, A. (2005) 'Källkritiken Måste Uppdateras för Att Inte Reduceras Till Kvarleva', *Historisk tidskrift*, 125 (2): 219–31.

Jennings, K.M. (2007) 'The Struggle to Satisfy: DDR through the eyes of ex-combatants in Liberia', *International Peacekeeping* 14 (2): 204–18.

JHSPH (Johns Hopkins Bloomberg School of Public Health) (2009) 'Review Completed of 2006 Iraq Mortality Study'. Online at: <http://www.jhsph.edu/publichealthnews/press_releases/2009/iraq_review.html> (accessed 15 April 2010).

Johnson, J.M. (2002) 'In-depth Interviewing', in J.F. Gubrium and J.A. Holstein (eds) *Handbook of Interview Research: Context and method*, London: Sage.

Johnson, N.F., Spagat, M., Gourley, S., Onnela, J.-P. and Reinert, G. (2008) 'Bias in Epidemiological Studies of Conflict Mortality', *Journal of Peace Research*, 45 (5): 653–63.

Kaarsholm, P. (2006) 'Violence in Signifier: Politics and generational struggle in KwaZulu-Natal', in P. Kaarsholm, (ed.), *Violence, Political Culture and Development in Africa*, Oxford: James Curry.

Kalyvas, S.N. (2006) *The Logic of Violence in Civil War*, Cambridge: Cambridge University Press.

Kant, I. (1795) *To Perpetual Peace: A philosophical sketch*, trans Ted Humphrey (2003), Indianapolis: Hackett.

Keeter, S. (2005) 'Survey Research', in D. Druckman (ed.) *Doing Research: Methods of inquiry for conflict analysis*, London: Sage, 121–62.

Kellstedt, P.M. and Whitten, G.D. (2009) *The Fundamentals of Political Science Research*, Cambridge: Cambridge University Press.

Kende, I. (1971) 'Twenty-five Years of Local Wars', *Journal of Peace Research* 8 (1): 5–22.

King, G., Keohane, R.O. and Verba, S. (1994) *Designing Social Enquiry: Scientific inference in qualitative research*, Princeton, NJ: Princeton University Press.

King, G., Keohane, R.O. and Verba, S. (2004) 'The Importance of Research Design', in H.E. Brady and D. Collier (eds) *Rethinking Social Inquiry: Diverse tools, shared standards*, Lanham, MD: Rowman & Littlefield.

Klandermans, B. and Smith, J. (2002) 'Survey Research: A case for comparative designs', in B. Klandermans and S. Staggenborg (eds) *Methods of Social Movement Research*, Minneapolis: University of Minnesota Press, 3–31.

Knodel, J. (1993) 'Design and Analysis of Focus Group Studies: A practical approach', in D.L. Morgan (ed.), *Successful Focus Groups: Advancing the state of the art*, Newbury Park: Sage.

Knox, C. (2001) 'Establishing Research Legitimacy in the Contested Political Ground of Contemporary Northern Ireland', *Qualitative Research*, 1 (2): 205–22.

Knox, C. and Monaghan, R. (2002) 'Fear of Reprisal: Researching intra communal violence in Northern Ireland and South Africa', in R.M. Lee and E.A. Stanko (eds), *Researching Violence: Essays on methodology and measurement*, London: Routledge: 157–76.

Korn, E.L. and Graubard, B.I. (1999) *Analysis of Health Surveys*, Hoboken, NJ: John Wiley.

Kreutz, J. (2006) 'The Nexus of Democracy, Conflict and the Targeting of Civilians, 1989–2005', in L. Harbom (ed.) *States in Armed Conflict 2005*, Uppsala: Universitetstryckeriet.

Kuklinski, J.H., Sniderman, P.M., Knight, K., Piazza, T., Tetlock, P.E., Lawrence, G.R. and Mellers, B. (1997) 'Racial Prejudice and Attitudes toward Affirmative Action', *American Journal of Political Science*, 41 (2): 402–19.

Kumar, N. (2007) 'Spatial Sampling Design for a Demographic and Health Survey', *Population Research Policy Review*, 26 (5): 581–99.

Lee, R.M. (1995) *Dangerous Fieldwork*, Qualitative Research Methods Series 34, London: Sage.

Le Monde (1999) 'Ce plan "fer à cheval" qui programmait la déportation des Kosovars', Vernet, Daniel, April 8.

Lieberman, E.S. (2004) 'Introduction: The promise and pitfalls of field research', *Qualitative Methods: Newsletter of the American Political Science Association Organized Section on Qualitative Methods*, 2 (1): 2–3.

Lilja, J. (2010) *Disaggregating Dissent: The challenges of intra-party consolidation in civil war and peace negotiations*, Uppsala University: Department of Peace and Conflict Research.

Lohr, S. (1999) *Sampling: Design and analysis*, Pacific Grove: Duxbury Press.

Loquai, H. (2000) *Der Kosovo-Konflikt : Wege in einen vermeidbaren Krieg: die Zeit von Ende November 1997 bis März 1999*, Baden-Baden: Nomos-Verl-Ges.

Lund, M.S. (1996) *Preventing Violent Conflicts. A strategy for preventive diplomacy,* Washington DC: United States Institute of Peace Press.

Lynch, J. (2004) 'Tracking Progress While in the Field', *Qualitative Methods: Newsletter of the American Political Science Association Organized Section on Qualitative Methods,* 2 (1): 10–15.

McCarthy, J.D., Titarenko, L., McPhail, C., Rafail, P.S. and Augustyn, B. (2008) 'Assessing Stability in the Patterns of Selection Bias in Newspaper Coverage of Protest during the Transition from Communism in Belarus', *Mobilization: The International Quarterly* 13 (2): 127–46.

McEvoy, S. (2000) 'Communities and Peace: Catholic youth in Northern Ireland', *Journal of Peace Research* 37 (1): 85–103.

McFarlane, A.C. and van der Kolk, B.A. (1996) 'Trauma and its Challenge to Society', in B.A. van der Kolk, A.C. McFarlane and L. Weisaeth (eds) *Traumatic Stress: The effects of overwhelming experience on mind, body, and society,* New York: Guilford Press.

McKeganey, N. (2001) 'To Pay or Not to Pay: Respondents' motivation for participating in research', *Addiction,* 96 (9): 1237–8.

McNeill, P. (1997) 'Paying People to Participate in Research: Why not?', *Bioethics,* 11 (5): 390–6.

Macmillan, M. (2003) *Paris 1919,* New York: Random House.

Mahoney, J. (2010) 'After KKV: The new methodology of qualitative research.' *World Politics* 62 (1): 120–47.

Marshall, M. and Jaggers, K. (2009) *Polity IV Project: Political regime characteristics and transitions, 1800–2007,* Center for Systemic Peace, George Mason University. Online at: http://www.systemicpeace.org/polity/polity4.htm (accessed 26 July 2010).

Melander, E. (1999) *Anarchy Within. The security dilemma between ethnic groups in emerging anarchy,* Uppsala University: Department of Peace and Conflict Research.

Melander, E. (2005) 'Political Gender Equality and State Human Rights Abuse', *Journal of Peace Research,* 42 (2): 149–66.

Melman, S. (1974) *The Permanent War Economy,* New York: Simon & Schuster.

Mertus, J.A. (2009) 'Maintenance of Personal Security: Ethical and operational issues', in C.L. Sriram, J.C. King, J.A. Mertus, O. Martin-Ortega and J. Herman (eds) *Surviving Field Research: Working in violent and difficult situations,* London: Routledge.

More, T. [1516] (1997) *Utopia,* Mineola, NY: Dover Publications

Morgan, D.L. (1997) *Focus Groups as Qualitative Research,* 2nd edn, Thousand Oaks: Sage.

Morgan, D.L. and Krueger, R.A. (1993) 'When to Use Focus Groups and Why', in D.L. Morgan (ed.), *Successful Focus Groups: Advancing the state of the art,* Newbury Park: Sage.

Morgan, D.L. and Scannell, A.U. (1998) *Focus Group Kit. Vol. 2, Planning focus groups,* Thousand Oaks: Sage.

Mvukiyehe, E. and Samii, C. (2009) 'Laying a Foundation for Peace? A quantitative impact evaluation of the United Nations operation in Côte d'Ivoire. Technical Appendix', unpublished manuscript, Columbia University. Online at: <http://www.columbia.edu/~cds81/docs/unoci/> (accessed 3 April 2010).

Myers, G. (1998) 'Displaying Opinions: Topics and disagreement in focus groups', *Language in Society,* 27 (1): 85–111.

Nilan, P. (2002) '"Dangerous Fieldwork" Re-examined: The question of researcher subject position', *Qualitative Research,* 2 (3): 363–86.

Nilsson, A. (2008) *Dangerous Liaisons: Why ex-combatants return to violence. Cases from the Republic of Congo and Sierra Leone,* Uppsala University: Department of Peace and Conflict Research.

Nilsson, D. (2006) *In the Shadow of Settlement: Multiple rebel groups and precarious peace,* Uppsala University: Department of Peace and Conflict Research.

Nincic, M. and Cusack, T.R. (1979) 'The Political Economy of US Military Spending', *Journal of Peace Research,* 16 (2): 101–15.

Nordstrom, C. and Robben, A.C.G.M. (eds) (1995) *Fieldwork under Fire: Contemporary studies of violence and survival,* Berkeley, CA: University of California Press.

Norman, J.M. (2009) 'Got Trust? The challenge of gaining access in conflict zones', in C.L. Sriram, J.C. King, J.A. Mertus, O. Martin-Ortega and J. Herman (eds) *Surviving Field Research: Working in violent and difficult situations*, London: Routledge.

Nye, J.S. (2004) *Soft Power: The means to success in world politics*, New York: Public Affairs.

Öberg, M. and Sollenberg, M. (2003) 'Teaching Conflict Analysis: Suggestions on the use of media as a resource for conflict analysis', in M. Aguirre and F. Ferrándiz (eds) *The Emotion and the Truth: Studies in mass communication and conflict*, Bilbao: HumanitariaNet.

Öberg, M., Möller, F. and Wallensteen, P. (2009) 'Early Conflict Prevention in Ethnic Crises, 1990–98: A new dataset', *Conflict Management and Peace Science*, 26 (1): 7–91.

Oliver, P.E. and Maney, G.M. (2000) 'Political Processes and Local Newspaper Coverage of Protest Events: From selection bias to triadic interactions', *The American Journal of Sociology*, 106 (2): 463–505.

Olsson, L. (2007) *Equal Peace: United Nations peace operations and the power-relations between men and women in Timor-Leste*, Uppsala University: Department of Peace and Conflict Research.

Osgood, C.E. (1962) *An Alternative to War or Surrender*, Urbana, IL: University of Urbana Press.

Paluck, E.L. (2009) 'Methods and Ethics with Research Teams and NGOs: Comparing experiences across the border of Rwanda and Democratic Republic of Congo', in C.L. Sriram, J.C. King, J.A. Mertus, O. Martin-Ortega and J. Herman (eds) *Surviving Field Research: Working in violent and difficult situations*, London: Routledge.

Paris, R. (2004) *At War's End: Building peace after civil conflict*, Cambridge: Cambridge University Press.

Pearson, R.W., Ross, M. and Dawes, R.M. (1992) 'Personal Recall and the Limits of Retrospective Questions in Surveys', in J.M. Tanur (ed.) *Questions About Questions: Inquiries into the cognitive bases of surveys*, New York: Russell Sage.

Pfetsch, F.R. and Rohloff, C. (2000) 'KOSIMO: A new databank on political conflicts', *Journal of Peace Research*, 37 (3): 379–91.

Philpott, D. and Powers, G.F. (eds) (2010) *Strategies of Peace*, Oxford: Oxford University Press.

PJSA (2010) 'Global Directory of Peace Studies and Conflict Resolution programs'. Online at: <http://www.peacejusticestudies.org/> (accessed May 2010).

Pontara, G. (1978) 'The Concept of Violence', *Journal of Peace Research* 15 (1): 19–32.

Pope, K. and Vasquez, M. (2007) *Ethics in Psychotherapy and Counseling: A practical guide*, 3rd edn, San Francisco, CA: John Wiley.

Post-Conflict and Ex-Combatant Surveys (2010) Online at: <http://www.columbia.edu/~mh2245/XCSURVEYS/> (accessed 12 April 2010).

Przeworski, A. and Teune, H. (1970) *The Logic of Comparative Social Inquiry*, New York: Wiley-Interscience.

Raleigh, C., Linke, A. and Hegre, H. (2010) 'Introducing ACLED – Armed Conflict Location and Event Data', *Journal of Peace Research*, 47.

Ranke, L. von and Wines, R. (1981) *The Secret of World History: Selected writings on the art and science of history*, New York: Fordham University Press.

Rapoport, A. (1961) *Games, Fights, and Debates*, Ann Arbor, MI: University of Michigan Press.

Rautalinko, E., Lisper, H.-O. and Ekehammar, B. (2007) 'Reflective listening in counseling: Effects of training time and evaluator social skills', *American Journal of Psychotherapy*, 61 (2): 191–209.

RDC (Research and Documentation Centre) (2007) *Bosnian Book of Dead*, Research and Documentation Centre: Sarajevo.

Regan, P.M. and Aydin, A. (2006) 'Diplomacy and Other Forms of Intervention in Civil Wars', *Journal of Conflict Resolution*, 50 (5): 736–56.

Reilly, J, Muldoon, O.T. and Byrne, C. (2004) 'Young Men as Victims and Perpetrators of Violence in Northern Ireland: A qualitative analysis', *Journal of Social Issues*, 60 (3): 469–84.

Richards, D. (1996) 'Elite Interviewing: Approaches and pitfalls', *Politics*, 16 (3): 199–204.

Richardson, L.F. (1960) *Statistics of Deadly Quarrels*, Chicago, IL: Quadrangle Books.

Richmond, O. (2009) 'A Post-liberal Peace: Eirenism and the everyday', *Review of International Studies*, 35 (3): 557–80.

Roberts, A. (1986) *Nations in Arms: The theory and practice of territorial defence*, 2nd edn, Basingstoke: Macmillan.

Roberts, L. (2000) 'Mortality in Eastern DRC: Results from five mortality surveys by the International Rescue Committee', International Rescue Committee. Online at: <http://www.theirc.org/special-reports/congo-forgotten-crisis> (accessed April 8, 2010).

Rogers, C.R. (1975) 'Empathic: An unappreciated way of being', *Counseling Psychologist*, 5 (2): 2–10.

Rogers, C.R. (2008) *Counseling and Psychotherapy*, reprint edn, Cambridge, MA: The Riverside Press.

Rossman, G.B. and Rallis, S.F. (2003) *Learning in the Field: An introduction to qualitative research*, London: Sage.

Rubin, H.J. and Rubin, I.S. (2005) *Qualitative Interviewing: The art of hearing data*, 2nd edn, London: Sage.

Rummel, R.J. (1997) *Death by Government*, London: Transactions Publishers.

Rummel, R.J. (2004) 'One-thirteenth of a Data Point Does Not a Generalization Make: A response to Dulić', *Journal of Peace Research*, 41 (1): 103–4.

Rundquist, B.S. (1978) 'On Testing a Military Industrial Complex Theory', *American Politics Research*, 6 (1): 29–53.

Russett, B.M. (1993) *Grasping the Democratic Peace: Principles for a post-cold war world*, Princeton, NJ: Princeton University Press.

Russett, B.M. and Oneal, J.R. (2001) *Triangulating Peace: Democracy, interdependence, and international organizations*, New York: Norton.

Salganik, M.J. and Heckathorn, D.D. (2004) 'Sampling and Estimation in Hidden Populations Using Respondent-driven Sampling', *Sociological Methodology* 34 (1): 193–240.

Samii, C., Gilligan, M. and Eck, K. (2009) 'Nepal Peacebuilding Survey: Study design', unpublished manuscript, Columbia University. Online at: <http://www.columbia.edu/~cds81/docs/nep/nep09_sampling_design091210.pdf> (accessed 3 April 2010).

Sartori, G. (1970) 'Concept Misformation in Comparative Politics', *American Political Science Review*, 6 (4): 1033–53.

Scacco, A. (2008) 'Who Riots? Explaining individual participation in ethnic violence', unpublished manuscript, Columbia University. Online at: <http://www.columbia.edu/~als2110/files/Scacco_Who_Riots.pdf> (accessed 8 April 2010).

Schelling, T. (1960) *The Strategy of Conflict*, Cambridge, MA: Harvard University Press.

Schmid, H. (1968) 'Politics and Peace Research', *Journal of Peace Research*, 5 (3): 217–32.

Schnabel, A. (2001) 'One Size Fits All? Focused comparison and policy relevant research in violently divided societies', in M. Smyth and G. Robinson (eds) *Researching Violently Divided Societies: Ethical and methodological issues*, London: Pluto Press: 193–206.

Seligmann, L. (2005) 'Ethnographic Methods', in Druckman, D (ed.), *Doing Research: Methods of inquiry for conflict analysis*, Thousand Oaks, CA: Sage: 229–54.

Sharp, G. (1973) *Politics of Nonviolent Action*, Boston, MA: Sargent.

Singer J.D. (1969) 'The Incompleat Theorist: Insight without evidence', in K. Knorr and J.N. Rosenau (eds) *Contending Approaches to International Politics*, Princeton, NJ: Princeton University Press.

Singer, J.D. and Small, M. (1972) *The Wages of War*, New York: John Wiley.

Sluka, J.A. (1995) 'Reflections on Managing Danger in Fieldwork: Dangerous anthropology in Belfast', in C. Nordstrom and A.C.G.M. Robben (eds) *Fieldwork under Fire: Contemporary studies of violence and survival*, Berkeley, CA: University of California Press: 276–94.

Small, M. and Singer, J.D. (1982) *Resort to Arms: International and civil wars, 1816–1980*, Beverly Hills, CA: Sage.

SMART (Standardized Monitoring and Assessment of Relief and Transitions) (2006) *Measuring Mortality, Nutritional Status, and Food Security in Crisis Situations: SMART METHODOLOGY.* Online at: <http://www.smartindicators.org/SMART_Methodology_08-07-2006.pdf> (accessed 12 April 2010).

Smith, J. (2007) *Social Movements for Global Democracy*, Baltimore, MD: Johns Hopkins University Press.

Smith, T.W. (1984) 'Recalling Attitudes: An analysis of retrospective questions on the 1982 GSS', *Public Opinion Quarterly*, 48 (3): 639–49.

Smyth, M. and Darby, J. (2001) 'Does Research Make Any Difference? The case of Northern Ireland', in M. Smyth and G. Robinson (eds), *Researching Violently Divided Societies: Ethical and methodological issues,* London: Pluto Press: 34–54.

Smyth, M. and Robinson G. (eds) (2001) *Researching Violently Divided Societies: Ethical and methodological is*sues, London: Pluto Press.

Söderström, J. (2010) 'Ex-Combatants at the Polls: Exploring focus groups & electoral meaning', *Anthropology Matters*, 12 (1).

Söderström, J. (forthcoming) 'Dissent & Opposition among Ex-Combatants in Liberia' (working title), *Democratization*.

Sorokin, P.A. (1937) *Social and Cultural Dynamics*, vol. 3, New York: Bedminster Press.

Spagat, M. (2010) 'Ethical and Data-Integrity Problems in the Second *Lancet* Survey of Mortality in Iraq', *Defense and Peace Economics*, 21 (1): 1–41.

Spagat, M., Mack, A., Cooper, T. and Kreutz, J. (2009) 'Estimating War Deaths: An arena of contestation', *Journal of Conflict Resolution*, 53 (6): 934–50.

Sriram, C.L. (2009) 'Maintenance of standards of protection during writeup and publication' in C.L. Sriram, J.C. King, J.A. Mertus, O. Martin-Ortega and J. Herman (eds) *Surviving Field Research: Working in violent and difficult situations*, London: Routledge.

Sriram, C.L., King, J.C., Mertus, J.A., Martin-Ortega, O. and Herman, J. (eds) (2009) *Surviving Field Research: Working in violent and difficult situations*, London: Routledge.

Stephan, M.J. and Chenoweth, E. (2008) 'Why Civil Resistance Works. The strategic logic of nonviolent conflict', *International Security*, 33 (1): 7–44.

Tabeau, E. and Bijak, J. (2005) 'War-related Deaths in the 1992-1995 Armed Conflicts in Bosnia and Herzegovina: A critique of previous estimates and recent results', *European Journal of Population*, 21 (2–3): 187–215.

Tabyshalieva, A. (2001) 'Researching Ethnic Conflict in Post-Soviet Central Asia', in M. Smyth and G. Robinson (eds.) *Researching Violently Divided Societies: Ethical and methodological issues*, London: Pluto Press: 130–47.

Thomson, S.M. (2009) '"That is not what we authorised you to do ...": Access and government interference in highly politicised research environments', in C.L. Sriram, J.C. King, J.A. Mertus, O. Martin-Ortega and J. Herman (eds) *Surviving Field Research: Working in violent and difficult situations*, London: Routledge.

Thorne, B. (1980) 'You Still Takin' Notes – Fieldwork and problems of informed consent', *Social Problems*, 27 (3): 284–97.

Tillema H.K. (1989) 'Foreign Overt Military Intervention in the Nuclear Ages', *Journal of Peace Research*, 26 (2): 179–95.

The Times (1999) '"Ethnic Cleansing" Plans Laid Years Ago', Susan Bell, April 9.

Tourangeau, R. (2000) 'Remembering What Happened: Memory errors and survey reports', in A.A. Stone, J.S. Turkkan, C.A. Bachrach, J.B. Jobe, H.S. Kurtzman and V.S. Cain (eds) *The Science of Self-report: Implications for research and practice*, Mahwah, NJ: Lawrence Erlbaum.

Tuckman, B. (1962) *The Guns of August*, New York: Macmillan.

UN (United Nations) (2005) *Household Sample Surveys in Developing and Transition Countries.* Online at: <http://unstats.un.org/unsd/hhsurveys/> (accessed 21 April 2010).

Upadhyaya, P. (2009) 'Peace and Conflict: Reflections on Indian thinking', *Strategic Analysis*, 33 (1): 71–83.

Urlacher, B.R. (2009) 'Wolfowitz Conjecture: A research note on civil wars and news coverage', *International Studies Perspective* 10 (2): 186–97.

Vick, K. (1999) 'Africa Has Refugees, Kosovo Gets Money', *Washington Post,* 8 October.

Vultee, F. (2009) 'The Second Casualty: Effects of interstate conflict and civil conflict on press freedom', *Media, War & Conflict,* 2 (2): 111–27.

Wallace, M. (1979) 'Arms Races and Escalation: Some new evidence', in J.D. Singer (ed.) *Explaining War*, Beverly Hills, CA: Sage.

Wallensteen, P. (1988) 'The Origins of Peace Research', in P. Wallensteen (ed.) *Peace Research: Achievements and challenges*, Boulder, CO: Westview Press; 7–29.

Wallensteen, P. (2003) 'The Uppsala Conflict Data Program 1978–2003: How it all began, how it matured and where it is today', in M. Eriksson (ed.) *States in Armed Conflict 2002*, Uppsala: Uppsala Publishing House.

Wallensteen, P. (2008) 'Global Governance and the Future of United Nations', in B. Hettne (ed.) *Human Values and Global Governance: Studies in development, security and culture,* vol 2, Basingstoke: Palgrave Macmillan, 198–219.

Wallensteen, P. and Sollenberg, M. (1998) 'Armed Conflict and Regional Conflict Complexes, 1989–97', *Journal of Peace Research*, 35 (5): 621–34.

Wehr, P. (1979) *Conflict Regulation*, Boulder, CO: Westview Press.

Wehr, P. (1985) 'Conflict and Restraint: Poland 1980–1982', in P. Wallensteen, J. Galtung and C. Portales (eds) *Global Militarization*, Boulder, CO: Westview Press.

Weinstein, J.M. (2005) 'Resources and the Information Problem in Rebel Recruitment', *Journal of Conflict Resolution*, 49 (4): 598–624.

Wiberg, H. (1988) 'The Peace Research Movement', in P. Wallensteen (ed.) *Peace Research. Achievements and challenges*, Boulder, CO: Westview Press.

Wilkinson, M. and Moore, A. (1997) 'Inducement in Research', *Bioethics*, 11 (5): 373–89.

Wolpe, H. (2003) 'Burundi: Facilitation in a regionally sponsored peace process', unpublished manuscript, The Africa Program, Woodrow Wilson International Center for Scholars, 38–44; 48–9.

Wood, E.J. (2006) 'The Ethical Challenges of Field Research in Conflict Zones', *Qualitative Sociology*, 29 (3): 373–86.

Wright, Q. (1942) *A Study of War*, Chicago, IL: University of Chicago Press.

Yin, R.K. (1994) *Case Study Research: Design and methods*, 2nd edn, London: Sage

Zartman, I.W. (2000) 'Mediating Conflicts of Need, Greed and Creed', *Orbis*, 44 (2): 255–66.

Политика (2007) 'Мистерията "подкова"'. Пройчев, Тодор, November 2.

Index

University of Maryland, 10, 106
University of Michigan, 19, 11
Unsystematic errors, 99, 102
Uppsala Code of Ethics, 13, 127
Uppsala Conflict Database, 52, 66
Uppsala Conflict Data Program
    (UCDP), 10–11, 19, 27, 91–106,
    109–112
  Peace agreement dataset, 103
Uppsala University, 28
  Department of Peace and Conflict
    Research, 6, 16, 92
USA (see 'United States of America')
Utopian ideas, 14–16, 21, 28, 30

V

Validity, 7, 35, 44, 60, 82, 91, 97–102,
    106, 111–112, 119, 134–135, 165,
    185–187, 191
Victim, 27, 29, 77, 119–120, 190
Victimization, 173
Victimization studies, 170
Vietnam War, the, 23–24, 31
Violence, 4, 9, 14–20, 23, 26–27, 29, 43,
    46, 54–55, 59, 77, 79, 83, 94–97, 104,
    110, 114, 116–123, 125, 139, 144, 150,
    165, 171, 181, 186, 190, 197
  Communal, 94, 117, 120
  Definition of, 15–16, 98
  Direct, 15, 95
  Electoral, 118
  Ethnic, 62, 81
  Indirect, 16, 95
  Local, localized, 43–44, 125
  Manifestations, 38, 119
  Non-state, 52
  Organized, 11, 15, 92–93, 96–97, 100,
    104–106, 110, 112, 179, 186
  One-sided, 52, 92, 94, 96, 103–105,
    112–113
  Political, 114–115, 199, 125
  Sectarian, 62
  Sexual, 8, 15
  Structural, 16

W

War
  Causes of, 15–20, 22, 27–28, 31
  Civil, 16, 75, 109, 112, 114, 117
  Concept of, 62, 93
  Correspondent, 49, 55
  Crimes, 39, 44, 46
  Definition of, 93, 99, 101, 186
  Diaries, 47
  Ethnic, 4
  Interstate, 19, 93, 122
  Intrastate. 93
  Internal, 28, 30
  International, 28
  Just war, 4, 14
  Micro foundations of, 165
  Nuclear, 16
  On terrorism, 29
  Tribal, 120
Warlords, 175
Websites, 8, 50, 52–53, 73, 129,
    190–191
West Bank, 58, 61
Wilson, Woodrow, 19
Within-case analysis, 116
Written narratives, 7–8, 11, 74–76,
    78–87, 190
Wolpe, Howard, 75–76, 78, 85
World Bank, 176, 194
  Data, 52, 110
World News Archive, 68, 104
World Trade Center (WTC), 58,
    62–63
World Values Survey, 10
World war, 4, 16, 28, 129
World War I, 1, 15, 17–18, 20, 27–28,
    31
World War II, 19–20, 22, 31, 39, 41–42,
    93
WTC (see 'World Trade Center')

X

Xinhua News Agency, 50
Xinjiang, 55